THE BIRDS OF NEBRASKA

PAUL A. JOHNSGARD

SCHOOL OF BIOLOGICAL SCIENCES
UNIVERSITY OF NEBRASKA-LINCOLN
LINCOLN, NE 68588-0118

Revised edition, 2013

TABLE OF CONTENTS

Part 1
Birdwatching Through the Year in Nebraska

Many Nebraskans are unaware that they are actually residing in one of the prime locations in the entire world for observing and enjoying some of the most aesthetically appealing of all the world's biological attractions. The area around Kingsley Dam and Lake McConaughy, for example, is known to have attracted more than 300 bird species, including 104 breeders (plus 17 probable breeders) making it the third-most species-rich bird location in the interior U.S.A. (after Laguna Atascosa National Wildlife Refuge in southern Texas and Cheyenne Bottoms Wildlife Management Area in central Kansas). More impressively, the spring congregations of cranes and waterfowl along the Platte River Valley have recently been ranked by Roger Pasquier (writing in *Forbes Magazine,* 1997) as the greatest bird spectacle on earth.

It has been estimated that bird-watching activities in the U.S.A. have increased 155 percent during the past decade, or at a more rapid rate than all other outdoor sports including walking, skiing and hiking, whereas fishing, hunting and tennis have all actually declined in popularity. Moneys now spent on wildlife recreation (over $100 billion) now exceeds total cash receipts from all livestock sales ("Wildlife Recreation," in *The Main Street Economist,* April, 2004), and in 2006 birders added $36 billion to the U.S. economy. About 63 million people in the U.S.A. feed or watch birds at home, and there are at least 48 million adult bird-watchers. In Nebraska alone an estimated 23.1 million dollars per year are spent by the public on non-consumptive bird-related activities, and about 800 people are employed in jobs supported by non-consumptive bird-related areas (*Bird Conservation*, spring, 1997, pp. 6-8).

Every month of the year has its own bird-related attractions in Nebraska, as the following monthly breakdown will suggest.

January

January in Nebraska is our coldest and dreariest month, and a good time for feeding birds and enjoying them through the windows. White-throated and white-crowned sparrows are welcome visitors to feeders now, as are American goldfinches and other typical finches, such as purple finches (rarely) and (increasingly) house finches. Dark-eyed juncos and eastern or spotted towhees scratch industriously in the snow for food, and in the countryside species such as horned larks, American tree sparrows, Harris' sparrows, and sometimes Lapland longspurs gather in open fields to search for seeds. During some years red-breasted nuthatches appear at suet feeders to join wintering downy, hairy and (in the east) red-bellied woodpeckers, and even less often red crossbills and (rarely) evening grosbeaks make their appearances, especially in western parts of the state. In the Panhandle and Pine Ridge other winter visitors might include Steller's jays, Bohemian waxwings, Clark's nutcrackers, mountain chickadees, Cassin's finches and gray-crowned rosy-finches. Northern cardinals now begin to sense the lengthening days, and by mid-January a few males may begin sing, to be joined later in the month by European starlings and sometimes a few precocious house finches.

For the adventurous birders, this month offers the temptation to drive to Kingsley Dam near Ogallala for the annual spectacle of several hundred bald eagles that annually gather there, and the chance– see some rare waterfowl, loons or gulls as well. This is the best time for seeing rough-legged hawks and other uncommon to rare northern visitors, such as snowy owls.

February

By February the days are perceptibly lengthening, and the end of winter seems almost in sight. Winter birds still gather at feeders, but American crows are on the move northward, as are vanguard individuals of American robins, red-winged blackbirds, and bluebirds.

By shortly after Valentine's day the first sandhill cranes can be expected to arrive on the Platte river, at least if it has become ice-free. They usually arrive on a south wind and with clearing skies, probably having flown from their wintering areas in Texas and New Mexico in a single day. Common mergansers begin to appear on the Platte too, as well as on larger reservoirs. Almost simultaneously common goldeneyes start to appear in these same locations.

As lakes and reservoirs slowly become ice-free bald eagles appear throughout the state's waterways. They feast on winter–killed fish that become available, often perching on ice blocks or on trees along the shoreline. Harlan County reservoir and Sutherland reservoir, in south-central Nebraska, are good places to look for eagles, as well as Lake McConaughy in the Panhandle and larger eastern reservoirs, such as Lewis and Clark Lake, Branched Oak Lake, and Cunningham Lake. DeSoto National Wildlife Refuge often has good numbers of bald eagles in February, and its visitor center allows for easy and comfortable eagle watching, as does the J-2 power plant near Lexington.

Great horned owls begin nesting in February, and should not be disturbed by playback of owl calls from this point onward through their nesting period.

March

March is perhaps the most exciting month of the year for Nebraska's birders. By the first week or two hundreds of thousands if not millions of geese (snow, Ross', Canada, cackling, and greater white-fronted) will have arrived in the eastern Rainwater Basin of southeastern Nebraska (centering on Clay County), and on a few basins farther west, such as Funk Lagoon. Unbelievable hordes of geese, as well as early duck migrants such as northern pintails and mallards crowd these marshes and the skies above, performing dizzying courtship flights and endless feeding flights to nearby fields for foraging. These great flocks of waterfowl usually peak by the middle of March.

During March the sandhill cranes begin to build up to a peak of about a half million birds in the central Platte Valley, spending the daylight hours feeding in cornfields and wet meadows, and roosting in shallow water around sandbars and islands in the wider portions of the river. Flights to and from their roosts occur at about sunset and sunrise, although cloudy skies may cause earlier evening flights and later morning departures, just as clear skies and a full moon may allow the birds to remain in fields for a longer period.

Mid-March is the target date for the Audubon Society's annual Rivers and Wildlife Conference at Kearney, drawing birders from around the country and the world. Finding space in one of the several crane-observing blinds is difficult then, but crane viewing from the road or from viewing platforms near Alda, Gibbon, and a hike-bike bridge near Fort Kearny are all options for the less lucky individuals. All of these experiences are memorable, but watching cranes land nearby at a blind near an evening roost, or seeing them depart at sunrise, provides a thrill unmatched anywhere in the world.

As March draws toward a close the second wave of duck migrants arrive, including American wigeon, gadwall, wood ducks, green-winged teal, redhead, canvasback, ring-necked duck, bufflehead, and hooded merganser. The final wave, with blue-wing teal, northern shoveler, ruddy duck, and perhaps cinnamon teal, complete the roster. Other water birds also arrive in March, including American coot, pied-billed and eared grebes, and western grebes, plus American white pelicans and double-crested cormorants.

The resident red-tailed hawk population is now supplemented by migrant red-tails as the rough-legged hawks begin to head north, and northern harriers (males first) begin to appear in the state. This is a good time to watch male harriers perform their circular territorial display flights (from which their generic name *Circus* derives), and to start looking for nest-building behavior in red-tails. Ospreys begin to funnel through the state in locations where bald eagles have been prevalent, and prairie grouse (sharp-tailed grouse and greater prairie-chickens) begin to assemble at their traditional display grounds, or leks.

April

The first half of April marks the mass departure of sandhill cranes from the Platte Valley, the arrival of whooping cranes, and the peak of mating activities by the prairie grouse. Seeing the great flocks of sandhill cranes rise up from the river one clear morning, circling while calling excitedly, gradually gaining altitude, and finally disappearing from view even though their great trumpeting voices still drift down like a vast but unseen angelic chorus, is an experience of a lifetime

Whooping cranes drift into the state in small family groups or flocks of up to about ten in size, stopping in the Platte Valley or in other wetland areas such as rivers in the Nebraska Sandhills or the Niobrara Valley. Rarely they may feed in the company of sandhill cranes, or roost among them at night.

The second week of April (often the third week in northern portions of Nebraska) is the best period for seeing prairie grouse display, for during this rather short time the majority of females visit the leks for mating. This sets off a frenzy of display activity and fighting among the males, to determine which will gain the opportunity to fertilize the suddenly available females. Somehow the females can determine the identity of the most virile and dominant male of each lek, and seek out this individual for their mating. Their leks are usually in areas of native grassland that are well away from tall trees, and often on shortgrass-covered hilltops. Blinds at locations such as at Halsey and McKelvie national forests, Crescent Lake, Valentine and Fort Niobrara national wildlife refuges, and Burchard Lake State Recreation Area, provide excellent sites for watching these activities.

The second half of April usually coincides with the peak of shorebird migration in Nebraska, as well as the arrival of the first insectivorous songbirds, such as the swallows, vireos, and warblers. This is an exciting period, as waves of plovers and sandpipers arrive at wetlands, and the skies overhead become clotted with Franklin's gulls, swallows of several species, and the blooming wild plums begin to reverberate with the songs of house wrens, rose-breasted grosbeaks, brown thrashers, and early-arriving warblers such as yellow-rumps.

May

May is simply magical in Nebraska. During the first two weeks of this month the peak of songbird migration occurs, with gorgeously plumaged warblers and plainer sparrows of infinite variety frustrating the observer by quickly scurrying about among tree canopies or skulking in the grass. Often one beautiful species will be present in a woodland or prairie on one day, only to be replaced on the next day with a new and equally interesting one. Butterflies and early spring flowers begin to appear, and persons tending their bluebird nest boxes can expect to peer in one day and see the female huddled down on a brood of squirming youngsters. Broods of Canada geese start to materialize on farm ponds and in city park lagoons, and in city backyards house wrens are simultaneously singing and feeding new broods.

Early May marks the International Migratory Bird Day and the time of the annual Audubon Birdathon in Nebraska. Then participating birders may compete to try produce the largest single-day bird list possible, with donors providing challenges by donating moneys to the local Audubon chapters. These funds aid prairie preservation and the purchase of instructional materials dealing with nature for distribution to grade schools.

June

June is the perfect time to be in the field in Nebraska; the long days allow for after–work birding, and this too is the month when Breeding Bird Surveys need to be carried out. People monitoring bluebird trails are busy then too; first or even second broods of bluebirds and tree swallows are likely to be out, and boxes need to be patrolled to try prevent depredations by raccoons or invading house wrens or house sparrows.

By the first of June the tardiest of the spring migrants, the common nighthawk and the black-billed and yellow-billed cuckoos, will have arrived in Nebraska, and the last arctic-breeding shorebirds should have departed. (By the end of June the appearance of any such arctic shorebirds in the state may actually represent early fall migrants, namely those individuals that were unsuccessful breeders and are already heading back south.) Summer evenings will be enriched by the distinctive territorial calls of nighthawks, chuck-will-widows, whip-poor-wills, and (in western Nebraska) poor-wills. The cuckoos (often called "rain crows" in Nebraska) may call from their hidden locations as evening twilight or afternoon thunderstorms approach. Generally, however, singing by birds diminishes in June, as the birds become preoccupied with nesting, and only such multiple-nesting species as house wrens, or those males that lost their initial mates and must quickly acquire new ones, are likely to be singing at full strength.

July

July is too hot for most outside activities in Nebraska, and birding activities are best confined to early morning walks, when a few die-hard songsters such as house finches may still be active. Second broods of many species will now be appearing, and early fall migrants such as long-billed curlews and cliff swallows will be starting to gather for migration. It amazing that the young of birds such as these can be ready to undertake flights of up to several thousand miles only a few weeks after hatching in the case of the swallows. Some multiple-brooding birds such as mourning doves and barn swallows will still be industriously fledging early broods and starting new ones soon thereafter, producing four or perhaps even five broods in a single season before running out of time. On the other hand trumpeter swan cygnets being reared in Sandhills marshes will only be about half-grown by July, and the approximate 100-day fledging period will require most of the summer before the cygnets are able to take their first flights.

By early July the brown-headed cowbird females, who may have already laid 40 or more eggs in the nests of unlucky hosts, will finally have become too exhausted for further laying. Thus, late-nesting sparrows and warblers may be spared the fate of having to raise a cowbird chick with their own young, which often results in the starvation of the host's chicks as a result of the cowbird's gluttonous appetite.

August

With the arrival of August the first sense that summer is almost over begins to take hold; the cooler mornings and the gathering flocks of swallows along telephone lines provides an early warning system that the good times are nearly over. This is a period when arctic-nesting shorebirds begin to filter into wetlands having muddy and sandy shorelines, and a chance for the birder to test his or her skills at identifying the maddeningly similar immature and fall-plumaged "peep" sandpipers, or the equally frustrating "confusing fall warblers." This is a perfect time for 10-power binoculars or spotting scopes and tripods, with their magnifications set at maximum power, and all the available field guides close at hand.

September

The blue skies of September bring not only occasional cumulus clouds to Nebraska, but also clouds of early fall migrant "blackbirds" (red-winged blackbirds ad well as grackles, cowbirds, and starlings). As the trees begin to turn color the first frosts send insect-eaters such as warblers and vireos scurrying southward, and set the stage for the great migrations of the larger birds. Migratory hawk species, such as Swainson's hawks, some non-residential red-tailed hawks, as well as Mississippi kites and turkey vultures begin to assemble and ghost southwardly. A keen observer may scan the sky with binoculars for skeins of geese or ducks, or perhaps may train a spotting scope on the face of a full moon some evening, and see fleeting silhouettes of distant birds crossing in front of it.

This is a good time to wander aimlessly through the woods; mosquitoes and chiggers are no longer a problem, and the dying leaves begin to allow a better look into the upper levels of the forest canopy. Escaping into the country also permits one to avoid the screaming hordes of football fans that are attracted to stadiums like ants to honey, mostly wholly unaware that the greatest visual spectacle on earth is passing by overhead.

October

October is the most colorful month of the year in Nebraska; the peak of fall color occurs about the middle of the month, and many wonderful birds are moving through the state's woodlands at the same time. Not long ago the peak of the arctic goose migration occurred in October, as several million snow geese would funnel down the Missouri Valley, and Canada and greater white-fronted geese would appear in the central and western parts of the state. Recently, however, the fall migrations of these geese have peaked later, often during the first week of November, perhaps as a reflection of global warming trends.

Nevertheless, October brings with it a major movement of larger migrants, from hawks to the early duck migrants such as blue-winged teal and shovelers, and many of the more tardy shorebirds. Sandhill cranes begin to appear in marshes of the Nebraska Sandhills. Few of them use the Platte Valley, since intensive waterfowl hunting activities there make the area unsafe for cranes, herons, cormorants or other birds bearing even a distant similarity to waterfowl.

November

During November the good birding season comes almost to a close; a few northern shrikes and rough-legged hawks are now arriving, and migratory sparrows such as American tree sparrows and Harris' sparrows start to materialize in shrubbery and thickets. Eagles start to invade the state in good numbers, tagging along with the flocks of ducks and geese, and occasionally snagging a sick or wounded one. On clear and calm evenings great flocks of geese can be heard overhead bound for unknown destinations using clues that we can only try to imagine.

Owls begin to announce their breeding territories now. Hardy birders will find that this is a good time for playing recordings of various owls after dark, then listening for responses. Barred owls respond especially well, often flying into a tree directly above the tape recorder.

December

December is in many ways the cruelest month; the days are so short that there is little time after work to go afield, and few birds to see when one does so. Yet it is a month for planning a Christmas Bird Count with close friends, and perhaps making out a Christmas list of bird-related gifts to present to friends and family, or perhaps hope to receive from them.

December is also the time to make out summaries of yearly bird lists, at least for people who keep such lists, and a time to start planning bird-watching trips for the following year. It is also not a bad time to consider a trip to Florida, southern Texas or even the tropics of Costa Rica, for a chance to get a flavor of how rich the bird life can be in places such as these. It is a time to look back on all the wonderful experiences of the previous year, such as that stunning scarlet tanager singing in the treetops, the spine-chilling sounds of sandhill cranes approaching their roosts, or a ruby-throated hummingbird that danced momentarily in the sunlight like a tiny sprite before it disappeared in the twinkling of an eye.

Fundamentals of Birdwatching

In recent decades bird watching has in recent decades has become one of the major recreational activities engaged in by Americans, with over sixty million persons now participating in this combination of intellectual activity, exercise, sport, and, in its most academic form, science. Its attractions include the facts that it can be equally enjoyed by absolute novices or lifelong devotees, it can be practiced by people ranging in age from a few years to elder citizens, and it requires very little in terms of special equipment. Finally, it is essentially of inexhaustible interest, given the fact that there are over 9,000 species of living birds in the world, and nobody could ever live long enough to learn about or even observe more than a small proportion of them.

Many birdwatchers are determined to see as many species as possible, and develop "life lists" that may be subdivided into state lists, yearly lists, or other categories. Such persons tend to call themselves "birders," and for them "birding" often has a competitive aspect, in which a maximum number of species that can be detected (seen or heard) and identified in a single day or year has a particular attraction.

Others are content simply to enjoy the birds attracted to nest boxes, feeders or water sources set up in their back yards, thus reveling in the fascinating behaviors, diverse plumages, nesting activities, or other facets of bird life that may visible from their patio deck or through their windows. Still others become avid bird-banders, engaging in a kind of avian lottery, and trying to recapture birds already banded by themselves or others. By banding and releasing birds they hope that, like placing a message in a bottle, somebody in the future may find the bird's carcass or perhaps recapture it, and by reporting it provide evidence of the bird's movements and longevity following its banding.

Finally, there are the professional ornithologists who, like other kinds of zoologists, might be interested in anatomy, genetics, physiology, classification, ecology, behavior, or any of the other branches of biological science, and tend to be educators or museum scientists. There are only a few thousand such persons, and perhaps a few hundred additional bird-related professionals who lead bird-watching tours all over the world. Still others may write about or photograph birds for a living, or perhaps draw, paint, sculpt, carve, or otherwise depict birds in some art-related field.

Optical Equipment and Acoustic Aids

Depending on one's area of interest, differing kinds of equipment and resource materials may be needed. The most popular type of bird appreciation, field observation and identification, requires only a minimum of equipment. Probably the most important of these are a pair of binoculars and an identification reference, or "field guide."

All binoculars are identified as to their magnification power and the diameter of their front ("objective") lenses; thus a pair of 8 x 40 binoculars have eight-power magnification and a front-lens diameter of 40 mm. Doubling the diameter of the objective lens quadruples the light transmission of the lens, but also increases its weight; the magnification of the binoculars does not influence their weight. Generally, to insure adequate light-gathering power under dim-light conditions, the objective lens should be at least five times greater than the magnification. This ratio (which would be 5.0 in 8 x 40 binoculars) is called the "exit pupil" index, since it is a measure of the diameter of the circle of light exiting the rear of the binocular and thus entering one's pupil. "Relative brightness" is calculated as the square of the exit pupil index. However, this index (the larger the better for maximum brightness under dim conditions) provides only a general guide to actual image brightness, and unless one is using the glasses in dark forests it is not a major consideration in choosing binoculars.

Often of greater interest than the exit pupil index is the binoculars angle of view, or maximum visual field, which is usually indicated in degrees. Binoculars typically have fields of view ranging from five degrees (263 feet at 1,000 yards) to 8.5 degrees (446 feet at 1,000 yards)."Wide-angle" binoculars (with fields generally of seven degrees or more) are generally better choices, but often are heavier than standard binoculars because of their larger prisms. Wide-angle binoculars sometimes also have increased distortion at the edges of the field of view.

Choosing a suitable pair of binoculars requires special care. Not only because a substantial outlay of money is involved, but also the choice made plays a large role in determining how effectively one will be able to locate and identify birds. These may be moving rapidly, mostly hidden by foliage, or so far away that considerable magnification is needed to observe their critical identification features. The subject of binocular choice is thus a complex topic, dictated in part by one's budget, an in part by the kind of primary bird-watching that is contemplated (for example, in forests, along lakes, or under dim-light conditions). Price ranges of binoculars range from less than $50 to several thousand dollars; my own two favorites have included one that I bought at a tag sale for $19.00, and another (a Vortex model) that was purchased new for $150.00. Several friends have pairs costing close to $1,000.00, and at times I envy them, but generally one can find a suitable pair for less than $200.00. The Bushnell Birder 7 x 35, at about $75.00, is acceptable for starting birders on a strict budget. Birder magazines such as *Birders World* often rank binoculars for usability and value, and Eagle Optics (www.eagleoptics.com) is a reliable source for both information on and purchase of quality binoculars at reasonable cost (see below).

When handling a pair of binoculars a prospective buyer should test for double images (produced when the paired optics are out of perfect alignment), colored fringes around the surfaces of objects visible at the edges of the field (a sign of chromatic aberration), apparent curvature of straight-line objects such as rooftops or utility poles (a sign of optical defects), and distortion, fuzziness, or light flare at the edge of the field when looking at a bright point of light such as a star. The ease of turning the focusing wheel (especially in cold weather) may be important, but the adjustment hinge for maintaining proper inter–pupillary distance (to correspond with the width of one's eye spacing) should not be too loose. A comfortable grip and weight, and ease of turning the focusing wheel especially in cold weather) are also considerations, and the neck-strap should be sturdy and comfortable as well. Better quality binoculars have anti-reflection coatings on all internal surfaces, are water–resistant, and may be internally "purged" with gasses that prevent fogging in wet weather.

For eyeglass-wearers the eye-relief distance (the distance between the binoculars rear lens and the farthest point behind the lens at which the binoculars entire field is visible) is more important than the binoculars' actual field of view. An eye relief of about 20 mm is needed for the eyeglass user to see the entire field and avoid "tunnel-vision" vignetting effects. This eye-relief measure is rarely indicated in the binoculars specifications, but possible vignetting effects should always be personally checked by prospective buyers who wear eyeglasses. Long eye-relief binoculars are usually limited to lower–power models and generally lack wide-angle features, so there is a trade-off in making such selections.

My own preferences are either 8-power or 10-power binoculars; the higher power glasses tend to be heavier, have a reduced field of view, and are harder to hold steady, but are excellent for viewing distant objects. Seven-power binoculars with a large exit-pupil ratio of at least 6.0 may be favored by those people who usually bird-watch in dense forests and require maximum light transmission capabilities. Armored binoculars (with a rubber coating) are more resistant to water and physical shocks than regular ones, and may be easier to hold, but are about two ounces heavier than non-armored models. Binoculars with roof-prisms are straight-tube in shape; those with regular prism design ("porro prisms") are usually wider at the front than in back, but occasionally in very small glasses are wider at the rear than in front. Roof-prism models are always more expensive, and often have narrower fields of view than porro-prism models. Yet, they average somewhat lighter and are less likely to go out of alignment, a condition that results in a double-image visual effect that will produce eyestrain.

One should strictly avoid zoom binoculars having variable power; they are always heavy and tend–have terrible optics. One should also avoid binoculars with tilt-lever focusing; they usually don't focus very closely, and, being generally cheap, tend to be loosely and poorly constructed. Similarly, avoid "universal focus" or "focus-free" optics that are pre-focused for moderate distance; it is impossible to adjust focus for close or extremely distant objects. Similarly, birders should buy binoculars that focus at least as close as about 15 feet or so; some models now focus down to less than 10 feet. Other binocular types to be avoided are those with individual-focus (as opposed to central-focus), and those that are either too small or too large to be easily hand-held and focused. Persons with small hands or children may, however, find small glasses more comfortable than standard-size ones.

Many "hard-core" bird-watchers own at least two pairs of binoculars of varied designs and powers, and some also invest in "spotting scopes" rather than using very high-power binoculars. These scopes usually are of 20-power to 30-power, with front lens diameters of at least 70 mm. and when used with a sturdy tripod are wonderful for identification of birds at great distances. However, they are quite expensive; the better models usually costing $500-$1,000 or more, and weigh several pounds. Zoom optics on the best of these scopes can be excellent, but there is a reduction in light transmission at the higher magnifications. Various models of Kowa scopes (TSN-2, TSN-4) are especially favored by birders, but are fairly expensive. Celestron calls theirs "long view" eyepieces and Kowa's are called "LER" eyepieces. A solid tripod, such as the 8-pound Bogen 3021 or the lighter Davis & Sandford RTS, is essential for use with spotting scopes.

Binoculars and other optics are often reviewed in the periodical "Better View Desired", published by Whole Life Systems, P.O. Box 162, Rehoboth, NM 87322; free sample issues are sent on request, and back-issues are available. Binoculars and telescopes can be purchased in many sporting-goods and discount stores, but wise shoppers will investigate mail-order sources. B. & H. Photo of New York (213/807-7474) is one of the trustworthy New York discount houses, but considerable care should be exercised when dealing with any of these outlets, which are notorious for their bait-and-switch tactics. An excellent catalog, with good prices and much technical information on choosing binoculars and spotting scopes, including comparative weight, field-of-view, eye-relief and near-focus data, is available from Eagle Optics, 716 S. Whitney Way, Madison, WI 53711 (608/271-4751). Their staff also provides excellent advice. The American Birding Association's (A.B.A.) sales catalog (800/578-0607) is quite informative, but their prices are not quite so competitive as are those of Eagle Optics. Other reliable mail-order houses that provide informative catalogs are Christophers, Ltd. 2401 Tee Circle, Suite 106, Norman, OK 73069 (800/356-6603) and National Camera Exchange, 9300 Olsen Highway, Golden Valley, MN 55427 (800/624-8107).

Besides optical equipment, many bird-watchers use cassette tape-recorders or tape-players. The A.B.A. sales catalog (see phone number above) has a very good selection of bird-songs on cassette tapes and CD recordings. Pre-recorded tapes are extremely useful for learning bird songs and other vocalizations, and may also be valuable tools for playback in the field, to stimulate responses from species that are normally difficult to see, such as rails or owls. Indeed, for such birds playback of vocalizations may be the only practical means of detecting the species' presence in an area.

Various recorded "field guides" to bird songs are now commercially available, including both CDs and DVDs. There are also CD-ROMs that provide both vocalizations and illustrations, usually along with individual range maps and other information on each species. One of these is "Birds of North America" by Thayer Birding Software (for Windows only) that not only provides quizzes and side-by-side species comparisons, but also includes the entire text of *The Birder's Handbook* by Paul Erlich et al. (see below). Another, the "National Audubon Society Interactive CD-ROM Guide to North American Birds" also includes quizzes, and is available in either Windows or Macintosh versions.

Some CD-ROMs offer convenient regional checklists for personal record-keeping, or provide national, continental, or even world-wide checklists or distributional information in computerized form. The A.B.A. catalogs list many of these, as well as variety of videos on field identification.

Reference Materials

Besides optical equipment, every person interested in birds needs some references for aid in identifying birds and, depending on level of interest, learning more about them than their names. At minimum, a field guide suitable for carrying along in a pocket or pouch is needed. Since the development of the first modern field guide by Roger T. Peterson in the 1930s, a veritable host of field guides have been published.

Persons in Nebraska are faced with the fact that our state lies in the transition zone between North American eastern and western avifaunas, and as a result neither R. T. Peterson's eastern or western field guide is entirely adequate for this region. Based on 40 years of teaching ornithology, I have come to recommend that beginning students use *Birds of North America*, by Chandler Robbins and others, published by Golden Books. It is relatively inexpensive, easy to use, and covers all North American birds. Its paintings and range maps are adequate, and its organization is excellent. For more advanced birders I recommend the National Geographic Society's *Field Guide to the Birds of North America*. It is larger and considerably more expensive (about $22.00) than the Golden Books guide, but has better paintings and range maps, and shows a much larger number of plumage variations (races, plumage "morphs" such as melanistic or leucistic variants), and has better descriptive captions. However, it is somewhat daunting for beginning birders, and is thus not a good "starter" choice.

One easily used photo-based guide (2001) is Ken Kaufman's *Birds of North America*, and excellent for birding newcomers, as it is small, well organized, and comprehensive. Another popular book by Fred Sibley is "*The Sibley Guide to Birds,*" and is notable for its many painted views of diverse plumages and different viewing angles. It is published by the National Audubon Society and A. A. Knopf. Eastern and western versions are also available.

Bird-finding guides to many states are now becoming increasingly popular; many of these are described in a catalog sold by the American Birding Association (see address below). There are more than 400 Nebraska birding sites posted on the following website: http://www.nebraskabirdingtrails.com, which was primarily written by the present author for the Nebraska Partnership for Bird Conservation and duplicates much of the information here. The locations on the website do include some not on this hard-copy version, and often have detailed site maps and tourism-related information such as nearby accommodations.

In 2004 the Nebraska Game and Parks Commission published a special 178-page issue of *Nebraskaland* titled "Birding Nebraska," which details over 60 major birding sites in the state, and has a fairly complete checklist of the state's birds. The Game & Parks website also has much useful information for birders; including a photo gallery of Nebraska birds: http://www.ngpc.state.ne.us/homepage.html. The Patuxent Wildlife Research Center has a valuable website, "Patuxent Bird Identification InfoCenter", with photos, songs, videos, maps and life history information on most North American birds: http://www.mbr-pwrc.usgs.gov/Infocenter/infocenter.html. A corresponding and equally useful identification guide is available through Cornell University's Laboratory of Ornithology website: http://www.birds.cornell.edu/programs/AllAboutBirds/BirdGuide/

Bird enthusiasts in Nebraska have traditionally had a very limited choice of state and regional references to exploit. The 200-plus breeding species occurring in Nebraska have been documented in my book *The Birds of the Great Plains: The Breeding Species and their Distribution* (University of Nebraska Press). A county-by-county historical summary of the breeding birds of the state may be found in James Ducey's *Nebraska Birds: Breeding Status and Distribution* (see references for complete citation). A new book, *Birds of Nebraska*, by Roger Sharpe and others, is out of print but often available through used-book dealers (Sharpe *et al.* 2001). Breeding bird surveys done in Nebraska during the 1980s (1984-1989) have been published (Mollhoff, 2001). Up-to-date information on the sightings of unusual birds in Nebraska (and other states or regions) is available on the Internet via the general birding website *www.birdingonthe.net/*

Magazines and other periodicals offer a more up-to-date source of information than do books, and there are several to choose from. One of the best bird magazines for amateur birders is *Birder's World,* a beautifully illustrated monthly magazine published by Birder's World Inc. 44 E. 8th St Suite 410 Holland, Michigan 49423-3502. Another attractive magazine is published for members by the American Birding

Association (A.B.A.), Box 6599, Colorado Springs, CO. 80904. As noted earlier the A.B.A. also sells a large variety of bird-oriented books, optical equipment, and recordings of natural sounds, with member discounts. The bimonthly *Bird Watcher's Digest,* published in Marion, Ohio, is produced in a format similar to *Reader's Digest,* and has less in the way of colored illustrations but many interesting articles. An attractively illustrated quarterly magazine, *The Living Bird,* is sent to members of the Laboratory of Ornithology, 159 Sapsucker Woods Road, Ithaca, N.Y. 14850. It is similar to *Birder's World* in format, but often includes updates on the laboratory's various research and bird-monitoring programs, such as Project Feederwatch, Project Tanager, and the Nestbox Network. Members of the National Audubon Society can subscribe to the bimonthly *American Birds* (previously titled *Audubon Society Field Notes*), which summarizes seasonal bird sightings across North America, and also publishes results of the annual Christmas Count bird surveys.

For more serious-minded readers there are several organizations and related journals from which to choose. In Nebraska one may wish to join the Nebraska Ornithologists' Union (current treasurer Elizabeth Grenon, 1409 Childs Rd. East, Bellevue, NE 68005; annual dues $15.00), and receive the quarterly *Nebraska Bird Review,* which emphasizes observations on Nebraska bird species and populations. The N.O.U. also publishes a periodic newsletter and has spring and fall "field days". Its homepage website is *http://www.noubirds.org/Birds/Birds.aspx,* which includes bird checklists for all 93 counties. And lists of relevant publications There are also several national organizations for serious birders, such as American Ornithologist's Union (P.O. Box 1897, Lawrence, KS 66044-8897). The AOU publishes *The Auk,* a very technically written quarterly journal containing research papers.

Vernacular and Technical Names of Birds

In scanning any field guide or other reference on birds, the reader will soon encounter two sets of names. One will be the English vernacular or "common" name, such as American robin. Such names (often capitalized in bird books and magazines), are the official names given the species by a group such as the American Ornithologists' Union or the American Birding Association. Such uniform names are needed to avoid confusion, such as that caused by having several commonly used names for a single species such as the red-tailed hawk (*e.g.* the eastern red-tailed hawk, western red-tail, Harlan's hawk, Krider's hawk, Fuertes' red-tail and even, in rural areas, the inappropriate name "chicken hawk"). Occasionally there are necessary changes in vernacular names, as when what had been considered a single species (such as the previously recognized northern oriole) is "split" into two species (namely, the Baltimore and Bullock's orioles). Conversely, what had been two or more previously recognized species (such as the slate-colored, white-winged, gray-headed and Oregon juncos) are "lumped" into a single species (the currently recognized dark-eyed junco). This may cause some confusion to readers, but is sometimes necessary in order to keep the vernacular names of birds in line with current ornithological research.

Even more confusing to most readers are the "scientific" or technical names of birds. These Latin or Latinized names are needed for scientists around the world who speak diverse national languages to be able to communicate effectively. Thus, the European robin is known as the *Rotkelchen* in Germany and the *rouge-gorge* in France, but is recognized by scientists as *Erithacus rubecula* in all these countries. Even in English-speaking countries potential confusion exists. Thus, the European robin is a quite different species from the American robin (*Turdus migratorius),* and in Australia the so-called magpies (*Gymnorhina*) are totally different from the magpies (*Pica*) of North America. To avoid such confusion and to provide a basis for a universal nomenclature, scientists have given all of the "kinds" of animals and plants names. These names are a combination of a general or "generic" name (singular = genus, plural = genera) and a specific name (the species, which is the same in singular and plural). The combination of a generic name and specific name represents a unique two-part or "binomial name," such as *Turdus migratorius* for the American robin and *Erithacus rubecula* for the European robin. Of these two components, the generic name comes first and is always capitalized, and the specific name comes second and is never capitalized. Sometimes a third name is added, which designates a recognizable geographic race or subspecies. Like the species, this name is never capitalized and sometimes is exactly the same as the species' name. as in the eastern race of the American robin *Turdus migratorius migratorius.* and its western race *Turdus migratorius propinquus.* Such triple names are called trinomials.

There may also be plumage variations that are not given formal recognition in the scientific name, such as genetically variable plumage morphs (commonly also called "phases"). Thus the "blue goose", a genetically-controlled morph of the lesser snow goose is not now recognized as a separate subspecies, although it once was. Occasionally distinctive subspecies or genetically recognizable morphs are given separate but unofficial vernacular designations, such as the greater and lesser races of the snow goose and sandhill cranes, or the variably melanistic (Harlan's) and albinistic (Krider's) morphs of the red-tailed hawk, the latter is sometimes considered an endemic Great Plains subspecies.

At "higher" levels of scientific nomenclature representing categories "above" that of the genus, one encounters progressively larger classification categories containing varied numbers of species and genera, such as the subfamily (which consistently ends in the suffix "inae"), the still larger family (which always ends in "idae"), and the even larger order (which generally ends in "iformes"). Although learning scientific names may seem daunting, at least by knowing that all the species within a single genus are believed by scientists to be close relatives, some understanding of basic bird relationships may be gained. The same applies to genera within a family or families within an order.

National and international committees on biological nomenclature make recommendations as to the most appropriate sequence for listing all such categories and naming their component subdivisions. Complete agreement on these matters and their adoption has yet to be reached by the appropriate committees of all the world's ornithological organizations. Nevertheless, the familiar so-called "Wetmore" (after its originator, Alexander Wetmore) sequence, beginning with flightless birds and loons, and ending with the sparrows and finch-like birds, is generally used in North America and is followed by most field guides and species lists.

Backyard Birding Opportunities

For those persons not interested in traveling far afield to do their bird-watching many opportunities exist for backyard observations. Feeding wild birds is an increasingly popular pastime, and usually allows for close-up viewing of many species, especially during winter. Most feeders allow for seeds such as sunflower seeds (for cardinals and other sparrow-like birds with crushing bills); house sparrows can be deterred from using such feeders by attaching free-hanging monofilament lines around their perimeters. There are also feeders designed to hold small seeds such as thistles (suitable for goldfinches and other small-billed finches) and sugar-water dispensers for hummingbirds. Few hummingbirds stop in Nebraska except along the Missouri River, but once they start to visit a feeder they are likely to remember its location from season to season. Several good books on bird feeding exist, such as *Birds at Your Feeder*, by Erica Dunn & D. Tessaglia-Hymes (W.W.Norton & Co.), and *Wild About Birds: The DNR Bird Feeding Guide* by C. L. Henderson, published in 1995 by the Minnesota Dept. of Natural Resources, St. Paul, MN. Project Feeder-Watch of Cornell's Laboratory of Ornithology (address given earlier) provides a way of contributing useful information on backyard birds to a national database.

Just as important as regularly maintained feeders is a clean water source, such as a birdbath or pool. Heated birdbaths, fountains and pools that provide a source of constantly dripping or flowing water are especially attractive to birds. Moving water provides a seemingly irresistible attraction for many birds, especially during migration periods. Although "drippers" and "misters" (which spray a fine mist on nearby leaves) are commercially available, simple but effective drippers can be easily made by using a gallon or two-gallon jug, poking one or two tiny holes in its lid, filling it with water, and hanging it above a bird-bath, so the water slowly drips down to the basin below. Different species (such as hummingbirds) seem to be attracted to misters than those favoring drippers, but both are very effective as bird attractants.

Nest boxes offer an additional way of attracting birds during the breeding season. These include not only the traditional wren houses, but also (especially on acreages) bluebird houses, owl houses, wood duck houses, and other nest sites for hole-nesting birds. Although wren houses can be readily purchased, these larger houses often have to be made. Various books on attracting birds to artificial nest sites, such *as How to Attract Birds*, published by Ortho Books and often sold in garden supply houses, will provide directions. The Wild Bird Habitat Stores of Lincoln, Nebraska and elsewhere, usually have this or similar publications, and also offer a wide array of bird foods and other reference materials. It is important to know that attracting house wrens to one's property will likely cause severe nest losses to other small bird species, especially cavity nesters such as bluebirds. This is a result of the wrens' tendency to take over other birds' nests, often piercing their eggs or even killing the young or adults. Because of this, attracting house wrens on one's property is discouraged, especially if bluebirds, chickadees, tree swallows and similar cavity-nesting species are desired.

Brush piles of dead branches and twigs are also attractive to many small birds, since these piles offer protection from the cold and from certain predators, such as accipiter hawks. Likewise dead trees, although they may be an eyesore or potential hazard on a small lot, are favored by cavity-nesters, and on large acreages can be very attractive. An excellent habitat-related booklet is *Landscaping for Wildlife,* published by the Minnesota Dept. of Natural Resources, 500 Lafayette Rd, Box 7, St. Paul, MN 55155(800-657-3757). This department has also published *Woodworking for Wildlife* , with many nest box designs and construction diagrams. Both are collectively available for $9.95.

Monitoring Bird Populations

Bird-banding data have proven abundantly that birds often have rather short lives; a five-year old American robin is unusual, and a ten-year-old is almost unheard of. A few groups of birds, generally larger species that are effectively protected by habitat or law, such as many seabirds, swans, cranes, and some others, may have life spans that approach those of humans. Yet, accidents, diseases, predators, starvation and inclement weather all take their toll on wild bird populations, regardless of human efforts to help. In many areas of North America the brown-headed cowbird, a "brood parasite" that lays its eggs in other species' nests and reduces the breeding success of its unwitting hosts, has had devastating effects on many native songbirds as it has expanded its range out of its native Great Plains. Although adapted to prairie and forest edge habitats, forest fragmentation caused by lumbering, road construction, and similar activities has placed many forest-adapted species at risk to such parasitism. Based on Breeding Bird Surveys, the breeding species that are most increasing in Nebraska are the wild turkey, Canada goose, and merlin, whereas the most declining grassland-adapted species are the Henslow's sparrow, grasshopper sparrow, short-eared owl, greater prairie-chicken, field sparrow, eastern meadowlark, Brewer's sparrow, chestnut-collared longspur and lark sparrow. Grassland-adapted species have declined greater nationally than have any other of the ecological categories recognized by the Fish and Wildlife Service, with 75 percent of the grassland species undergoing population declines. The four most common breeding species in Nebraska are the western meadowlark, house sparrow, mourning dove and red-winged blackbird; all appear to be declining.

Monitoring populations of legally hunted species is the responsibility of national conservation groups such as the U.S. Fish and Wildlife Service, but little effort is made by such groups to monitor populations of songbirds. Here the amateur birder can actively assist, by participating in annual Christmas Bird Counts or Breeding Bird Counts (National Audubon Society), doing Breeding Bird Surveys during June (Biological Resources Division, USGS), helping with systematic counts at bird feeders (Project FeederWatch of the Laboratory of Ornithology), or maintaining long-term records of the bird populations of a specific location. The Office of Migratory Bird Management of the U.S. Fish and Wildlife Service sponsors a Partners in Flight program that concentrates on needs for monitoring and conserving populations of migratory birds; its activities include organizing workshops, educational programs and bird-related outdoor activities. In conjunction with this program, The Nebraska Game and Parks Commission participates in the International Migratory Bird Day in May. This often occurs during the same weekend as the Audubon Society's annual Birdathon weekend, which encourages a variety of conservation and bird-awareness activities at the peak of spring migration. Bird-banding activities go on at various nature centers such as at Fontenelle Forest in Bellevue, Neale Woods in Omaha, and Lincoln's Pioneer Park Nature Center. Volunteers are sometime allowed to become trained in helping to remove captured birds from nets or traps, prior to their banding. Holding a wild bird and releasing it again is a rare and joyful experience for many people, and serves a valuable scientific purpose as well.

Bird diseases, such as the bacterial-carried eye disease that mainly affects the vision of house finches in eastern and central states, and the outbreaks of fowl cholera that regularly occur each spring among waterfowl in south-central Nebraska, are some of the conspicuous avian mortality factors that can be observed and documented fairly easily. For example, persons observing at bird feeders have helped to document the spread of eye disease among house finches in mid-western and eastern states. Accidents such as deaths caused by birds flying into windows can be avoided or at least ameliorated by affixing parallel strips of conspicuously colored tape along the inner surface of the window (silhouette cutouts of owls or hawks do little good), or by allowing similar plastic strips to hang down freely from the tops of window sills. Free-ranging cats kill millions of wild birds every year; de-clawing pet cats helps to reduce such needless mortality.

The Wachiska chapter also organizes birding outings, Christmas Bird Counts, Birdathons, rare bird alerts, bird-identification classes, prairie preservation and appreciation activities, and related conservation programs. In Omaha similar activities are performed by the Audubon Society of Omaha, (Center Mall, 1941 S. 42nd St #501, Omaha 68105, ph. 402/342-1345), and in Kearney the Big Bend chapter (P.O. Box 1575, Kearney 68848) helps organize the annual spring river conference each March. There is also a Wildcat Audubon chapter in Scottsbluff, and a Loess Hills chapter in Sioux City (P.O. Box 5133, Sioux City 51102). Phone numbers or contact people for these smaller groups can be obtained from the state office at Spring Creek Prairie: Audubon Nebraska, P.O. Box 117, Denton, Ne (402/793-2301).

Establishing and patrolling bluebird nest box trails has had a major effect on restoring the eastern bluebird as a breeding species in Nebraska, and has also similarly benefited tree swallows. The organization Bluebirds Across Nebraska is the sponsor of this program throughout the state, and in Lincoln it is coordinated through the local Wachiska chapter of the Audubon Society (402/486-4846). Many states have raptor rehabilitation centers that try to heal and release wild hawks and owls that have met with accidents or been shot by thoughtless hunters. In Nebraska the Fontenelle Forest Raptor Recovery Center is the state headquarters of these important activities. (402/731-3140)

The Audubon Society also sponsors the annual spring Rivers and Wildlife Conference during mid-March in Kearney. Other popular spring bird-related activities occurring during the same month are the Wing Ding celebration at Clay Center in early March, celebrating the waterfowl migration in the Rainwater Basin, and the Wings over the Platte activities in Grand Island during the latter part of March.

Sources of Information on Birding in Nebraska

Sets of individual county road maps (scale 1" or 1/4" per mile) are available from the Nebraska Roads Department (1500 Highway N-2, Lincoln 68509; 402/471-4567) are also extremely useful when exploring back-country areas. An atlas of 79 topographic maps of the entire state (scale 1:200,000, or ca. 1/3" per mile) is available for $16.95 in the *Nebraska Atlas and Gazetteer*, published by DeLorme, PO Box 298, Freeport, ME 04032 (207/865-4171). This atlas also shows state parks and recreation areas, national lands, campgrounds, wildlife viewing areas, fishing, hiking and other attractions.

The author's self-published "*A Nebraska Bird-finding Guide*" has nearly 50 county maps and lists over 400 pubic-access birding sites in the state. It is out of print but may be downloaded free at:. http://digitalcommons.unl.edu/biosciornithology/51. Much of the same information on bird-finding is also now freely available at: www.nebraskabirdingteails.com. This is an interactive web site, with many individual site maps, as well as regional and statewide maps and various searching modes. Other free downloads are:

Birds of the Cedar Point Biological Station Area, Keith and Garden Counties, Nebraska: Seasonal Occurrence and Breeding Data. 1996. (With C. R. Brown, M. B. Brown, J. Kren & W. C. Scharf) http://digitalcommons.unl.edu/biosciornithology/24

Birds of the Central Platte River Valley and Adjacent Counties. 2013. Mary B. Brown & Paul A. Johnsgard Lincoln, NE: Cons. & Survey Div., Inst. of Ag. & Nat. Resources, U. of Nebraska–Lincoln. 182 pp. digitalcommons.unl.edu/zeabook/15/

Birds of the Rainwater Basin, Nebraska. 2012. Joel Jorgensen. Nebraska Game and Parks Commission. http://outdoornebraska.ne.gov/wildlife/programs/nongame/NGBirds/pdf/Birds%20of%20the%2 0Rainwater%20Basin%20Version%201.0%20(May%202012).pdf

Wetland Birds of the Central Plains: South Dakota, Nebraska and Kansas, 2012. P. A. Johnsgard. 275 pp. pp. 2012. Lincoln, NE: Zea E-Books & Univ. of Nebraska Digital Commons http://digitalcommons.unl.edu/zeabook/8/

Wings over the Great Plains: The Central Flyway. 2013. P. A. Johnsgard. Lincoln, NE: Digital Commons, Univ. of Nebraska-Lincoln Libraries. With 7 maps, 49 drawings by P. A. Johnsgard. 249 pp.http://digitalcommons.unl.edu/zeabook/13.

Nebraska's rivers are publicly owned, but the adjoining shorelines are usually in private ownership. Birding from a canoe is possible on several rivers (Niobrara, Dismal, Calamus, Missouri, Platte, Republican), but access points are often limited. The longest stretch of river ideal for canoe-based birding is the 76-mile section of the Niobrara designated as a National Scenic River. The Platte is too shallow over much of its length for good canoeing. Some refuge lakes at Valentine National Wildlife Refuge also offer wonderful birding opportunities from a canoe. Those at Crescent Lake N.W.R. are closed to such activities.

The Nebraska Division of Travel and Tourism (301 Centennial Mall S., Lincoln, NE 68509) can provide free information on general tourist attractions (phone 402/471-3441 or 800/742-7595; from out of state call 800/228-43307. Their website is www.visitnebraska.org, and their email address is tourism@ded2.ded.state.ne.us.). Tourism information and free state highway maps are also available at most Interstate rest areas. Road information can be obtained in-state by calling 800/906-9069; if out-of-state call 402/471-4533. The emergency highway help line is 800/525-5555. State recreation areas usually offer more highly developed recreational facilities and modern camping. Annual park entry permits or more information can be obtained from the Parks Division, Game and Parks Commission, PO Box 30370, Lincoln, NE 68503, (800/826-PARK). District offices are also located in Alliance (308/762-5605), Bassett (402/684-2921), Norfolk (402/370-3374) and North Platte (308-535-8025). The Nebraska Game and Parks Commission's "Land Atlas" is a list of areas owned or leased by the Commission in each Nebraska county and that are available for public access and recreational use: http://sunfish.ngpc.state.ne.us/gpland/gpland.htmls. The Game & Parks website also has much useful information for birders; http://www.ngpc.state.ne.us/homepage.html.

Rare birds seen in Nebraska should be described and reported to the Nebraska Ornithologists' Union (NOU) for documentation in their quarterly journal *Nebraska Bird Review* (editor: Janice Paseka, 1585 Co. Rd. 14. Blvd., Ames Ne 68621: paseka@#tvsonline.net.) The NOU also publishes periodic newsletters for members. It has spring and fall meetings, usually in September and May, at locations favorable for seasonal birding. The NOU web site (address provided earlier in "Reference Materials") has a great deal of useful bird information. NEBirds is a list-serve for reporting recent Nebraska bird sightings and sharing bird information. It is accessible by free subscription by going–the following web site: http://groups.yahoo.com/group/NEBirds/. Click on the link labeled "Join This Group", and provide the requested information. You will have to become a Yahoo member before you can join any group. When you fill out the Yahoo membership information uncheck the boxes relating to receiving information from Yahoo if you want to avoid spam from Yahoo advertisers. Up-to-date information on the sightings of unusual birds in Nebraska (and other states or regions) is also available on the Internet via the general birding website www.birdingonthe.net/

Most federally-owned birding areas in Nebraska consist of national historic sites, national wildlife refuges and national monuments. Federally owned areas also include waterfowl production areas (WPAs). State owned sites include state parks, state recreation areas (SRAs), and wildlife management areas (WMAs). Typically no permit is needed to enter WPAs or WMAs, but annual (or daily) state park entry permits are needed for SRAs and all state parks and state historical parks. One regional national wildlife refuge (DeSoto) also charges a daily entry fee ($3.00). All state wildlife management areas offer free, unrestricted birding or other nature study opportunities. They sometimes provide primitive camping facilities, and most are open to seasonal hunting and fishing.

Nebraska has numbered its 93 counties relative to historic population size (1 = largest, 93 = smallest). The preliminary numbers on car licenses correspond to these numbers, except for a few eastern counties (Lancaster, Douglas & Sarpy), which have replaced these numbers with random three-letter

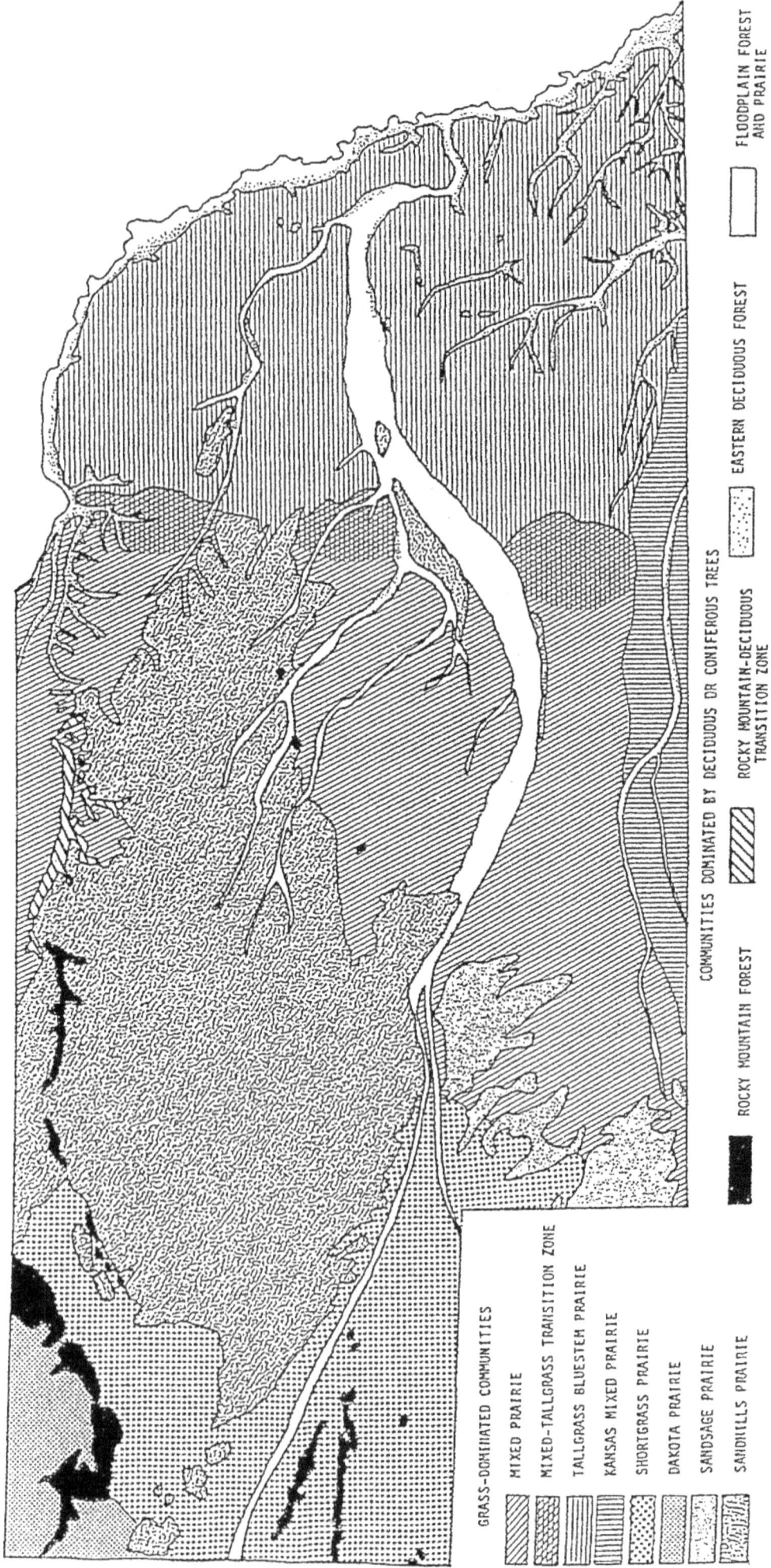

Figure 1. Native vegetation of Nebraska. After a map by Robert Kaul

GRASS-DOMINATED COMMUNITIES

MIXED PRAIRIE

MIXED-TALLGRASS TRANSITION ZONE

TALLGRASS BLUESTEM PRAIRIE

KANSAS MIXED PRAIRIE

SHORTGRASS PRAIRIE

DAKOTA PRAIRIE

SANDSAGE PRAIRIE

SANDHILLS PRAIRIE

COMMUNITIES DOMINATED BY DECIDUOUS OR CONIFEROUS TREES

ROCKY MOUNTAIN FOREST

ROCKY MOUNTAIN-DECIDUOUS TRANSITION ZONE

EASTERN DECIDUOUS FOREST

FLOODPLAIN FOREST AND PRAIRIE

Figure 2. Landforms of Nebraska. After a map by the U. of Nebraska Conservation and Survey Division

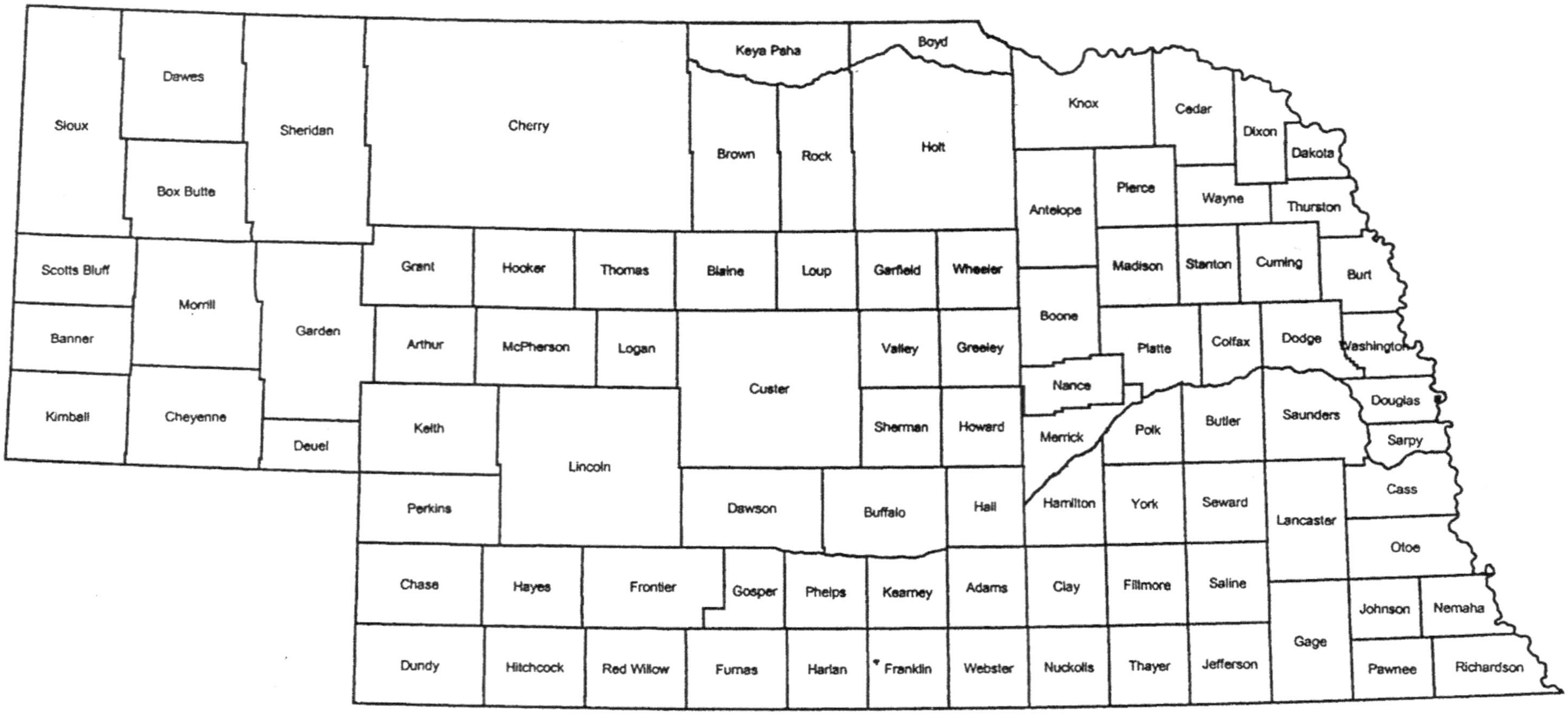

Figure 3. Nebraska county names

combinations. The state's emergency highway help line is 1-800-525-5555. Its cellular phone hotline is 55 (star 55). Road reports are available in-state via 1-800-906-9069. From Omaha dial 553-5000, and from out of state dial (402)471-4533. The State Patrol Citizen Band Call Letters are KNE 0911. The statewide Crime Stoppers number is 1-800-422-1494.

Part 2: The Birds of Nebraska

INTRODUCTION

This summary of the birds of Nebraska grew out of the research associated with the writing of my *Birds of the Great Plains: Breeding Species and Their Distribution* (University of Nebraska Press, 1979). Inasmuch as the only previous comprehensive summary of Nebraska's birds, the "Revised Check-list of Nebraska Birds" (*Occasional Papers of the Nebraska Ornithologists' Union*, 1958) was about 40 years old, and has since received only a minimal revision that covered the period to 1970, it seemed apparent to me that a completely new list of birds of the state should be prepared.

For my present purposes this list has been restricted to those species that have been convincingly reported at least once in Nebraska from historic time to the present. It has also been modified in its current revision to conform very closely in that regard to the most recent Nebraska Ornithologists' Union's "Official list of the birds of Nebraska" (Brogie, 2010; NOU Records Committee, 2011 and annual updates). Many important records of Nebraska's birds are published in the official journal of the Nebraska Ornithologists' Union (N.O.U.), the *Nebraska Bird Review*. Because of the amazing proliferation of records (and birders) since the early 2000s, it was impossible for me to summarize individually all of the post-2000 records published in the *Nebraska Bird Review* except for those I considered most important. I also excluded some records of exotic waterfowl that almost certainly were escaped from captivity. The seasonal reports in that journal are by far the most complete and most valuable record of current bird life in Nebraska, and fortunately this journal is now being archived in the University of Nebraska's Digital Commons website.

The N.O.U.'s official state list of birds (455 species as of 2013, including 329 "regular" species, 42 of "casual" occurrence, 68 accidentals, and six extinct or extirpated species) is based on actual specimen evidence or some other convincing basis of each species' proven occurrence in the state. I have followed the N.O.U. species list closely, although my terms of relative abundance and status often differ. Many of the recent state records (especially since 2005) of relatively rare species have not been individually mentioned in this present summary; these have been fully summarized through 2000 by Sharpe *et al.* (2001), and more recently in the periodic additions to the "Official" list as summarized in the *Nebraska Bird Review*. The latest American Ornithologists' Union taxonomy (*AOU Check-list of North American Birds*, 7th edition and later supplements) is followed here.

Many of Nebraska's birds are declining, and one of the best lines of evidences on population trends are the annual Breeding Bird Surveys, which began in 1966, Where there are statistically significant (95% p.) trend data available from the most recent summary (1966–2011), I have included this information, at least for the more typical Nebraska species. Migration data summaries here in most cases were based on published data from the 1930's to the mid-1980s,

Because of climate change, the spring medians should probably be adjusted to about 10 days earlier, and the fall medians to about 10-20 days later.

Vegetation and Topography of Nebraska

Lying near the center of the Great Plains of North America, Nebraska shows a variety of geographic and ecologic influences on its bird fauna. Of its approximately 200 breeding species, the largest single component is arboreal, or adapted to living in trees, woodlands and forests, while limnic (aquatic and shoreline-adapted) species make up the second largest component. Species primarily associated with grasslands comprise a still smaller breeding component, and xeric-adapted forms associated with semi-desert scrub are the least numerous *(Prairie Naturalist* 10: 97-112). Most of Nebraska's arboreal species of birds, which comprise about 45 percent of the state's total species, are eastern or northern in their geographic breeding affinities, while a small percentage are western or southern in origin. Of the limnic-adapted forms, which make up about 32 percent of the state's total avifauna, a considerable proportion are either northern or widespread (pandemic) in breeding distributional affinities, and many of these are only migrants in the state. Species especially associated with natural grasslands, which made up the largest single original vegetational component in the state, comprise only about 10 percent of the state's total avifauna, and the remaining species are mostly rather general in their ecological breeding requirements.

In its original state, probably close to 90 percent of the land area of Nebraska was covered by native grasslands. Of the total land area of 77,510 square miles, more than a fifth, or 19,000 square miles, are comprised of the Sandhills grasslands. Other major grassland components are the tallgrass bluestem prairie of the eastern third of the state, the mixed prairie generally lying to the west of the tallgrass prairies, the sandsage prairie of southwestern Nebraska, the Kansas mixed prairie of the southernmost counties of Nebraska, the Dakota prairie of the Pine Ridge area, and the shortgrass prairie of the high plains in western Nebraska.

The surface topography of Nebraska is primarily that of a slightly inclined plane, sloping from west to east at an average gradient of about nine feet per mile. The state's elevations range from more than 5,000 feet in the Panhandle region to about 825 feet in the extreme southeast. Precipitation likewise increases from the northwest to the southeast, from about 15–33 inches of total annual precipitation. The two largest river valleys in the state are the Missouri Valley and the Platte Valley, which both tend to be quite broad and fairly shallow, while the Niobrara Valley in the northern part of the state tends to be deeper and narrower, the shorelines often lined with steep bluffs. Bluffs and escarpments are also typical of the Pine Ridge area in the northern panhandle, the Wildcat Hills in Scotts Bluff and Banner counties, and the upper portions of the North Platte Valley.

Several species of Nebraska birds have become extirpated as an apparent result of human activities since settlement times, and many relatively specialized species have undergone considerable retraction of ranges as wetlands have disappeared and natural vegetation has given way to agriculture, urbanization, and other disturbances. Other generalist species, such as various "blackbirds" (including starlings and cowbirds) and crows, have benefited from these same changes. The increasing development of riparian woodlands along the Platte and other river systems crossing the plains has also facilitated east-to-west range changes in forest-adapted birds, and reservoirs such as Lake McConaughy have attracted many new species (especially gulls) to the state in recent years. The appearance of some of the other new species on the list has perhaps been influenced by increased bird-feeding activities by the general public, and new information resulting from increased recreational bird-watching.

Definitions of Terms Used in the Text
Terms of Temporal Occurrence

Permanent Resident. Present throughout the year and presumably breeding.

Summer Resident. Present during the summer, presumably breeding, but migrating out of the state for part of the year.

Migrant. Passing through the state in spring or fall or both, but normally not remaining through summer or winter. The term "straggler" is used for rare migrants, or individuals of regular migrant species that sometimes remain in the area beyond their normal period.

Vagrant. Refers to species normally resident or migratory in other areas, individuals of which sometimes stray well outside their range and are of accidental occurrence in the state.

Winter visitor. Species normally present in the area only between November 1 and May 1. The term "late winter visitor or spring migrant" refers to those species usually not appearing until mid-January and sometimes remaining until late May.

Terms of Relative Abundance

Abundant. Present in such quantity that large numbers are likely to be encountered daily during the proper season and in appropriate habitats.

Common. Present in such quantity that several are likely to be encountered daily during the proper season and in appropriate habitats.

Uncommon. A few are likely to be seen each year by visiting the appropriate habitats.

Occasional. Not observed every year, but reported more than 50 times in the state.

Rare. Up to 50 state records for the species exist.

Extremely Rare. Up to 25 state records for the species exist. "Very rare" is a comparable term, but is not based on a count of actual records.

Accidental. Up to 5 state records for the species exist.

Hypothetical. Evidence of occurrence in the state is still inadequate.

Extirpated. The species rarely if ever now occurs in the state, but once was more numerous.

Extinct. The species is no longer alive anywhere.

Terms of Geographic or Ecological Distribution

Arboreal. The species is associated with woodlands and forests.

Endemic. The species is essentially limited to a particular region or habitat.

Limnic. The species is associated with aquatic environments.

Montane. The species is associated with mountains.

Pandemic. The species has a wide distribution, sometimes throughout the continent.

Pelagic. The species is associated with open oceans.

Xeric. The species is associated with deserts or dry climates.

List of Species

Family Tinamidae

(Elegant (Crested) Tinamou)   *Eudromia elegans*

Unsuccessfully introduced into Nebraska. Birds of this species were released in Dundy County in 1970. There were no sightings after approximately five months following release (*Nebraska Bird Review* 39:39).

Family Anatidae

Black-bellied Whistling-Duck   *Dendrocygna autumnalis*
Extremely rare. A duck hunter killed a male of this species near Ong, Clay County, on October 29, l989 (*Nebraska Bird Review* 58:9l), and two were seen in Lancaster County in 1993 (*Nebraska Bird Review* 61:136). There were 14 records through 2011 (*Nebraska Bird Review* 80:89),.

Taiga Bean-Goose   *Anser fabalis*
Accidental. Photographed at DeSoto National Wildlife Refuge from December 29, l984–January 10, l985 (*Nebraska Bird Review* 53:3). Also reported April 4, 1998, Funk Lagoon (Brogie, 1999).

Pink-footed Goose   *Anser brachyrhynchus*
Hypothetical. Photographed at Harvard Marsh, January 30, 2006, but unproven to have been from a wild bird (*Nebraska Bird Review* 75:91).

Greater White-fronted Goose   *Anser albifrons*
A common spring and fall migrant throughout Nebraska, becoming abundant in the central Platte Valley and Rainwater Basin. Migrants occur throughout the Plains States, but are more common in western and central areas than toward the east.
Migration. Twenty-nine initial spring sightings are from February 12 to May 12, with a median of March 12. Seventeen final spring sightings are from March 23 to May 18, with a median of April 14. Nineteen initial fall sightings are from September 14 to November 21, with a median of October 23. Fifteen final fall sightings are from October 12 to December 29, with a median of November 6.
Habitats. Migrants are associated with large marshes, shallow lakes, wide rivers with bars and islands, and adjacent agricultural grain fields.
Comments. This fine goose, often called "specklebelly" by hunters, concentrates in the Platte Valley in spring, with estimates during the late 1900's of up to about 80 percent of the entire mid-continent population then concentrated in the state. More recently it has become much less common there in spring. It breeds in the high arctic, often near colonies of snow geese, but is not a colonial nester.

Snow Goose   *Chen caerulescens*
A spring and fall migrant throughout Nebraska, less common westwardly but abundant in the Missouri River Valley and, recently, the central Platte Valley. The bluish morph ("blue goose") and less common intermediate (heterozygotic) types comprise about a third of the total population in eastern Nebraska, but are much less frequent westward. Migrants are abundant throughout the Plains States during spring and fall, particularly in the Missouri River Valley, which supported a mid-continental population of about five million birds in the early 2000s.
Migration. Thirty-six initial spring sightings range from January 8 to March 28, with a median of March 9. Twenty-six final spring sightings are from March 6 to May 20, with a median of April 20. Forty initial fall sightings are from August 19 to December 16, with a median of October 4. Thirty-eight final fall sightings are from October 26 to December 31, with a median of December 2.
Habitats. Marshes, sloughs, river bottom meadows and croplands such as corn fields are used on migration. Lakes or reservoirs near croplands are also utilized.
Comments. Snow geese in the Great Plains have increased tremendously in the past few decades; current populations of about five million birds are more than their tundra breeding grounds can support The birds have also shifted their migration route somewhat farther west to the Central Platte Valley, especially during spring. Peak numbers during fall at DeSoto National Wildlife Refuge sometimes reached 800,000 birds about a decade ago, and more recently up to a million or more snow geese may stopover in March on large Rainwater Basin marshes, such as Harvard and Funk wildlife management areas.

Ross's Goose   *Chen rossii*

An increasingly common and regular spring and fall migrant in the state. It is present each spring in the Rainwater Basin wetlands, at Plattsmouth Game Management Area in Cass County and many other eastern and Platte Valley counties, typically in the company of large flocks of snow geese. Ross's geese comprised an estimated two percent of the carcasses among 1,200 white geese killed by a tornado passing near York, on March 13, 1990 (*Nebraskaland* 68(2): 34-41, 1991). As many as 5,600 birds have been seen at a single location, and Ross's geese now make up 2-3 percent of Nebraska snow goose flocks (Johnsgard, 2012). This goose is now a regular and uncommon migrant throughout the Plains States.

Migration. Six spring records are from March 10 to April 13, with a mean of March 29. Five fall records are from November 10 to December 22, with a mean of November 26.

Habitats. Found in the same habitats as snow geese.

Comments. These tiny geese are easily overlooked among the vast flocks of snow geese with which they associate. Apparent hybrids between the species have been seen often. A very few blue-morph Ross's geese have been seen recently in Nebraska (*Nebraska Bird Review* 66:19), the genes perhaps entering the gene pool via hybridization with blue-morph snow geese.

Emperor Goose   *Chen canagica*

Accidental. A specimen was found dead at Harvard Waterfowl Management Area during the spring of 1997 (*Nebraska Bird Review.* 66:149, 153).

Brant   *Branta bernicla*

Extremely rare. Besides some early records for Buffalo and Hamilton counties; recent sight records are for Webster, (1960), Nemaha, (1959), Adams (1957) and Kearney counties (1998). Rare fall migrant at Lake McConaughy (Brown, Dinsmore and Brown, 2012). There are records for both the eastern (*bernicla*) and western (*nigricans*) taxa, with four records for the latter (*Nebraska Bird Review* 79:49).

Cackling Goose.   *Branta hutchinsii.*

Common spring (early March to mid-April) and fall (early October to early December) migrant, especially in the central Platte Valley. Swenk (*Nebraska Bird Review* 2:103-116, 1934) classified 17 of 404 Nebraska-shot Canada goose specimens as *hutchinsii*. He classified the majority of the birds as intermediate *leucopareia,* which would probably include the forms represented by the present-day taxa *parvipes* and *taverneri* (the latter now part of *hutchinsii*). Typical *hutchinsii* types are very common in the Rainwater Basin (*Nebraska Bird Review*, 74:99–105), and some wintering may occur in southwestern Nebraska and adjacent western Kansas.

Canada Goose   *Branta canadensis*

A common to abundant migrant throughout Nebraska with widespread breeding and local overwintering. Canada geese have been released widely, and breeding now occurs throughout the state. Overwintering is now normal in the Platte Valley and some cities, especially the larger races. These larger birds include many intergrades of *B. c. maxima* and *B. c. moffitti*, and possibly *B. c. interior* (*Nebraska Bird Review* 74:99–105).

Migration. Forty-five initial spring sightings are from January 4 to April 3, with a median of March 27. Forty-one final spring sightings are from March 19 to May 30, with a median of April 28. Fifty-three initial fall sightings are from July 28 to December 20, with a median of October 13. Fifty-four final fall sightings are from October 18 to December 31, with a median of December 10.

Habitats. Migrant birds are found on large marshes, lakes or reservoirs, and nearby grain fields. Breeding is typical on prairie marshes, or sometimes on larger lakes with islands or muskrat houses.

Comments. These fine geese have become widespread breeders in Nebraska in recent years, having adapted to small farm ponds and city park lagoons as well as spreading through the Sandhills' wetlands. Smaller races that breed in Canada are also abundant migrants through the state, and up to 100,000 may winter in ice-free locations. Separating Canada from the newly recognized cackling goose in Nebraska under field conditions is often very difficult. Breeding Bird Surveys between 1966 and 2011 indicate that the species underwent a significant population increase (8.8% annually) during that period.

Barnacle Goose   *Branta leucopsis*
       Accidental. A specimen was shot in Otoe County during November of 1968 (*Nebraska Bird Review* 37:2). A likely escaped captive was seen in 1998 (*Nebraska Bird Review* 66:34).

(Mute Swan)   *Cygnus olor*
       Hypothetical, Many sightings have almost certainly been of escaped captives, and so far no breedings by seemingly wild birds have been noted (*Nebraska Bird Review* 76:132; 77:49). However, it is very likely that such will occur soon, if it has not already, since the feral Great Lakes population of mute swans has been substantially expanding and increasing.

Trumpeter Swan   *Cygnus buccinator*
       A rare spring and fall migrant and local summer resident in the Sandhills of Nebraska. Probable pair or family-group migrants have also been observed in many western and southern counties. This species originally nested in the state, but was extirpated and apparently absent until the late 1960s, when recolonization occurred as a result of releases made in South Dakota. Nesting has since occurred in many Sandhills lakes, mainly in Cherry and Grant counties, but with breeding-season usage also reported from marshes in Sheridan, Garden and Brown counties. by l995 the Nebraska population totaled about 150 birds. There were seven confirmed nestings during the 1984-1989 atlasing period (Mollhoff, 2001).
       Migration. Eight spring sightings are from January 24 to May 23, with a mean of March 28. Six fall sightings are from August 10 to November 7, with a mean of October 6.
       Habitats. Migrants are found on lakes, large marshes, and impoundments. Breeding occurs on large shallow marshes or lakes having abundant submerged vegetation, emergent plants, and stable water levels. Wetlands used during the breeding season average about 180 acres, with about 75 percent open water and having slight to (infrequently) medium salinity levels.
       Comments. This is the heaviest of all Nebraska's birds, and perhaps the most regal. These swans prefer to nest on large Sandhills marshes having a substantial amount of freedom from human disturbance. The birds are only slightly migratory, sometimes moving south as far as Kansas during winter. Birds seen in the eastern parts of Nebraska probably are associated with of the large Minnesota breeding population, which now extends south into Iowa.

Tundra Swan   *Cygnus columbianus*
       An uncommon or occasional spring and fall migrant in Nebraska, primarily to be expected in eastern and northeastern areas, but rarely observed as far west as Garden and Dawes counties. It is a regular and common migrant in the northern portions of the Plains States.
       Migration. Twenty springs sightings range from January 1 to May 15, with a median of March 27. Eleven fall sightings are from October 21 to December 14, with a median of November 22.
       Habitats. Shallow lakes, marshes and adjacent flooded fields are used by migrants.
       Comments. Previously known as the whistling swan, this species new name reflect a merger with the Bewick's swan of the Old World, and "tundra" describes its breeding habitat very well. Most tundra swans miss Nebraska while migrating, either turning east in Minnesota toward the Atlantic coast, or west in North Dakota toward the Great Salt Lake region of Utah.

Wood Duck   *Aix sponsa*
       An uncommon spring and fall migrant and summer resident in eastern Nebraska, but less common westwardly, and becoming infrequent in the Panhandle and Sandhills. Breeding was originally limited to the Missouri's forested valley and the lower portions of the Platte Valley, probably west to about Kearney. This species is significantly extending its range westwardly, and probable family groups have been seen as far west as Box Butte Reservoir, Dawes County, and the North Platte Valley, Garden and Scotts Bluff County. Breeding mainly occurs in the eastern half of the Plains States, and most migrants are also found in this region.

Migration. Sixty-nine initial spring sightings are from January 17 to June 7, with a median of March 28. Half of the sightings fall within the period March 13 to April 8. Thirty-five final fall sightings are from September 10 to December 31, with a median of October 21. Half of the records fall within the period October 3-30.

Habitats. Throughout the year this species is associated with tree-lined rivers, creeks, oxbows and lakes, and usually breeds near slow-moving rivers, sloughs or ponds where large trees are found.

Comments. Wood ducks have become much more widespread and common in Nebraska recently, both because of nest-box erection programs and also the increasing growth and maturation of riverine forests along major river systems. Breeding Bird Surveys between 1966 and 2011 indicate that the species underwent a significant population increase (2.1% annually) during that period.

Gadwall   *Anas strepera*

A common to abundant spring and fall migrant and a common summer resident in Nebraska, primarily breeding north of the North Platte River and especially in the Sandhills. It also nests south to the Rainwater Basin of Clay and adjacent counties. Breeding also occurs widely in the Dakotas and western Minnesota.

Migration. The range of 48 initial spring sightings is from January 3 to June 8, with a median of March 28. Half of the records fall within the period March 6 to April 8. Fifty final fall sightings range from October 4 to December 31, with a median of November 21. Half of the records fall within the period November 2 to December 2.

Habitats. Migrants are normally found in shallow marshes and sloughs, and sometimes on deeper waters such as lakes and reservoirs. Nesting occurs preferentially on shallow prairie marshes, especially those having grassy or weedy islands or surrounding weedy cover.

Comments. The common name "gray duck" is often used by hunters and fits the bird well, and it is often overlooked by birders whose eyes are first attracted to the more brilliantly plumaged duck species. Breeding Bird Surveys between 1966 and 2011 indicate that the species underwent a significant population increase (2.9 % annually) during that period.

Eurasian Wigeon   *Anas penelope*

Occasional migrant, at least during spring. Besides a single old specimen record from Cuming County (Bruner, Wolcott and Swenk, 1904), the species was reported in Adams County in March of 1955, in Lincoln County in November of 1966, and has also been observed at Valentine National Wildlife Refuge, Cherry County. It has also been reported from Cedar and, Clay counties (Brogie, 1997) and Thayer County (*Nebraska Bird Review* 73:81). One probable hybrid Eurasian x American wigeon has been reported (*Nebraska Bird Review* 66:35). Most records are for March and April, latest is May 2; fall plumages would be difficult to separate from those of the American wigeon. In recent years reports suggest the species to be a regular spring migrant, especially in the Rainwater Basin. As of 2011, there were at least 30 spring records (*Nebraska Bird Review* 79:49).

American Wigeon   *Anas americana*

A common to locally abundant spring and fall migrant throughout Nebraska, and a local and generally uncommon breeder, apparently mostly confined to the northwestern parts of the Sandhills (south and east to Garden and Holt counties). It is a migrant through the Plains States, and often breeds in the Dakotas and Minnesota.

Migration. Sixty-seven initial spring sightings range from January 9 to May 28, with a median of March 22. Half of the sightings fall within the period March 6–30. Thirty-four final spring sightings are from March 27 to June 6, with a median of May 3. Fifty initial fall sightings are from August 28 to December 17, with a median of September 30. Fifty final fall sightings are from October 9 to December 31, with a median of November 18.

Habitats. During migration these birds are sometimes found on large lakes or reservoirs, but forage where submerged plants can easily be reached from the surface or around the shoreline in grassy meadows. Breeding is usually done on marshes or lakes with abundant aquatic food at or near the surface, and especially those with adjacent sedge meadows or brushy, partially wooded habitats nearby.

Comments. This species, which was once called the "baldpate" because of the male's white forehead in breeding plumage, can be easily recognized in flight owing to the brilliant white forewing patches. It often associates with gadwalls, but is more inclined to feed on grassy vegetation along shorelines than are other surface-feeding ducks. Gadwalls and wigeon usually arrive about the same time as green-winged teal in spring, comprising a "second wave" of birds that appear after mallards and pintails. Breeding Bird Surveys between 1966 and 2011 indicate that the species underwent a significant population decline (2.6% annually) during that period.

American Black Duck   *Anas rubripes*

A rare migrant in the eastern half of Nebraska, very rare in the west. Breeding is regular in Minnesota and occasional in North Dakota, and migrants are most commonly encountered in those two states. It is commonly observed at the DeSoto National Wildlife Refuge, on the Washington County to Iowa boundary. It has been observed west to Dawson, Keith and Cherry counties.

Migration. Nine spring records range form March 1 to May 26, with a mean of March 26. There are fall records from August to December 22, and the species has been captured during winter banding operations in eastern Nebraska.

Habitats. Usually found among flocks of mallards in Nebraska, and using the same habitats during migration.

Comments. In Nebraska black ducks are seen only infrequently among mallard flocks, and many of these birds are actually mallard x black duck hybrids. Such hybridization by mallards has threatened the black duck's gene pool over nearly all of the eastern United States, with "pure" black duck populations now restricted to Canada's Atlantic coast.

Mallard   *Anas platyrhynchos*

An abundant migrant and a locally common summer resident throughout Nebraska. Wintering birds are common wherever open water occurs. Migrants occur throughout the Plains States, and breeding occurs locally in all but the southernmost portions. The "Mexican duck" *A. p. diazi* and the mottled duck *A. fulvigula* are both questionable in Nebraska. A specimen attributed to the former taxon was collected in Cherry County in October of 1921, and more recently a possible mottled duck was taken in Rock County in October of 1969 (*Nebraska Bird Review* 38:80). The 1921 specimen has since been proven to be a hybrid (*New. Mex. Dept. Game and Fish Bulletin* 16, 1977), and the mottled duck record is also suspect as to identity—mottled ducks are very hard to distinguish from female mallard x black duck hybrids.

Migration. Forty-three initial spring sighting are from January 1 to May 29, with a median of March 12. Half of the records fall within the period March 2 - April 3. Sixty-four final fall sightings are from August 25 to December 31, with a median of November 27. Half of the sightings fall within the period November 21 - December 28.

Habitats. Breeding birds favor fairly shallow waters, either still or slowly flowing, and surrounding dry areas of non-forested vegetation. Migrants are often found on large marshes, lakes or reservoirs, especially where nearby grain fields provide food.

Comments. The mallard is Nebraska's commonest duck, and probably the most popular species among hunters. It is a hardy bird, usually overwintering in large numbers, and breeding even in locations as unlikely as the heart of Lincoln and Omaha wherever urban lakes and streams allow. Breeding Bird Surveys between 1966 and 2011 indicate that the mottled duck underwent a significant population decline (3.1% annually) during that period. Declining estimates population trends in the mallard were not statistically significant.

Blue-winged Teal   *Anas discors*

An abundant spring and fall migrant and common summer resident throughout Nebraska. Migrants occur throughout the Plains States, and breeding is regular in all but the southernmost areas.

Migration. Sixty-eight initial spring sightings range from February 10 to June 1, with a median of April 2. Half of the sightings fall within the period March 28 to April 10. Eighty-eight final fall sightings are from August 19 to December 31, with a median of October 10. Half of the records fall within the period September 24 to October 23.

Habitats. Migrants are found on generally shallow ponds, ditches, marshes, and the like, and rarely occur in deep open water. Breeding is typically in marshes surrounded by native prairies and grassy sedge meadows.

Comments. This is the commonest migrant teal in the state, and one of the latest duck species to arrive in spring, owing to its long migration from wintering grounds sometimes as far away as northern South America. It is also probably the most common breeding duck in Nebraska, but few remain long in the fall, the birds usually departing shortly after the first freezing weather.

Cinnamon Teal   *Anas cyanoptera*

An uncommon spring and fall migrant in the western half of Nebraska, becoming rarer eastwardly but observed as far east as Sarpy and Dakota counties. Probably a local summer resident, but confusion with the blue-winged teal during summer makes the species' breeding status unclear. The birds are regularly present at Crescent Lake during summer, and there is a recent nesting record for Garden County (Mollhoff, 2001). Breeding has also been reported at Facus Springs, Morrill County. It has also bred in several other Plains States, especially toward the southwest.

Migration. Sixty-two initial spring sightings are from January 9 to June 6, with a median of April 26. Half of the sightings fall within the period April 8 to May 10. Six fall records are from July 13 to November 14, with a mean of September 19.

Habitats. This species occupies the same habitats as does the blue-winged teal in Nebraska, and usually are found in flocks of that species.

Comments. Persons wanting to see this beautiful little duck should consider visiting Crescent Lake National Wildlife Refuge in June, when as many as 6-8 males might be seen on a good day. Females are almost impossible to distinguish from female blue-winged teal, but have somewhat longer bills and are generally more uniformly brownish. Breeding Bird Surveys between 1966 and 2011 indicate that the species underwent a significant population decline (0.5% annually) during that period.

Northern Shoveler   *Anas clypeata*

A common to abundant spring and fall migrant, and a common to uncommon summer resident in Nebraska, with breeding most frequent in the Sandhills area, and decreasing southeastwardly. It is a migrant throughout the Plains States, and breeds locally except in the southern and southeastern portions.

Migration. Seventy initial spring sightings are from January 27 to June 6, with a median of March 23. Half of the sightings fall within the period March 11–30. Sixty-two final fall sightings range from September 5 to December 31, with a median of November 4. Half of the records fall within the period October 20 to November 20.

Habitats. Migrants utilize aquatic habitats rich in zooplankton and phytoplankton, and during the nesting season the birds favor shallow prairie marshes rich in those food sources. Non-wooded shorelines are preferred over wooded ones, and mud-bottom ponds are also apparently preferentially used.

Comments. Although generally despised by hunters because of their reputed poor taste and oversized bill, the shoveler's bill is a marvelously adapted structure, allowing the birds to extract plankton-sized materials from water. In spring the males are one of our most attractively plumaged waterfowl. They arrive late, at about the time the blue-winged teals also appear, and males are soon actively engaged in aquatic head-pumping displays and noisy display flights. Breeding Bird Surveys between 1966 and 2011 indicate that the species had a significant population increase (2.3% annually) during that period.

Northern Pintail   *Anas acuta*

An abundant spring and fall migrant and a common summer resident throughout Nebraska, breeding locally in suitable habitats. Frequently overwinters in considerable numbers where open water occurs. Migrants occur throughout the Plains States, and breeding is regular in all but the southernmost portions.

Migration. Sixty initial spring sightings range from January 18 to May 29, with a median of March 12. Half of the records fall within the period February 27 to March 20. Fifty-seven final fall sightings range from September 16 to December 31, with a median of November 19. Half of the records fall within the period November 6 to December 18.

Habitats. While on migration nearly all aquatic habitats are used, ranging from flooded fields to large lakes and reservoirs. Breeding is also near water areas ranging from small ponds to permanent marshes, but usually where the surrounding land is quite open and well drained.

Comments. Pintails are among the most graceful of all our waterfowl, and by early March usually rival mallards in abundance. They are also among the commonest breeding ducks in Nebraska, along with mallards and blue-winged teal. During spring their wonderful courtship flights are simply breathtaking to watch, and the males' accompanying fluty display whistles are among the sweetest sounds of nature.

Garganey   *Anas querquedula*

Accidental. A male was seen on March 28, 1998 in Kearney County, and probably the same bird was later seen in Hall County, March 29 to April 5, 1998 (*Nebraska Bird Review* 66:35, 149).

Green-winged Teal   *Anas crecca*

An abundant spring and fall migrant and an occasional summer resident. Breeding is essentially limited to the northern half of the state and is concentrated in the western Sandhills. There is at least one breeding record from south of the Platte River in the eastern Rainwater Basin (*Nebraska Bird Review* 76:138). Migrants occur throughout the Plains States, and breeding is regular in the Dakotas, western Minnesota and northwestern Iowa.

Migration. Fifty-eight initial spring sightings range from January 1 to June 4, with a median of March 20. Half of the records fall within the period March 12-30. Fifty-five final spring sightings are from April 4 to June 10, with a median of May 10. Forty-six initial fall sightings are from August 3 to October 18, with a median of September 12. Forty-nine final fall sightings are from September 20 to December 31, with a median of November 2.

Habitats. Migrants are associated with almost all standing or slowly-flowing aquatic habitats in Nebraska, and breeding normally occurs where ponds or sloughs are surrounded by a mixture of grassland, sedge meadows, and well drained areas supporting shrubby or tall woody vegetation.

Comments. In spite of its small size, the green-winged teal is a very early spring migrant, appearing soon after mallards and northern pintails make their appearance. Then the males' cricket-like display calls become quite apparent, and their animated courtship displays are a delight to watch. It is also a fairly late fall migrant, remaining long after the blue-winged teal have departed.

Canvasback   *Aythya valisineria*

An uncommon to locally common spring and fall migrant statewide, and a local summer resident in the western Sandhills (especially Valentine and Crescent Lake National Wildlife Refuges). Breeding also occurs in the Dakotas and western Minnesota, and migrants occur throughout the Plains States.

Migration. Sixty-eight initial spring sightings are from February 12 to May 21, with a median of March 18. Half of the records fall within the period March 7 to March 30. Thirty-nine final fall sightings are from October 12 to December 31, with a median of November 14. Half of the records fall within the period October 29 through November 23.

Habitats. On migration this species uses marshes, rivers and shallow lakes rich in submerged pond weeds and similar vegetation. Prairie marshes with abundant emergent vegetation and some areas of open water are favored for nesting.

Comments. Canvasbacks have traditionally been regarded as regal ducks; their long sloping bills and robust outlines set them apart from most other ducks, and they are reputed to be among the most edible of all waterfowl. They are larger than redheads and generally paler in both sexes, and lack the high rounded head profile of that species.

Redhead   *Aythya americana*

A common spring and fall migrant statewide and locally common summer resident in the Sandhills west to Garden County, as well as occasional breeding in the Rainwater Basin (*Nebraska Bird Review* 75:730. This is the southernmost area of regular breeding in the Plains States. Breeding is regular in the Dakotas, Minnesota and Northern Iowa, and migrants occur throughout the Plains States.

Migration. Sixty initial spring sightings range from February 9 to May 25, with a median of March 13. Half of the sightings fall within the period March 1 through March 20. Fifty-six final fall sightings are from October 9 to December 1, with a median of November 9. Half of the records fall within the period October 28 to November 19.

Habitats. Migrants are found on large prairie marshes, lakes and reservoirs, especially where submerged vegetation is abundant. Nesting typically occurs on marshes at least an acre in size, having both open areas and stands of emergent vegetation.

Comments. Redheads are considerably more common than canvasbacks in Nebraska, and can usually by seen during summer at Crescent Lake and Valentine refuges. Neck-stretching and head-throw displays are common in spring, accompanied by soft cat-like meowing calls.

Ring-necked Duck   *Aythya collaris*

An uncommon to common spring and fall migrant almost statewide, becoming less common in the Panhandle. It apparently has bred rarely in the Sandhills (reported by Oberholser [1920] to breed in Garden, Morrill, Cherry and Brown counties), but Nebraska is outside the regular breeding range of this species and there are no actual breeding records for Crescent Lake or Valentine refuges. Local breeding occurs in the Dakotas; breeding is regular in much of Minnesota. Migrants occur throughout the Plains States.

Migration. Forty-two initial spring sightings are from February 12 to May 25, with a median of March 21. Half of the records fall within the period March 7 to March 30. Twenty-six final spring sightings are from March 24 to May 30, with a median of April 21. Twenty-seven initial fall sightings are from September 17 to December 7, with a median of October 12. Twenty-three final fall sightings are from October 27 to December 31, with a median of November 17.

Habitats. Migrants are found on large prairie marshes, lakes and reservoirs, but prairie marshes are only secondary breeding habitats. Rather acidic swamps and bogs, surrounded by shrubby covers are the primary breeding habitat.

Comments. This species, often called the "ring-billed duck" is closely related to the redhead, as is obvious from its downy plumage. However, its breeding habitats are quite different from those of redheads, and it is believed to be only a migrant in Nebraska.

Tufted Duck   *Aythya fuligula*

Accidental. An male was found at Lake Keystone, Keith County, Nov. 3, 1999, was documented by many, and remained in the area until March or later. Several more recent sightings have since occurred there (Brown, Dinsmore and Brown, 2012).

Greater Scaup   *Aythya marila*

Apparently an occasional migrant and winter visitor in Nebraska, probably more common than the few published records would suggest. It is probably regular during late fall, winter, and early spring on larger reservoirs and lakes. Although migrants might appear anywhere in the Plains States, they are probably most common in the Missouri Valley impoundments.

Migration. Twenty-seven total spring records are from January 11 to May 18, with the largest number (12) for March, followed by April (8), and three each for February and May. There are fall records from October 27 to December 30.

Habitats. Migrants and wintering birds utilize lakes and reservoirs in the interior, but most birds winter coastally.

Comments. Males of the two scaup species are quite similar (and the females even more), but greater scaups have a greenish-glossed head (not purplish), and a much flatter crown profile, with no hint of a crest at the rear. The two species don't often associate because of their differing habitat preferences.

Lesser Scaup   *Aythya affinis*

A common to abundant spring and fall migrant statewide, and an occasional summer resident in the Sandhills (probably Garden, Morrill, Cherry and Brown counties). Known to have nested at Crescent Lake

National Wildlife Refuge, but not at Valentine Refuge. Overwinters locally where open water is present. Also breeds in the Dakotas and locally in Minnesota. Migrants occur throughout the Plains States.

Migration. Sixty-nine initial spring sightings are from February 12 to May 20, with a median of March 19. Half of the records fall within the period March 5 through March 25. Forty-three final spring records are from March 10 to June 6, with a median of May 11. Forty-five initial fall sightings are from July 20 to December 15, with a median of October 18. Thirty-one final fall sightings are from November 22 to December 31, with a median of December 14.

Habitats. Deeper marshes, reservoirs, borrow-pits and lakes are commonly used by migrating birds. Prairie marshes surrounded by partially wooded uplands are favored for breeding, especially those supporting large populations of amphipods (scuds).

Comments. This "bluebill" is a very common spring and fall migrant, and is perhaps the most abundant of the diving ducks in Nebraska. Males have bright blue bills in spring; like male ruddy ducks this blue coloration is probably caused by light refraction effects rather than blue pigmentation. Breeding Bird Surveys between 1966 and 2011 indicate that the species underwent a significant population decline (1,5% annually) during that period.

King Eider   *Somateria spectabilis*

Accidental. Photographed at DeSoto National Wildlife Refuge 10-24 November, 1985 (Bray *et al.*, 1986).

Common Eider   *Somateria mollissima*

Accidental. There is a specimen record for a female killed early December of 1967 in Lincoln County, which is of the Hudson Bay race *sedentaria* (*Nebraska Bird Review* 37:38).

Harlequin Duck   *Histrionicus histrionicus*

Accidental in Nebraska, with three early records from the Omaha area (one of which probably was from Burt County) (Bruner, Wolcott and Swenk, 1904). There were three documented records for the state as of 2001, plus four undocumented ones (*Nebraska Bird Review* 69:164). There has since been at least one more reported sighting. Harlequin ducks are rare even in Wyoming, where they locally breed on mountain streams.

Surf Scoter   *Melanitta perspicillata*

A rare migrant in Nebraska, occurring primarily in the fall. It has been seen at least twice in Lancaster, Keith and Douglas-Sarpy counties. Rare spring, fall and early winter migrant at Lake McConaughy (Brown, Dinsmore and Brown, 2012). Like the other scoters, most reports are of females or immature males that are easily overlooked or confused with other species. It has also been reported for the Dakotas, Kansas and Oklahoma. As of 2010 there were seven documented spring records, as compared to three for black scoters (*Nebraska Bird Review* 78:43).

Migration. Five spring records are from April 21 to May 15. Eight fall records are from October 7 to December 16, with a mean of November 6. Reported at Lake McConaughy from April 22 to May 15, and October 8 to January 20 (Brown, Dinsmore and Brown, 2012).

Habitats. Lakes, reservoirs and larger rivers are used by migrants. Most wintering is done coastally.

Comments. About as rare as the preceding species, birds seen in Nebraska have a distinctive head pattern, with whitish spots in front of and behind the eye, and lack white wing markings.

White-winged Scoter   *Melanitta fusca*

An occasional spring and fall migrant, more common in the fall than spring, and with most of the records from counties bordering the Platte or Missouri rivers. It has been recorded at least twice in Lincoln, Adams, Lancaster and Douglas counties. Uncommon spring, fall and early winter migrant at Lake McConaughy (Brown, Dinsmore and Brown, 2012). It is probably an annual visitor to the state, especially along the Missouri River and on the larger reservoirs. As of 2011 there were 26 spring records (*Nebraska Bird Review* 80:50).

Migration. Five total spring records are from March 31 to April 29, with a mean of April 7. Twenty-one fall records are from October 7 to December 10, with a median of November 10. Half of the records fall within the period October 28 to November 22. Reported at Lake McConaughy from Nov. 1 to May 28 (Brown, Dinsmore and Brown, 2012).

Habitats. Lakes, reservoirs and larger rivers are used by some migrants. Most birds migrate and winter in coastal areas.

Comments. This largest of the scoters is similar to the surf scoter in female or immature plumage, but has a large white patch on the inner wing feathers that allow for positive identification. It is the species most often seen in Nebraska, and once bred as close as northern North Dakota.

Black Scoter   *Melanitta americanq*

An extremely rare vagrant in Nebraska, occurring primarily in fall. It has been seen in a few scattered locations throughout the state, and seemingly is the rarest of the scoters in Nebraska. Rare fall and early winter migrant at Lake McConaughy (Brown, Dinsmore and Brown, 2012). It is rare or accidental in the Dakotas and Kansas, and has been reported from Oklahoma only as a few sight records.

Migration. Two spring records are for March 25 and May 4. Seven fall records range from September 28 to December 10, with a mean of October 28. Reported at Lake McConaughy from Oct. 12 to January 15 (Brown, Dinsmore and Brown, 2012).

Habitats. Lakes, reservoirs and larger rivers are used by migrants. Most wintering is done coastally.

Comments. This rare sea duck usually is seen in the female-like immature plumage while in Nebraska, when its two-tone brown head helps in identification. The rarest of Nebraska scoters, there were a remarkable six fall reports in 2010, as well as six reports for white-winged scoters and five reports for surf scoters (*Nebraska Bird Review* 78:134).

Long-tailed Duck   *Clangula hyemalis*

A rare fall and spring migrant statewide, but perhaps slightly more common eastwardly. Two or more records exist for Keith, Lancaster, Douglas and Washington counties, with at least eight for Douglas County. More common now than before the formation of large reservoirs. As of 1933 there were less than a dozen definite records for the state (*Nebraska Bird Review* 1:11), but the species was seen almost every year in the 1970s, and is now regular during early winter at Lake McConaughy/Ogallala (up to nine seen at one time in early December).

Migration. Thirteen total spring records are from February 3 to April 19, with a median of March 29. Ten total fall records are from October (no date) to December 11, with a median of November 27. Reported at Lake McConaughy from Nov. 3 to April 29 (Brown, Dinsmore and Brown, 2012).

Habitats. Lakes, reservoirs and larger rivers are used by migrating birds; most wintering is done in coastal habitats.

Comments. Long-tailed ducks nest higher in the arctic than almost any other duck, and mostly occur in Nebraska as late fall and winter vagrants.

Bufflehead   *Bucephala albeola*

A common to uncommon migrant statewide. Occasionally stragglers remain in the state through the summer, with one breeding record for Brown County. Breeding occurs locally in North Dakota, and migrates throughout the Plains States.

Migration. Fifty-three initial spring sightings are from February 21 to May 1, with a median of March 18. Half of the records fall within the period March 6 through March 24. Thirty-eight final spring sightings are from March 15 to May 29, with a median of April 21. Thirty-four initial fall sightings are from August 14 to December 16, with a median of October 19. Thirty-one final fall sightings are from October 29 to December 31, with a median of November 24.

Habitats. Lakes, reservoirs and deeper marshes are used by migrating birds.

Comments. Easily one of the most beautiful of Nebraska's ducks, these birds tend to appear on the same kinds of wetlands as goldeneyes and mergansers, the males sparkling like gigantic snowflakes on the water, and the tiny, drab females almost invisible by contrast. Nesting occurs in the cavities made by flickers and other small woodpeckers.

Common Goldeneye   *Bucephala clangula*

A common to uncommon spring and fall migrant statewide, occasionally overwintering where open water is available. Breeding occurs in Minnesota and locally in North Dakota. Migrants are regular throughout the Plains States.

Migration. Thirty-five initial spring sightings range from January 1 to April 12, with a median of March 5. Twenty-four final spring sightings are from March 9 to May 8, with a median of March 30. Thirty-four initial fall sightings are from October 10 to December 31, with a median of November 21. Thirty-one final fall sightings are from November 22 to December 31, with a median of December 14. Reported at Lake McConaughy from September 9 to June 13 (Brown, Dinsmore and Brown, 2012).

Habitats. Deeper marshes, rivers, lakes and reservoirs are used during migration.

Comments. This beautiful diving duck appears in spring at about the same time as do common mergansers, and both species can often be seen engaging in excited courtship displays, performing head-throws, backward kicks, vertical neck-stretching, and other remarkable male posturing, as the drab females either ignore the males or perhaps threaten them with bill-pointing gestures. The white plumages of male goldeneyes and common mergansers fairly glisten in the sun, and when in flight both species exhibit large while wing-patches.

Barrow's Goldeneye   *Bucephala islandica*

A rare winter and spring vagrant in Nebraska, probably mainly occurring westwardly, but with records extending to Douglas County. Rare to uncommon spring, fall and early winter migrant at Lake McConaughy (Brown, Dinsmore and Brown, 2012).   It has been observed two or more times in Garden, Lincoln, and Douglas counties, and there are at least ten records for Lake McConaughy (*Nebraska Bird Review* 66:11). It is apparently rare to accidental throughout the Plains States from North Dakota to Oklahoma.

Migration. Eight spring records range from February 15 to April 2, with a mean of March 19. Three fall records are from November 26 to December 21. Reported at Lake McConaughy from Nov. 14 to April 19 (Brown, Dinsmore and Brown, 2012).

Habitats. While on migration this species uses the same habitats as the common goldeneye, but is more prone to winter in coastal or brackish waters.

Comments. There is little chance of seeing this species in Nebraska, although it breeds in Wyoming's Teton Range and elsewhere in that state. A few hybrids with common goldeneyes have been recorded. Such hybrids, and even females of the two species, are difficult to recognize.

Hooded Merganser   *Lophodytes cucullatus*

An uncommon to occasional spring and fall migrant in eastern Nebraska, and an occasional to rare migrant in western parts of the state. Stragglers sometimes remain into summer, but there is little evidence of breeding in Nebraska at the present time. However, there are apparently valid early records of nesting from Lancaster, Gage, and Cuming counties (Bruner, Wolcott and Swenk, 1904), and the author observed a female and five newly fledged young at Twin Lakes, Seward County, in July, 1995. Two other breeding records for eastern Nebraska also exist (*Nebraska Bird Review* 73:50). As of 2010 there were only three confirmed state breeding records (*Nebraska Bird Review* 78:43).

Migration. Seventy-four initial spring sightings range from January 16 to May 30, with a median of March 26. Half of the records fall within the period March 13 to March 28. Fourteen final spring records are from March 19 to May 30, with a median of April 25. Sixteen initial fall sightings are from September 14 to November 27, with a median of November 5. Nineteen final fall sightings are from November 6 to December 17, with a median of November 22.

Habitats. Migrants are found on clear-water rivers, lakes, reservoirs and deeper marshes. Breeding is usually on rivers, creeks and oxbows bordered by woods and supporting good populations of fish.

Comments. This species seems to be increasing in Nebraska, as it was rarely observed by the author in the 60s and 70s, but now it is a regular spring migrant in eastern Nebraska. Perhaps it has benefited from nest-box erection programs for wood ducks, as it often will choose such places for laying its eggs.

Common Merganser   *Mergus merganser*

A regular spring and fall migrant statewide, varying in abundance from very common to occasional. Overwinters commonly where open water persists; stragglers sometimes remain through the summer. Summering birds are regular in the Lake Alice area of Scotts Bluff County, and nesting has been suspected. Evidence of breeding in the state includes a brood sighted in Custer County in 1968 (*Nebraska Bird Review* 37:45) and one reported from the North Platte Valley west of Lake McConaughy (*Nebraska Bird Review* 62:105). It regularly breeds in Minnesota, and migrates throughout the Plains States.

Migration. Fifty initial spring sightings are from January 14 to April 25, with a median of March 9. Half of the records fall within the period March 3 through March 27. Thirty-nine final spring sightings are from March 4 to May 30, with a median of April 6. Thirty-eight initial fall sightings are from September 18 to December 31, with a median of November 13. Thirty-six final fall sightings are from November 20 to December 31, with a median of December 17.

Habitats. Migrants and wintering birds are found on rivers, lakes, reservoirs, and any other large water areas supporting fish populations. Most nesting occurs on forest-lined lakes and ponds near rivers, but rarely nesting occurs in treeless areas in rock crevices or other natural cavities.

Comments. It is likely that more nesting records of this splendid species will accrue as time passes, since summering birds are increasingly common in Nebraska. The birds need clear waters with a good fish population; hunters and fishermen tend to hate this and other "sawbill" species because of their fishy taste and appetites. However, the birds generally eat slow-swimming prey rather than trout and other game fish.

Red-breasted Merganser   *Mergus serrator*

An occasional to rare spring and fall migrant statewide, more common westwardly than in eastern Nebraska. Perhaps overwinters rarely. It is a regular migrant throughout the Plains States.

Migration. Sixty-one initial spring sightings are from January 15 to May 12, with a median of March 29. Half of the records fall within the period March 19 to April 7. Twenty-four final spring sightings are from February 14 to May 18, with a median of April 20. Sixteen total fall sightings are from September 21 to December 31, with a median of November 18. Half of the records fall within the period November 4 through November 27. Reported at Lake McConaughy from August 7 to June 7 (Brown, Dinsmore and Brown, 2012).

Habitats. Lakes, reservoirs and large rivers are used by migrants; wintering more often occurs coastally.

Comments. The red-breasted merganser is less common in eastern Nebraska than the two other mergansers, which is too bad because it is a most attractive species. Like the common merganser it is dependent upon fish in clear-water habitats.

Ruddy Duck   *Oxyura jamaicensis*

A common spring and fall migrant statewide and an uncommon and very local summer resident in some of the deeper and more permanent marshes of the Sandhills and Rainwater Basin. It is considered a common breeder at both Valentine and Crescent Lake refuges. It is a regular breeding species in the Dakotas and Minnesota, and migrates throughout the Plains States.

Migration. Sixty-seven initial spring sightings are from February 12 to June 9, with a median of April 3. Half of the records fall within the period March 14 to April 19. Fifty-nine final fall records are from August 30 to December 31, with a median of November 27. Half of the records fall within the period October 10 to November 27.

Habitats. Migrants may be found on lakes, reservoirs, larger marshes and similar habitats offering considerable open water and mud-bottom feeding areas. Breeding is on prairie marshes having stable water levels and an abundance of emergent vegetation, along with some areas of open water.

Comments. This wonderful little duck is nearly everybody's favorite; from its sky-blue bill to its long, spiky tail it advertises its uniqueness. From the time it finally arrives in spring and begins its bizarre displays through the summer breeding period it is hard to imagine a more interesting bird to watch. Like other stiff-tailed ducks it feeds almost entirely on small fly larvae that live in the muddy bottoms of ponds, using its sensitive bill to locate its prey.

Family Odontophoridae

(Scaled Quail)   *Callipepla squamata*

Unsuccessfully introduced into Nebraska. Releases were made during the late 1950s, but there have been no observations since 1962. The nearest breeding area is southwestern Kansas and southeastern Colorado, and it also breeds in Oklahoma, Texas and New Mexico.

(California Quail)   *Callipepla californica*

Unsuccessfully introduced into Nebraska. An attempt to establish this species in 1939 was a failure. Also unsuccessfully introduced into South Dakota in 1961.

Northern Bobwhite   *Colinus virginianus*

A permanent resident almost statewide, becoming rarer westwardly. It breeds commonly in eastern and southern Nebraska, extending into the Sandhills along river drainages, and reaching the Wyoming and Colorado borders along the North Platte and South Platte Rivers, as well as the tributaries of the Republican River. The western range limits are highly variable, depending on yearly weather conditions. The northern range limits are in South Dakota and southern Minnesota.

Habitats. Throughout the year this species is normally found where there is a combination of grassy nesting cover, cultivated crops, and brushy cover or woodlands with a brushy understory. Nesting is typically done in open herbaceous cover consisting of rather short vegetation that does not obstruct easy entry and exit, but sufficient to provide concealment from above.

Comments. The familiar "*bob-white*" call of the male bobwhite is known to everybody, and is more a signal of a male's availability than a territorial proclamation. All of the New World quails are monogamous, and in all the male remains with his mate to help protect and raise the brood. Family broods become the basis for fall coveys, which usually are of about the right number (6 to 10 birds) to comprise an effective roosting ring at night. The group organizes itself into a tight circle, heads pointed outwardly, thus sharing body heat and remaining alert in all directions. Breeding Bird Surveys between 1966 and 2011 indicate that the species underwent a significant population decline (4.2% annually) during that period.

Family Phasianidae

(Chukar)   *Alectoris chukar*

Various attempts have been made to release this species in Nebraska, including the release of 700 birds in southern Scotts Bluff County in 1969. There have been subsequent observations as late as the 1990s. They were observed in Lincoln, Banner, Sheridan and Dawes counties to as late as the early or mid 1970s, and in Sioux Country in 1998. It is unlikely that a breeding population still persists in the state, but there have been persistent reports from the Redington area.

Gray Partridge   *Perdix perdix*

Uncommon and local in northern Nebraska, in recent years. Fairly common in South Dakota, and has been reported in Nebraska on numerous occasions since 1950, most often in the northern tier of counties, west to Sioux County. Currently centered in Knox, Cedar and Dixon counties (*Nebraska Bird Review* 77:51). It is a regular breeder from southern South Dakota northward, and some of the Nebraska records may represent fall wanderers, but nesting has been reported near West Point (*Nebraska Bird Review* 48:88). During 1984-1989 period there were four confirmed nestings, extending from Cherry County east to Cedar County (Mollhoff, 2001). Breeding Bird Surveys between 1966 and 2011 indicate that the species underwent a significant population decline (1.4% annually) during that period.

(Japanese Quail)   *Coturnix japonica*

Unsuccessfully introduced into Nebraska in 1957. The migratory tendencies of this species makes it an unsuitable game bird.

Ring-necked Pheasant   *Phasianus colchicus*

An introduced permanent resident, now fairly common almost statewide, but more common eastwardly. Also resident in the other Plains States, primarily in the Dakotas and Kansas.

Habitats. Throughout the year a combination of small grain croplands and adjacent heavier covers such as weedy ditches, sloughs, wooded areas or shelterbelts provide optimum habitat. Nesting is often done in roadside ditches, in alfalfa or sweet clover fields, or in heavy grass cover.

Comments. The ring-necked pheasant perhaps represents the most successful of the many efforts to introduce exotic game birds into North America. These efforts begin in the early 1900s, and by mid-century the species was established over much of the country, especially in the grain belt of the northern plains, Evidently it fit into our avifauna without displacing our native grouse, although it gradually replaced prairie-chickens as the loss of prairie habitats caused the gradual disappearance of these native birds.

Ruffed Grouse   *Bonasa umbellus*

Extirpated from Nebraska. Previously a permanent resident of the Missouri's forested valley. Releases during 1968 in Nemaha County were evidently unsuccessful, with no records since 1973. The nearest breeding area is the Black Hills. Nesting also occurs in North Dakota and Minnesota.

Greater Sage-Grouse   *Centrocercus urophasianus*

Probably extirpated from Nebraska. Apparently once bred in extreme northwestern Nebraska, but no actual nesting records exist. Displaying birds are sometimes seen in Sioux County, so rare nesting within Nebraska is still possible. It still breeds in adjacent South Dakota, Wyoming, and southwestern North Dakota.

Sharp-tailed Grouse   *Tympanuchus phasianellus*

A locally common permanent resident over much of Nebraska, primarily north of the Platte River, and with the eastern limits approximating those of the Sandhills. Once much more widespread, and probably including the entire state. Breeding also still occurs in the Dakotas and Minnesota.

Habitats. Open grassland habitats, where trees are absent or nearly so, is the typical Nebraska habitat. Brushy cover covering from 5 to 30 percent of the land is used in more northerly areas, especially where winter snow accumulation is considerable.

Comments. Sharp-tailed grouse are still surprisingly common in Nebraska, and like prairie-chickens offer early risers a chance to witness the visual poetry of several males dancing in nearly perfect synchrony on their traditional leks, or display grounds. In some areas of the Sandhills both species display on the same grounds, and hybrids occasionally result. The displays and vocalizations of the two species are quite different, but evidently females sometime are attracted to the "wrong" male for mating.

Greater Prairie-Chicken   *Tympanuchus cupido*

A locally common to uncommon permanent resident, especially in the eastern half of the Sandhills, southwestern Nebraska and a few southeastern counties. Rare in the Panhandle and absent from some Missouri Valley counties. The species' range is discontinuous and probably declining as native grasslands disappear, but the Nebraska populations are perhaps the best of all the remaining ones.

Habitats. Greater prairie-chickens are primarily associated with native grasslands, and where native grasslands and grain croplands interdigitate. Nesting usually occurs in grassy open habitats such as ungrazed meadows or hayfields, usually in rather dry sites, but sometimes nests are placed in brushy vegetation or in open woods or at the edge of woods.

Comments. Nebraska is one of the few states in which prairie-chickens are still sufficiently common as to be major game birds. The eastern edge of the Sandhills probably represents the prime prairie-chicken habitat; here a mixture of native grasses and grain crops such as corn provide both nesting cover and winter foods for these birds.

Lesser Prairie-Chicken   *Tympanuchus pallidicinctus*
      Extirpated from Nebraska. Three 1924 and 1925 specimens from Red Willow County are known. This species is resident in southwestern Kansas.

Wild Turkey   *Meleagris gallopavo*
      Originally native to Nebraska but extirpated, and now re-established as a resident in many areas, especially in the Pine Ridge and along all of the major river systems. It has also been re-introduced into the Dakotas, and indigenous populations persist from Kansas southward.
      Habitats. Although various races differ greatly in habitats utilized, in Nebraska the birds in most parts of the state are found in floodplain forests having a variety of hardwood trees, especially those bearing acorns or other large and edible seeds. In the Pine Ridge area the birds are associated with pines, cedars, running water and a fairly rugged topography. Nesting occurs in forested areas, with the nests being well concealed, often under a log or at the base of a tree.
      Comments. Wild turkeys scarcely differ from domestic "bronzed" ones in their general appearance (their tail-tips are usually tan rather than white), but are much more wary and more slim-bodied. Yet, their calls and display postures are identical, and at times wild birds will mate with domestic ones, producing feral individuals of varied wildness. Breeding Bird Surveys between 1966 and 2011 indicate that the species underwent a significant population increase (8.0% annually) during that period.

Family Gaviidae

Red-throated Loon.   *Gavia stellata*
      An extremely rare spring and fall migrant. There have been at least 14 sightings of this species in the state. Most are for Douglas and Lancaster counties, but it has also been observed once each in Buffalo, Sarpy, Frontier, Keith and Washington counties. It has been reported in Kansas and Oklahoma, and once (1989) in South Dakota.
      Migration. Five spring records are from April 17 to May 7, with a mean of April 28, and eight fall records are from October 31 to December 2, with a mean of November 17. There is also one mid-June record.
      Habitats. Larger rivers, lakes and reservoirs while on migration.
      Comments. This is the smallest of the loons, and the only one lacking the black-and-white back patterning when in breeding plumage. It is also the only loon that can take off from small tundra ponds, as are common on its arctic nesting grounds.

Pacific Loon   *Gavia pacifica*
      Extremely rare. There were at least 14 Nebraska records for this species as of 1997. A specimen was collected before 1900 in Frontier County (Bruner, Wolcott and Swenk, 1904), one was observed in November of 1961 in Sarpy County (*Nebraska Bird Review* 40:40), one was seen in October, 1971 in Scotts Bluff County. Other records to 1985 are listed by Bray *et al.* (1986) and through 1996 by Brogie (1997). Many of the records are for November;. As of 2010 there were only four spring records (*Nebraska Bird Review* 78:43 Rare spring, fall and winter migrant at Lake McConaughy (Brown, Dinsmore and Brown, 2012).

Common Loon   *Gavia immer*
      Uncommon spring and fall migrant throughout Nebraska. This species has been observed in at least 33 counties, being recorded ten or more times in Douglas, Lincoln and Lancaster counties, at least five times in Scotts Bluff and Keith counties. Most of the sightings have occurred in the eastern half of the state. Also migrates through other Plains States, becoming rarer southwestwardly, and breeds in Minnesota and North Dakota.
      Migration. Excepting two January records, 55 initial spring sightings range from March 18 to May 27, with a median of May 7. Fourteen final spring sightings are from April 12 to May 28, with a median of

May 16. Twenty-five initial fall sightings are from July 20 to November 2, with a median of October 24. Seventeen final fall sightings are from October 25 to December 7 with a median of November 2. Of a total of 135 records, the largest number (37) are for April, followed by May (35), November (26), and October (15). Records exist for all months except February.

Habitats. Larger rivers, lakes and reservoirs while on migration.

Comments. This is much the most common species of loon seen in the state, and the plumage patterns seen here vary greatly, but usually are of the winter or immature type. Calling occurs only rarely while the birds are in Nebraska, and nearly all birds seen are single individuals.

Yellow-billed Loon   *Gavia adamsii*

Accidental. An adult was photographed on Branched Oak Lake, Lancaster County, in November 1996 (Brogie, 1997). An immature was seen on Lake McConaughy August 8-October 20, 1998 (Brogie, 1999), one at Lake McConaughy in September, 2003 (*Nebraska Bird Review* 72:61) and one in Rock County, November 29, 2009 (*Nebraska Bird Review* 77:142). As of 2009 there had been four state records, all in fall.

Family Podicipedidae

Pied-billed Grebe   *Podilymbus podiceps*

A common spring and fall migrant and local summer resident throughout Nebraska. It breeds almost throughout the Plains States, excepting the drier areas of the southwestern states.

Migration. A total of 116 initial spring sightings range from February 27 to June 10, with a median of April 5. Half of the sightings fall within the period March 24 to April 22. Eighty-four final fall sightings are from August 21 to December 6, with a median of November 6. Half of the sightings fall within the period October 10 - November 16.

Habitats. Breeding occurs on small ponds, river impoundments and lakes, ranging from quite small to large, but always those having extensive stands of heavy emergent vegetation and adjacent areas of open water.

Comments. This grebe is the commonest species in the state, and one that rarely strays far from reedy or weedy shorelines. It often dives by sinking vertically when alarmed, with at most its head remaining above water. Its bill is adapted for eating crustaceans and other invertebrates rather than fish, and it is never seen in flocks like the other Nebraska grebes. Breeding Bird Surveys between 1966 and 2003 indicate that the species underwent a significant population increase (0.3% annually) during that period.

Horned Grebe   *Podiceps auritus*

An uncommon spring and fall migrant throughout Nebraska, and an accidental resident. It has reportedly bred in Cherry County, but the closest area of regular breeding is in central South Dakota. It also breeds in North Dakota and northwestern Minnesota.

Migration. Sixty-two initial spring sightings range from February to June 4, with a median of April 16. Twenty four final spring sightings are from April 14 to May 22, with a median of May 6. Seventeen initial fall sightings are from September 5 to November 11, with a median of October 8. Seventeen final fall sightings are from October 9 to November 27, with a median of November 11.

Habitats. Rivers, lakes and reservoirs while on migration. Breeding occurs on ponds and marshes ranging in size from less than an acre to several hundred acres, which may be seasonal or permanent. Submerged aquatic vegetation is typically abundant, but emergent growth may be rather sparse.

Comments. Slightly larger than the eared grebe, this is much less common, and lacks that species' black neck. There are no modern nesting records for this attractive species.

Red-necked Grebe   *Podiceps grisegena*

An extremely rare spring and fall migrant in Nebraska. There have been sightings of this species in at least six counties, with most of the reports for Douglas-Sarpy, and nearly all from counties bordering the

Platte or Missouri rivers. It is considered rare in Kansas and Oklahoma, but a regular migrant in the Dakotas. It breeds in Minnesota and North Dakota.

Migration. Seven spring records are from March 13 to May 17, with a mean of April 9, and eight fall records are from September 30 to December 21, with a mean of October 30.

Habitats. Rivers, lakes and reservoirs while on migration.

Comments. The red-necked grebe is a large, robust species that seems to prefer rather large bodies of water, and has a sharp bill well adapted to fish-eating. Like the eared grebe, it also occurs widely in Europe.

Eared Grebe   *Podiceps nigricollis*

An uncommon spring and fall migrant throughout Nebraska, and a fairly common summer resident, especially in the Sandhills, but locally also in the Rainwater Basin south of the Platte River. It also breeds in the Dakotas, Minnesota and Iowa.

Migration. A total of 105 initial spring sightings range from February 19 to June 5, with a median of April 22. Half of the sightings fall within the period of April 11 to May 5. Twenty three final fall sightings are from August 23 to November 15, with a median of October 16. Half of the sightings fall within the period October 8-30.

Habitats. Rivers, lakes and reservoirs during migration. Breeding occurs on ponds, marshes, and shallow river impoundments that are usually rich in submerged aquatic plants. Large, open ponds providing abundant feeding areas but also some sheltered locations with emergent aquatic plants for nesting sites seem to be favored.

Comments. This beautiful little grebe is a colonial nester, and one of the summer attractions of Crescent Lake National Wildlife Refuge during mid-June is watching families of eared grebes with several chicks on the backs of nearly every adult. Scattered nestings have occurred in states to the south of Nebraska, including Kansas, Oklahoma, Texas and eastern Colorado.

Western Grebe   *Aechmophorus occidentalis*

A common spring and fall migrant in the western part of Nebraska, rarer eastwardly, and a summer resident in western areas. Breeding occurs primarily on the larger Sandhills marshes, including Crescent Lake and Valentine refuges, which represent the southeastern limit of breeding of this species in the Plains States. Many apparent non-breeders and a few breeders occur during summer on Lake McConaughy. It also breeds in the Dakotas and southwestern Minnesota.

Migration. Seventy-seven initial spring sightings range from March 10 to June 10, with a median of May 6. Half of the sightings fall within the period April 19 - May 18. Forty-three final fall sightings are from September 10 to December 7, with a median of October 3. Half of the sightings fall within the period October 1 - 24.

Habitats. Rivers , lakes and reservoirs while on migration. Breeding is on ponds and lakes that usually have large expanses of open water, and on some marshes that are at least 50 acres in area.

Comments. The western grebe is perhaps the most spectacular of all the North American grebes, and during April as many as 14,000 of these splendid birds aggregate on Lake McConaughy. Breeding is common on several large marshes at Crescent Lake and Valentine refuges. The species' spectacular courtship displays are perhaps best seen during May.

Clark's Grebe   *Aechmophorus clarkii*

Occasional; probably a regular breeder. The state's first record was of an adult in breeding plumage found dead at Lake Keystone, Keith County on June 1, 1986, and since then a considerable number of sightings have been reported in western Nebraska, including adults with young at the western end of Lake McConaughy in late July, 1993 (Rosche, 1994). Up to 16 birds have been reported there, and some have also been seen at Crescent Lake National Wildlife Refuge. Sightings have occurred east to Lancaster County. In 1998 and 2002 breeding was noted at Willy Lake, Sheridan County

Comments. Probably this poorly distinguished species is more common in Nebraska than generally appreciated, since is very easily overlooked among flocks of western grebes. An apparent hybrid has also been seen (*Nebraska Bird Review* 65:161). Wintering birds were first seen in 1997-98 (*Nebraska Bird Review* 66:19).

Family Phaethontidae

(White-tailed Tropicbird)   *Phaethon lepturus*
Hypothetical. A highly questionable sight record for this species exists for Lincoln County (*Nebraska Bird Review* 41:59, 79). There are no other regional records.

Family Ciconiidae

Wood Stork   *Mycteria americana*
Accidental. Although there is a good early sight record (Sarpy County, 1925) the only specimen known is one from Hamilton County in the 1880s (Bruner, Wolcott and Swenk, 1904). Wood storks have recently been seen as close to Nebraska as northern Missouri.

Family Fregatidae

(Magnificent Frigatebird)   *Fregata magnificens*
Hypothetical. There is a sight record for this species by Lawrence Bruner in Cuming County in the spring of 1884. A frigate-bird of uncertain species was seen in Knox County, September 7 to 8, 2007 (*Nebraska Bird Review* 75:103). Specimens have been collected in Kansas and Oklahoma.

Family Phalacrocoracidae

Neotropic Cormorant   *Phalacrocorax brasilianus*
Very rare The first specimen was obtained 2 October, 1982, at Sutherland Reservoir *(Nebraska Bird Review* 51: 18). Since photographed at Hackberry Lake, Cherry County, September 4, 1993 *(Nebraska Bird Review* 64:31), seen at Valentine National Wildlife Refuge, Cherry County, July 19, 1995 *(Nebraska Bird Review* 63:71) and at Chambers, Holt County, May 20-30, 1996 (*Nebraska Bird Review* 64:44). Also recorded several times between 1998 and 2010, totaling 16 reports by 2010 (*Nebraska Bird Review* 66:33; 67:72; 68:108, 78:135; 79:122). This species in apparently slowly moving north into the central Great Plains.

Double-crested Cormorant   *Phalacrocorax auritus*
An uncommon spring and fall migrant throughout Nebraska, becoming more common westwardly. It is a summer resident in several locations in the western half of the state, east to Cherry County and the vicinity of North Platte. It also breeds locally in Minnesota and the Dakotas.
Migration. Of 102 initial spring sightings, the range is March 14 to May 29, and the median is April 12. Half of the records fall during the period April 14-25. Thirty-nine final spring records range from April 17 to June 2, with a median of May 1. Thirty-one initial fall sightings are from August 7 to October 20, with a median of September 21. Thirty-one final fall sightings are from September 17 to December 14, with a median of October 23
Habitats. Migrating birds use deeper marshes, lakes, rivers and reservoirs. Breeding occurs on islands, trees, or cliffs near water, and within about 10 miles of an adequate fish supply.
Comments. During the past few decades this cormorant has increased in the U.S.A., benefiting from fish farms in the south and better protection on its nesting grounds. Nesting may occur in partly submerged bushes or trees, or on nesting platforms set out for Canada geese, as well as on sandy or gravely islands.

Family Anhingidae

Anhinga   *Anhinga anhinga*

Accidental. Recorded in Buffalo County in September 1913, in Hamilton County during May 1955, in Greeley County in April 1975, on the Platte River in October 1976, reported from Sarpy County in April 1978, and at Indian Cave State Park in 2005 (*Nebraska Bird Review* 73:50).

Migration. The few available records for this species range from April 27 to October (no date). There are also records for May and September.

Habitats. Normally associated with lagoons, lakes, rivers, and swamps with quiet or sluggishly flowing fresh water that is clear and supports fish.

Comments. This is essentially a tropical fish-eating species that stalks its prey underwater, spearing it in a heron-like manner while wholly submerged. The nearest known nesting has occurred in southeastern Oklahoma.

Family Pelecanidae

American White Pelican   *Pelecanus erythroryhnchos*

A common migrant throughout Nebraska, especially in central and western counties. Non-breeders commonly occur through the summer on Harlan County Reservoir and Lake McConaughy, but there are no breeding records for the state. It breeds locally in Minnesota and the Dakotas.

Migration. Eighty-four initial spring sightings range from February 21 to May 22 with a median of April 28. Half of the records fall within the period May 10-24. Thirty final spring sightings are from April 12 to June 1, with a median of April 28. Twenty-eight initial fall sightings range from August 5 to November 21, with a median of September 24. Twenty-eight final fall sightings are from September 16 to November 10 with a median of October 16.

Habitats. Deeper marshes, lakes and reservoirs are used by migrating and non-breeding birds.

Comments. The nearest breeding site for this species is at LaCreek National Wildlife Refuge near Martin, South Dakota, and probably many of the birds seen in Nebraska are migrants going to and from this site or others farther north, or are non-breeders spending their summers away from the crowded breeding colonies. Breeding Bird Surveys between 1966 and 2011 indicate that the species underwent a significant population increase (3.9% annually) during that period.

Brown Pelican   *Pelecanus occidentalis*

Extremely rare. Vagrants of this species have been seen in Nebraska on various occasions. Swenk (1934) summarized five early records, and since then the species has been reported in Lincoln County in 1937, in Cherry and Keya Paha counties in 1955, and in Custer County in 1977. There are records for Dodge and Dakota counties (*Nebraska Bird Review* 59:150), DeSoto National Wildlife Refuge, Harlan County Reservoir (*Nebraska Bird Review* 73:81) and Lake Babcock (*Nebraska Bird Review* 77: 52;162). As of 2008 there were six spring and one fall record (*Nebraska Bird Review* 76:139).

Migration. The few available records for this species range from April 10 to October 10. There are records for April, May, July and October.

Habitats. Normally associated with coastal beaches and shorelines.

Comments. Unlike the white pelicans of the world, the brown pelican dives from the air for its prey, and is almost entirely limited to coastal waters.

Family Ardeidae

American Bittern   *Botaurus lentiginosus*

A common spring and fall migrant throughout Nebraska, and a locally common summer resident. It breeds throughout the state in suitable habitats, with the Sandhills marshes providing optimum habitat. It also breeds widely elsewhere in the Plains States, except in the drier southwestern regions.

Migration. The range of 109 initial spring sightings is from March 26 to June 10, with a median of May 3. Half of the records fall within the period April 23 to May 11. Forty-four final fall sightings are from July 14 to December 17, with a median of October 6. Half of the sightings fall within the period October 1 to 27.

Habitats. Normally this species is found in marshes, swamps and bogs having heavy emergent vegetation or with adjacent wet swales or tall grassy meadows.

Comments. This strange heron, often called (obscenely) a "shitepoke" by native Nebraskans, often goes unseen by casual observers, who fail to notice it standing erect and motionless among cattails and reeds near water. Its booming courtship call is responsible for its alternative vernacular name, "thunderpump."

Least Bittern   *Ixobrychus exilis*

An uncommon spring and fall migrant and seemingly rare summer resident. It breeds locally in the eastern half of the state, and perhaps has its western nesting limits in Garden County, where it has been observed during summer at the Ash Hollow marshes and Crescent Lake National Wildlife Refuge. It breeds widely elsewhere in the Plains States, excepting the drier western portions.

Migration. Thirty-nine initial spring sightings range from March 30 to June 4, with a median of May 15. Half of the records fall within the period May 4-24. Ten final fall sightings are from July 28 to September 19, with a median of August 17.

Habitats. In Nebraska this species is usually found in freshwater or slightly brackish marshes or lake edges having extensive stands of emergent vegetation, and with scattered bushes or similar woody growth.

Comments. This is the smallest of the American herons, and a miniature relative of the American bittern. It builds a distinctive nest of materials organized like the spokes of a wheel in marshy vegetation.

Great Blue Heron   *Ardea herodias*

A common migrant and a local summer resident, breeding in colonies in various locations throughout Nebraska, but especially along major rivers and locally in the Sandhills. It also breeds locally elsewhere throughout the Plains States.

Migration. The range of 87 initial spring sightings is from January 6 to June 6, with a median of April 2. Half of the records fall within the period March 26 - April 30. Of 103 final fall sightings, the range is August 8 to December 30, and the median is October 13. Half of the records fall within the period September 23 - November 7.

Habitats. Migrants are found around all water areas supporting a fish population and having shallows for foraging. Nesting usually occurs among groves of tall trees, but sometimes also has been reported on the ground, on rock ledges, among bulrushes, or other elevated situations. Cottonwood groves seem to be a favored nesting location in Nebraska.

Comments. Commonly but incorrectly called "cranes" by Nebraskans, great blue herons differ from cranes in many ways, including their tree-nesting behavior, their flight profile (flying with kinked-necks rather than outstretched necks), and their strongly fish-dependent diet. However, they are beautiful and graceful birds, and often nest colonially in areas where fish are plentiful. Breeding Bird Surveys between 1966 and 2011 indicate that the species underwent a significant population increase (0.8% annually) during that period.

Great Egret   *Ardea alba*

An occasional spring and fall migrant, or summer visitor. It is most common in eastern counties, but observed as far west as Box Butte and Garden counties. There was an attempted nesting in Sarpy County in 1960 (*Nebraska Bird Review* 28:55), and another nesting by about seven birds in that county in 2008 (*Nebraska Bird Review* 76:98). It is a regular breeder in Oklahoma, Iowa, and southern Minnesota, and occasional in eastern Kansas.

Migration. Sixty-two initial or only spring records are from March 26 to June 1, with a median of April 29. Half of the records fall within the period April 16 to May 10. Ten final spring sightings are from April 6 to June 8, with a median of May 9. Twenty-one total fall records are from August 2 to October 21, with a median of September 1. Of 95 total records, the largest number (34) are for May, followed by April (30), August (10) and September (8).

Habitats. Associated with streams, swamps, and lake borders, and usually found near trees during the nesting season.

Comments. The range of several egrets seems to have expanded in recent years, and that is certainly the case with the great egret. There are influxes of the birds into Nebraska just prior to breeding (perhaps of birds headed toward Minnesota and western Iowa), and again following the breeding season. Breeding Bird Surveys between 1966 and 2011 indicate that the species underwent a significant population increase (2.4% annually) during that period.

Snowy Egret   *Egretta thula*

A rare vagrant or summer visitor throughout Nebraska; most of the records are for counties bordering the Platte or Missouri Rivers, especially Scotts Bluff, Lincoln, Platte, Douglas-Sarpy and also Lancaster. There are breeding records from Lancaster, Scotts Bluff and (more recently) Hall counties (Mollhoff, 2001). It regularly breeds in Oklahoma and South Dakota, and has also bred in Kansas.

Migration. Twenty-four total spring records are from April 13 to June 10, with a median of May 7. Ten total fall records are from July 30 to October 1, with a median of August 17. Of 34 total records, the largest number are for May (17) followed by April (6) and August (4).

Habitats. Nonbreeding birds occur over a wide array of aquatic habitats supporting fish. During the breeding season fairly sheltered habitats with shrubby or low tree growth are favored. Nesting often occurs among other heron species.

Comments. This beautiful little egret can be easily recognized by its "golden slippers" and its all-black bill. In the spring it exhibits beautiful filmy white "aigrette" plumes that once were the high-fashion rage, and nearly spelled the species' doom before federal protection was enacted.

Little Blue Heron   *Egretta caerulea*

An occasional to uncommon spring and rare fall vagrant, primarily in the eastern half of Nebraska. There are records from at least 18 counties, but the largest numbers of sightings are for Adams, Platte, Lancaster, and Douglas-Sarpy. Up to 15 have been seen near Nebraska City. It breeds regularly in Oklahoma and Kansas, is a rare breeder in South Dakota, and is an accidental breeder in North Dakota.

Migration. A total of 55 spring records range from April 4 to June 1, with a median of May 8. Fifteen fall records are from July 23 to October 20, with a median of August 19. Of 80 total records, the largest number (37) are for May, followed by April (16), June (8) and July (7).

Habitats. Migrants are associated with freshwater marshes, swamps and upland meadows.

Comments. Breeding Bird Surveys between 1966 and 2003 indicate that the species underwent no significant population changes during that period.

Tricolored Heron   *Egretta tricolor*

Accidental. There are at least five records, including one shot in Kearney County in November of 1918, another collected in Clay County in August 1918, and a sight record from Clay County in August of 1971 (*Nebraska Bird Review* 41:14). Seen in Hitchcock County in 2001 (*Nebraska Bird Review* 71:98).

Reddish Egret.   *Egretta rufescens*

Accidental. One photographic record for Lake McConaughy, September to October, 2000. (*Nebraska Bird Review* 68:146). A second bird was seen at Funk Wildlife Management Area, June 12, 2008 (*Nebraska Bird Review* 76:99; 77:83).

Cattle Egret   *Bubulcus ibis*

An occasional spring and fall vagrant, first reported in Nebraska in 1965, and observed with increasing frequency since then. It has been seen west as far as Dawes County, but most records are for Lancaster, Otoe, and Douglas-Sarpy. Nesting has been documented for Keith County (*Nebraska Bird Review* 63:89) and Cherry County (Mollhoff, 2001). It has been reported in all of the other Plains States.

Migration. Twenty-one total spring records range from April 12 to June 3 with a median of May 9. Eleven total fall records are from July 23 to October 20, with a median of August 29. Of 32 total records, the largest number (11) are for May, followed by April (8) and August (5).

Habitats. Migrants are associated with upland meadows and pastures.

Comments. Since this species found its way to America from Africa via the West Indies, it has spread widely, Feeding on insects disturbed by foraging cattle on the American plains is seemingly little different from feeding around the feet of zebras and wildebeest on the savannas of East Africa. Breeding Bird Surveys between 1966 and 2003 indicate that the species underwent a probable population decline (1.0% annually) during that period.

Green Heron   *Butorides virescens*

A common migrant, and a summer resident, breeding over most of Nebraska excepting the panhandle and the western Sandhills. It also breeds locally in the other Plains States, primarily in the eastern portions.

Migrations. The range of 93 initial spring sightings is from March 10 to June 7, with a median of April 27. Half of the records fall within the period April 15 - May 6. The range of 50 final fall sightings is from July 23 to November 9, with a median of September 18. Half of the records fall within the period September 4-25.

Habitats. Migrating birds occur almost anywhere small fish (such as minnows) can be captured. Breeding usually occurs near trees, but some nesting is in marshlands well away from tree cover.

Comments. This widespread little heron is notable for the fact that it has been seen catching small minnows, disabling them, and then releasing them to serve as bait for attracting larger fish. Breeding Bird Surveys between 1966 and 2011 indicate that the species underwent a significant population decline (1.5% annually) during that period Until recently it has also been called the "green-backed heron" and "little green heron, " in part because of some Latin American populations of uncertain taxonomy.

Black-crowned Night-Heron   *Nycticorax nycticorax*

A common migrant throughout Nebraska, breeding locally in suitable habitats throughout most of the state except perhaps the driest portions of western Nebraska. It also breeds widely elsewhere in the Plains States, excepting the drier areas.

Migration. Eighty initial spring sightings range from March 29 to June 9, with a median of April 25. Half of the records fall within the period April 18 to May 10. Fifty-four final fall sightings are from July 22 to November 15, with a median of September 6. Half of the records fall within the period August 18 to September 29.

Habitats. This is a highly adaptable species, found in a wide array of aquatic habitats, with nesting occurring in swamps, marshes, and sometimes even city parks or orchards where water is nearby.

Comments. The night-herons are called thus because of their large eyes and associated abilities to forage late into the evening hours, when it is almost dark. This species is a fairly common breeder at Crescent Lake and Valentine refuges, and it is a startling sight to have one of these herons suddenly take flight from just a few feet away while walking through heavy marsh vegetation.

Yellow-crowned Night-Heron   *Nyctanassa violacea*

An uncommon spring and fall migrant and occasional summer visitor in Nebraska, mainly the eastern half of the state. There is a single 1963 record of unsuccessful breeding in Sarpy County (*Nebraska Bird Review* 32:9), and young fledglings have twice been seen near Lincoln. Breeding is regular in Oklahoma, local in Kansas, and occasional in northwestern Missouri.

Migration. Forty-three total spring sightings range from April 2 to June 10, with a median of May 6. Half of the records fall within the period April 29 to May 14. Twelve total fall records are from August 1 to October 24, with a median of September 5.

Habitats. Non breeding birds occupy a wide range of aquatic habitats, but in Nebraska the birds are often found along tree-lined rivers.

Comments. This beautiful night-heron mostly nests to the south of Nebraska, but occasionally finds its way into our state. Young birds resemble those of black-crowned night-herons, but are somewhat darker on the back and wing-coverts.

Family Threskiornithidae

(White Ibis) *Eudocimus albus*
    Accidental. Observed over a period of several days in Rock County in August of 1963 *(Nebraska Bird Review* 32:12). Also reported July 5, 1999, at Kissinger Lagoon (*Nebraska Bird Review* 67:88), and at Funk Lagoon August 9, 2001 (*Nebraska Bird Review* 69:162, 71:98*).

Glossy Ibis *Plegadis falcinellus*
    Rare. More than 50 spring records have been noted for this species through 2011, most since 2004 (*Nebraska Bird Review* 80 to 52). Various immature and non-breeding examples of this species have been reported for Nebraska. Records extend from April to August. Apparent hybrids with the following species have also been seen.

White-faced Ibis *Plegadis chihi*
    A rare spring vagrant and summer visitor throughout Nebraska. Local breeding has occurred in Garden County and (more recently) in Cherry County (Mollhoff, 2001). It has been observed at least three times in Sioux, Scotts Bluff, Garden, Lancaster and Douglas-Sarpy counties, and once or more in Dawes, Cherry, Keith, Lincoln, Brown, Adams, Antelope, Platte and Dakota counties. Six state nesting records were known as of 2003, and some recent ones have occurred in the Rainwater Basin.
    Migration. Thirty two total records range from April 9 to October 14. The largest number (14) of the sightings are for May, followed by April (9), and there are two records each for June, August, September and October.
    Habitats. Non-breeding birds may occur in almost any wet or moist habitat, including marshes, flooded fields, wet meadows, and other areas having shallow water for foraging. Nesting usually occurs in shallow marshes having extensive emergent vegetation.
    Comments. This somewhat exotic-looking bird has become regular at Crescent Lake refuge; I have seen groups of up to 14 birds there in recent years. It is difficult to distinguish from the following species, and they often hybridize. Breeding Bird Surveys between 1966 and 2011 indicate that the species underwent a significant population increase (3.2% annually) during that period.

Roseate Spoonbill *Platalea ajaja*
    Accidental, There is a Nebraska specimen record from Buffalo County, obtained in June of 1932. There is also a sight record of two seen near Hastings, Clay County, in August 1966 (*Nebraska Bird Review* 34:77), and a single individual was seen near Nebraska City on August 5 & 14, 1997 (*Nebraska Bird Review* 65:162).

Family Cathartidae

Black Vulture *Coragyps atratus*
    Accidental. There is a single old specimen record, and more recently there have been sightings in January of 1950 (Keith County), April of 1951 (Logan County), April of 1955 (Keya Paha County), and March of 1963 (Hamilton County).

Turkey Vulture *Cathartes aura*
    An uncommon to common spring and fall migrant statewide, and a little-documented summer resident. It is a local breeder along some of the major river systems (Republican, Missouri and Niobrara), and in the Pine Ridge area, but there are few actual published records (*Nebraska Bird Review* 39:19; 64:47). Mollhoff (2000) reported only six confirmed nestings during the Breeding Bird Atlasing years. Raptor Recovery Nebraska has raised several chicks rescued from various locations. It is a local but regular breeder in all of the Plains States, and a migrant throughout.
    Migration. Ninety initial spring sightings are from January 12 to June 10, with a median of April 14. Half of the records fall within the period April 1–24. Nineteen final spring sightings are from April 11

to June 10, with a median of May 18. Eleven initial fall sightings are from July 20 to September 25, with a median of September 6. Thirty-five final fall sightings are from August 6 to December 30, with a median of September 26. Half of the records fall within the period September 16 to October 4.

Habitats. Migrants or non-breeders are found widely over open plains, sandhills or other areas offering visual foraging. At the northern end of its range the species is mostly associated with brushy woodlands adjoining open grasslands or croplands during the breeding season. Cliffs, crevices, abandoned buildings or other cavities are needed for nesting sites.

Comments. Once associated largely with the remote deserts of the west, the turkey vulture has become yet another urbanized species. More than 60 now roost nightly during summer in the heart of Lincoln, moving out to the country during the day to scavenge for carrion along roadsides, and often nesting in abandoned barns or farmhouses. Breeding Bird Surveys between 1966 and 2011 indicate that the species underwent a significant population increase (2.3% annually) during that period.

Family Pandionidae

Osprey   *Pandion haliaetus*
An uncommon to occasional spring and fall migrant statewide, probably most common eastwardly, where more large rivers and reservoirs exist. Nesting has occurred since 2008 in the Panhandle, near Scottsbluff and Keystone (*Nebraska Bird Review* 76:57; 80:91).

Migration. The range of 102 initial spring sightings is from January 1 to May 25, with a median of April 21. Half of the records fall within the period April 12 to May 1. Twenty-one final spring sightings are from April 7 to May 27, with a median of May 5. Twenty-two initial fall sightings are from August 28 to November 30, with a median of September 15. Half of the records fall within the period September 14-24. Seventeen final fall sightings are from September 17 to December 26, with a median of October 9.

Habitats. While on migration this species occurs along rivers, lakes and reservoirs that support fishes and have fairly clear water for foraging.

Comments. It is more than likely that ospreys will begin nesting in Nebraska again, considering the many new reservoirs that have been formed in recent decades. The birds are now regular spring and fall migrants at Lake McConaughy and other larger reservoirs in the state, and watching them dive into water to capture prey is an exciting event. Breeding Bird Surveys between 1966 and 2011 indicate that the species had a significant population increase (2.3% annually) during that period.

Family Accipitridae

Swallow-tailed Kite   *Elanoides forficatus*
Extirpated. Previously bred in eastern Nebraska (Greenwood [Cass County], Rockport [Douglas or Washington counties], and Calhoun [Washington County] according to Bruner, Wolcott and Swenk, 1904), but disappearing sometime after 1900. A 1960 sighting for Douglas County was later retracted.

White-tailed Kite   *Elanus leucurus*
Accidental. Reported Sarpy County, August-September, l983, and Polk County May 6, 1995 (*Nebraska Bird Review* 51:91; 63:60). Four total records to 2004 (*Nebraska Bird Review* 73:52). The fifth ands sixth records were from southeastern Lincoln County, in the summers of 2007 and 2008 (*Nebraska Bird Review* 77:99).

Mississippi Kite   *Ictinia mississippiensis*
Rare. In addition to some old records for Adams and Douglas counties, there have been three sightings between 1975 and 1977 in Douglas-Sarpy counties, two during 1974 in Lincoln County, one in 1978 in Lancaster County, one in 1950 in Antelope County, one in 1944 in Adams County, and one in 1948 in Webster County. Since 1991 breeding attempts have occurred regularly in the city of Ogallala (*Nebraska Bird Review* 63:89; 65:88-89, 164), and more recently in Red Cloud (*Nebraska Bird Review* 73:52) Benkleman (*Nebraska Bird Review* 78:136), and Imperial (*Nebraska Bird Review* 80:91).

Migration. Eight total spring records are from April 15 to May 30, with a mean of May 15. Four fall records are for September 9 (2), 11 and 19. Kansas's records extend to late October.

Habitats. Associated with scrub and open woodlands near water. The Ogallala nestings have been in a large tree in a residential area. Parks and golf courses are also used for nesting by these birds.

Comments. Breeding by this attractive little kite has occurred for more than a decade in Ogallala, but has not spread out, in spite of several broods that have been reared successfully there. The breeding range in Kansas has slowly advanced northward, so additional nesting locations in Nebraska should be expected.

Bald Eagle   *Haliaeetus leucocephalus*

An uncommon spring and fall migrant and locally common winter resident in Nebraska, especially along the major rivers and reservoir areas, such as Lewis and Clark Lake, Lake McConaughy, Johnson Lake and Harlan County Reservoir. Although it once bred regularly in eastern Nebraska, the first known modern-era nesting attempt was in 1973 in Cedar County (*Nebraska Bird Review* 41:76). In more recent years nesting efforts have occurred every year, often along the Platte River or other larger bodies of water. By 1998 nesting efforts were known from Douglas, Sherman, Garden, Gage, Nemaha, Pawnee and Boyd counties. By 2005, 35 nests were occupied, mostly along larger rivers. During winter bald eagles appear at lakes, reservoirs or larger rivers throughout the Plains States. Between 1991 and 2009 49 young had fledged from 440 nests with known outcomes (*Nebraska Bird Review* 78:121 to 126).

Migration. Sixty-five initial fall sightings range from September 16 to December 31, with a median of November 29. Half of the records fall within the period November 16 to December 16. Eighty-eight final spring sightings are from January 8 to May 12, with a median of March 19. Half of the records fall within the period March 17 to April 2.

Habitats. Bald eagles in Nebraska utilize ice-free areas of larger tree-lined rivers and reservoirs during winter periods. Perching is usually done in tall cottonwoods near water.

Comments. Bald eagle winter populations have greatly increased in recent years; now an average of more than 1,000 birds winter within the state. Lake McConaughy is especially favored, but Johnson and Harlan County reservoirs, the J-2 hydroplant near Lexington, the central Platte River, and the Republican and Missouri Rivers are also important areas. Usually about 25-30 percent of these birds are immatures, suggesting that favorable reproduction is occurring. Breeding Bird Surveys between 1966 and 2011 indicate that the species underwent a significant population increase (4.9% annually) during that period.

Northern Harrier   *Circus cyaneus*

A common migrant and permanent resident throughout Nebraska. Although in cold winters most birds may leave the state, in most areas and years the species can be regarded as a resident. It is probably most common as a breeder in the Sandhills and the Rainwater Basin. It breeds locally almost throughout the Plains States, and is a regular throughout during migration.

Migration. Thirty-nine initial spring sightings range from January 1 to June 2, with a median of March 13. The wide spread of the records suggest it is a resident over much of the state. Thirty-six final fall records are from September 14 to December 31, with a median of December 9.

Habitats. This species occurs in open habitats such as native grasslands, prairie marshes and wet meadows. Nesting is done in grassy or woody vegetation ranging from upland grasses and shrubs to emergent vegetation in water more than two feet deep.

Comments. Northern harriers are graceful predators that are usually seen sweeping low over marshes and fields, and showing white rump patches in both sexes. Adult males are otherwise silvery gray with black wingtips, whereas females and young males are mostly chocolate brown. Breeding Bird Surveys between 1966 and 2011 indicate that the species underwent a significant population decline (0/9% annually) during that period.

Sharp-shinned Hawk   *Accipiter striatus*

An uncommon to occasional winter visitor and spring migrant throughout Nebraska. Although the only recent breeding records are for the northwest (Sioux County and the Niobrara Valley, Brown County), the species may also nest in the Missouri River's forested valley. It probably nests locally in the Dakotas and Minnesota, and has nested in Kansas and Oklahoma, and migrates throughout the Plains States.

Migration. A total of 142 initial spring records range from January 1 to June 1, with a median of March 29. Half the records fall within the two periods January 1 to 9 and March 17 to April 27, indicating that this species is probably a winter visitor and early spring migrant. Forty-one initial fall records are from July 26 to December 30, with a median of September 16. Half of the records fall within the period September 3 -19. Thirty-five final fall sightings are from August 20 to December 31, with a median of November 10.

Habitats. Throughout the year this species is associated with fairly dense forests, especially mixed woods with some coniferous trees. During winter it often enters wooded yards and hides near feeders to wait for possible prey.

Comments. This is the smallest and most common of the accipiter hawks, noted for their rounded wings, long tails, and swift flight abilities. Sharpshins specialize on catching small birds, often around bird feeders, and they can cause the rapid evacuation of the area by their sudden appearance.

Cooper's Hawk   *Accipiter cooperii*

An uncommon winter visitor and spring migrant throughout Nebraska, and probably a local permanent resident. It is perhaps a rare nester in the Missouri River forests of eastern Nebraska, and there are some recent summer records for the Pine Ridge area, as well confirmed nestings in Hitchcock and Frontier counties during the breeding bird atlasing period of 1984-1989 (Mollhoff, 2001). It is a local but probably regular breeder in suitable habitats throughout the Plains States, especially in eastern and southeastern areas.

Migration. A total of 164 initial spring sightings range from January 1 to June 10, with a median of March 16. Half of the records fall within the two periods Jan. 1–9 and March 13 to April 26, suggesting that the species is a winter visitor and early spring migrant. Thirty-four initial fall records are from August 7 to December 27, with a median of September 16. Half of the records fall within the period September 4 to October 1. Thirty-five final fall sightings are from September 8 to December 31, with a median of October 30.

Habitats. Throughout the year this species is associated with mature forests, especially hardwood forests.

Comments. A larger relative of the sharp-shinned hawk, the Cooper's preys on larger birds, but is even more fearless in its attacks. These two similar species are best distinguished by size, the Cooper's nearly crow-sized. Breeding Bird Surveys between 1966 and 2011 indicate that the species underwent a significant population increase (2.3% annually) during that period.

Northern Goshawk   *Accipiter gentilis*

An occasional winter visitor and spring migrant nearly statewide. Probably less common now than earlier, but there have been recent observations from Box Butte, Cherry, Custer, Saunders, and Lancaster counties according to Game and Parks Commission records. The only areas of breeding in the Plains States are the Black Hills and northern Minnesota, but it is a migrant throughout.

Migration. Forty-eight spring records range from January 1 to June 1, with a median of March 15. Half of the records fall within the two periods January 1–11 and April 14 to May 16, suggesting this species is both a winter visitor and late spring migrant. Twenty-two total fall records are from September 16 to December 31, with half of the records occurring within the two periods September 21–October 17 and December 25-31.

Habitats. Throughout the year this species is rarely found far from wooded to heavily forested areas.

Comments. The Latin name of the goshawk may suggest it is "gentle", but the name really refers to the royal appearance of the bird. The common name goshawk refers to the species' ability to attack and kill geese and similar-sized birds.

Harris's Hawk   *Parabuteo uncinctus*

Accidental. The main evidence of occurrence in the state is a specimen reportedly collected at Elkhorn, Douglas County, on October 28, 1922, and now in the Hastings Museum (*Nebraska Bird Review* 45:52). Also observed in Scotts Bluff County on January 13 and 27, 1995 (*Nebraska Bird Review* 64:134).

Red-shouldered Hawk   *Buteo lineatus*

An uncommon to occasional spring and fall migrant in eastern counties and a rare permanent resident in southeastern Nebraska; very rare in other parts of the state. It has been observed west to Lincoln, Garden and Cherry counties, and reported rarely in the Pine Ridge, but known breeding is limited to the Missouri Valley. It apparently bred in Douglas County in 1958 and again in 1964 (*Nebraska Bird Review* 47:38) and in Fontenelle Forest in 1995. Fontenelle Forest and Indian Cave State Park. are likely potential breeding sites In 2009 a nesting attempt was made at Pawnee Lake, Lancaster County (*Nebraska Bird Review* 77: 99; 143). It also breeds in eastern Kansas and eastern Oklahoma.

Migration. Forty-nine initial spring sightings are from January 1 to June 10, with a nearly random temporal distribution, suggesting that the species is perhaps a resident in its limited Nebraska range. Eleven final fall sightings are from September 25 to December 27, with a median of November 16, and no clear indication of migratory movements.

Habitats. Throughout the year this species is found in relatively moist woodlands, especially floodplain forests, with adjacent open country for foraging.

Comments. This attractive hawk has declined in the Midwest in recent years, probably at least in part because of forest fragmentation trends. Eastern Nebraska represents the western edge of its historic breeding range. Breeding Bird Surveys between 1966 and 2011 indicate that the species underwent a significant population increase (2.9% annually) during that period.

Broad-winged Hawk   *Buteo platypterus*

An uncommon spring and fall migrant in eastern Nebraska, and occasional summer resident in the Missouri's forested valley and the panhandle. Nesting has occurred in eastern Nebraska, but there seem to be no recent records, although Fontenelle Forest and Indian Cave State Park are likely sites. Breeding has occurred for several years since 2008 in North Platte (*Nebraska Bird Review* 76:100; 80:92). It still breeds locally in Minnesota, Kansas, and Oklahoma, and has bred in South Dakota.

Migration. Excluding a single January record, the range of 82 initial spring sightings is from March 4 to June 6, with a median of April 26. Half of the records fall within the period April 17 to May 1. Nineteen final spring sightings are from April 12 to June 8, with a median of May 15. Eleven initial fall sightings are from August 8 to October 3, with a median of September 12. Sixteen final fall sightings are from August 25 to November 19, with a median of October 5.

Habitats. Associated with mature deciduous forests, especially those near water, during the breeding season. Migrant birds are sometimes seen in flocks over open country.

Comments, Like the red-shouldered hawk, this little woodland-nesting buteo has regionally declined in population, and shows little sign of recovery. It is a highly migratory species, and like the Swainson's hawk is perhaps exposed to pesticides on its wintering grounds. Breeding Bird Surveys between 1966 and 2011 indicate that the species had a significant population increase (0.9% annually) during that period.

Swainson's Hawk   *Buteo swainsoni*

A common to uncommon spring and fall migrant and summer resident almost statewide, becoming less common eastwardly, and with the eastern limits of regular breeding probably west of a line from Gage to Burt counties. Largest numbers occur during the fall migration period in late September, but none overwinter. It also breeds elsewhere in the Plains States excepting the easternmost areas, and migrates throughout the region.

Migration. Ninety-three initial spring sightings are from January 1 to June 8, with a median of April 18. Half of the records fall within the period April 3 to May 3. Sixty-five final fall sightings are from August 4 to December 27, with a median of September 26. Half of the records fall within the period September 14 to October 1.

Habitats. While this species occurs in Nebraska it is associated with open country, especially high plains and sandhills with only scattered trees for nesting sites.

Comments. This a plains-adapted, largely insect-eating hawk that is still quite common in western Nebraska, although in recent years mass poisoning by pesticides on wintering areas of South America has done great damage to populations. West of about Kearney most of the buteos seen from roadsides are likely to be Swainson's hawks, whereas east of Grand Island red-tailed hawks increasingly comprise the majority. Breeding Bird Surveys between 1966 and 2011 indicate that the species underwent a significant population increase (0.4% annually) during that period.

Zone-tailed Hawk   *Buteo albonotatus*

Accidental. A single bird was seen and photographed near Cedar Point Biological Station, Keith County, April 25, 2007 *(Nebraska Bird Review*76:118).

Red-tailed Hawk   *Buteo jamaicensis*

An uncommon summer or permanent resident statewide, but more common eastwardly, and a common spring and fall migrant. It is a breeder and migrant throughout the Plains States.

Migration. Thirty-two initial spring sightings range from January 1 to May 21, with a median of March 22 and a nearly random temporal distribution, suggesting that the species is essentially a permanent resident. Twenty-three final fall sightings are from September 29 to December 31, with a median of November 26.

Habitats. A combination of extensive open habitat for visual hunting and scattered clumps or groves of tall trees for nesting provide the year-round needs for this species.

Comments. The red-tailed hawk is the most familiar of Nebraska's buteo hawks. It is present all year, but migrants also move through the state during September to October and again in March and April. Nesting is done in tall hardwoods near the edges of woodlands, and the birds are highly effective predators of rodents, rabbits, and snakes such as bull snakes. Not all red-tailed hawks have rusty tails; first-year birds have barred brown tails, and the Harlan's race often has grayish tails with little or no rufous tinting. The pale Krider's hawks often have pinkish tails, but some pale red-tails are thought to be leucistic (semi-abinistic) versions of the Harlan's hawk. Typical Harlan's hawks are fairly frequent (ca. 2 percent of the population) during winter in Nebraska. Breeding Bird Surveys between 1966 and 2011 indicate that the species has undergone a significant population increase (1.7% annually) during that period.

Ferruginous Hawk   *Buteo regalis*

An uncommon to occasional permanent resident in western Nebraska. It is apparently migratory and a summer visitant only in northwestern Nebraska, but is a permanent resident or winter visitor elsewhere. Regular breeding occurs west of a line from Dundy to Keya Paha counties, and there are recent records of breeding from Banner, Cherry, Chase, Furnas and Lincoln counties. Elsewhere in the Plains States it nests widely in the drier and short-grass plains region, and may be seen on migration somewhat farther east.

Migration. Seventy initial spring sightings range from January 1 to May 25, with a median of March 1. The wide spread of the records (half falling between January 17 and April 12) suggest that the species is essentially residential in Nebraska. Twenty final fall records are likewise widely spread between August 26 and December 31.

Habitats. While in Nebraska, this species is normally found in grassland habitats having scattered trees or clay buttes or bluffs for nesting sites.

Comments. This majestic buteo is almost eagle-sized, and like the golden eagle is able to prey on prairie dogs and rabbits very effectively. It has a very broad gape, causing it to have a somewhat froglike appearance when its beak is opened. At times its pale rusty tail may cause confusion with pale-morph red-tailed hawks, but the rusty thighs and white "panels" in its outer wing feathers help with identification. Breeding Bird Surveys between 1966 and 2011 indicate that the species underwent a significant population increase (1.3% annually) during that period.

Rough-legged Hawk   *Buteo lagopus*

An uncommon migrant and winter visitor statewide, becoming more common westwardly. It also occurs throughout the entire plains region.

Migration. Eighty-five initial fall records range from September 30 to December 30, with a median of November 2. Half of the records fall within the period October 9 to November 22. A total of 73 final spring sightings range from January 8 to May 20, with a median of March 26. Half of the records fall within the period March 10 to April 12.

Habitats. Open prairies, plains and other grassland habitats are used while on migration and during wintering in the Plains States.

Comments. This is one of Nebraska's winter buteos, for only then does it move south from arctic breeding grounds and share the plains with red-tailed and ferruginous hawks. Like the ferruginous hawk its tarsi are fully feathered (hence the name "rough-legged'), but is a somewhat smaller and is adapted to preying on lemming-sized rodents.

Golden Eagle   *Aquila chrysaetos*

An uncommon migrant and winter resident throughout Nebraska, becoming more common westwardly, and a permanent resident in western Nebraska, especially the Pine Ridge area. There are recent breeding observations from Sioux, Dawes, Sheridan, Box Butte, Scotts Bluff, Banner, Morrill, Garden, Cheyenne and Lincoln counties according to Game Commission records. It also breeds in the western portions of the Dakotas and from Colorado southward, and during winter appears farther eastwardly.

Migration. This species is evidently a resident in western Nebraska and a winter visitor elsewhere, and thus the records are not susceptible to ready statewide analysis. Late winter sightings seem to follow closely the temporal pattern of the bald eagle.

Habitats. Throughout most of the year this species is associated with arid, open country, often with buttes, mountains or canyons that offer remote nesting sites and large areas of grassland vegetation for foraging. In winter it is sometimes found near rivers or reservoirs, but not nearly to the extent that is true of the bald eagle.

Comments. Breeding Bird Surveys of golden eagles in Nebraska suggest that they are widely distributed in western counties, with no special areas of concentration. This is not surprising, since jackrabbits and cottontails are probably important parts of the diet, but there is no attraction to localized sources of fish. Good places to look for nesting birds include the Pine Ridge region.

Family Rallidae

Yellow Rail   *Coturnicops noveboracensis*

Apparently an extremely rare spring and probably fall migrant in Nebraska. Most of the records are for eastern counties. There are at least two June records, suggesting possible breeding (*Nebraska Bird Review* 41:24), but the nearest area of kn0own breeding is southern Minnesota. It also breeds in eastern North Dakota and perhaps in South Dakota and Iowa.

Migration. Eight total spring records are from April 26 to June 10, with a mean of May 6. There apparently are no fall records for the species in Nebraska, but it has been seen as late as August 26 in South Dakota and to September 30 in North Dakota.

Habitats. During migration this species is likely to be found in marshes with extensive grassy or sedge vegetation. When they occur in the same marshes with Virginia and sora rails they tend to occupy the densest areas of sedges, while the other species are more often found in areas of cattails and bulrushes.

Comments. Yellow rails are among the most elusive of birds, and even the most avid birders often fail to add this species to their life lists. Most have to settle for hearing responses to playbacks of the species' calls.

Black Rail   *Laterallus jamaicensis*

Apparently an extremely rare spring and fall migrant. There are two specimen records from Nemaha County for September of 1873, one was seen in the Omaha Market, and an early sight record for

Cuming County (Bruner, Wolcott and Swenk, 1904). Recent records include one possibly seen at Lake 11 near Omaha, Douglas County, September 20, 1979, and one reported on May 13, 1979, from Phelps County (*Nebraska Bird Review* 47:67). Also reported from Crescent Lake National Wildlife Refuge between May 31 and September 6 (*Nebraska Bird Review* 63:73). Nebraska is slightly outside its known breeding range. Reported from Lancaster County in May, 1980 (*Nebraska Bird Review* 48:88), and (a calling bird) from Verdigre, Knox County, Nov. 1, 2002 (*Nebraska Bird Review* 71:138*)*.

Migration. The few Nebraska records extend from May 13 to September 20. In Kansas it has been reported from as early as March 18to as late as September 26.

Habitats. In the Great Plains this species occupies marshy meadows that are heavily overgrown with sedges and grasses. Like the yellow rail, it is much more likely to be heard than seen.

Comments. This species is even less frequently seen than the yellow rail, although some people have told stories of sitting still beside a dense marsh and seeing a black rail suddenly appear and nearly walk across their feet! Playback of recordings of black rail calls at Crescent Lake Refuge have suggested that a breeding population may occur there, but this remains to be proven.

Clapper Rail   *Rallus longirostris*

Accidental. A single specimen record exists for Stapelton, Logan County, resulting from a bird captured in a trap January 20, 1951. Also observed near Brule, May 9, 1954 (Brown, Dinsmore and Brown, 2012).

King Rail   *Rallus elegans*

A rare summer resident in eastern Nebraska. There are few sightings, but it probably breeds locally and rarely east of a line from Jefferson to Knox counties. It possibly also nests in the Clear Creek marshes **at** the west end of Lake McConaughy. Most recent sightings are from eastern North Dakota and southern Minnesota southward to eastern Texas. Nests rarely in South Dakota.

Migration. Nine total spring records are from April 2 to June 9, with a mean of May 6. Five fall records are from July 10 to September 11, with a mean of August 7.

Habitats. During the breeding season this species is associated with freshwater marshes, up to four feet deep, with abundant shoreline and emergent vegetation.

Comments. This large rail has been seen several times in the Lincoln area, but no definite recent nesting records have been established for Nebraska. An old nesting record does exist for Douglas County.

Virginia Rail   *Rallus limicola*

An uncommon spring and fall migrant and summer resident almost statewide. It is less common in the Panhandle, but is regular in southern Sioux and Dawes counties. It breeds widely in the Plains States excepting the drier western areas and also the southeastern portion, and occurs throughout during migration.

Migration. Thirty-six initial spring sightings are from February 14 to June 1, with a median of May 8. Half of the records fall within the period April 29-May 16. Thirteen final fall sightings are from July 21 to October 13, with a median of September 16.

Habitats. The primary breeding habitats are marshes with extensive stands of emergent vegetation such as taller grasses, bulrushes and sedges. Nests are built over wet ground or in shallow water among emergent vegetation.

Comments. Virginia rails probably nest regularly in the state, especially in the Sandhills, but actual nesting records seem to be limited to Sheridan, Garden, Arthur, Lincoln, Cherry, Holt and Lancaster counties. Until Lake Ogallala was modified to allow for increased hydro power capabilities for Kingsley Dam in the 1980s, a regular veritable chorus of sora and Virginia rails could be heard on summer evenings.

Sora   *Porzana carolina*

A common spring and fall migrant and locally common summer resident nearly statewide. It is more local in the Panhandle. It breeds very widely in the Plains States excepting the southern and southwestern regions, and occurs throughout during migration.

Migration. Of 108 initial spring records, the range is from March 10 to June 3, and the median is May 6. Half of the records fall within the period April 30 to May 12. Twenty-five final fall sightings are from July 27 to November 27, with a median of September 30.

Habitats. Habitats are apparently almost identical to those of the Virginia Rail, namely marshlands with extensive stands of dense emergent vegetation, especially grasses and grassland plants. Nesting tends to occur in deeper water than is true of the Virginia rail, often in water 9 to 12 inches deep and well concealed in cattails, bulrushes, or sedges.

Comments. This species is the commonest of the rails in Nebraska, but even so nesting records are rather few and far between. During the atlasing period there was only a single confirmed nesting, in Lincoln County (Mollhoff, 2001) The eggs and nests of sora and Virginia rails are nearly identical.

Purple Gallinule   *Porphyrio martinica*

Accidental. One was observed in Cuming County in the summer of 1884 or 1885, and a second one was observed in Gage County on March 28, 1962 (*Nebraska Bird Review* 38:50). There are records for at least ten Kansas counties, and breeding occurs in Oklahoma.

Common Gallinule   *Gallinula galeata*

An occasional migrant in eastern Nebraska and a rare summer resident. There are a few old and scattered breeding records (Cherry, Lincoln and Douglas counties), and more recent (1984-1989) ones in Lancaster and Fillmore counties (Mollhoff, 2001). As of 2009 there had been about ten breeding records (*Nebraska Bird Review* 77:144). It breeds regularly in Minnesota, Iowa, Kansas and Oklahoma.

Migration. Sixteen initial spring records are from March 23 to June 1, with a median of May 11. Half of the records fall within the period May 1 to 29. Three final fall sightings are from July 26 to September 29, with a mean of August 22.

Habitats. The favored summer habitat of this species consists of freshwater ponds and marshes having an abundance of emergent vegetation. Nests are usually placed above water or on land surrounded by water.

Comments. Common gallinules (called "common moorhens" in Britain) are moderately common birds, but are nearly as elusive as rails in most locations. Yet, in England, where they are fully protected, they are as fearless as coots and can be easily seen in park lagoons, such as in the heart of London.

American Coot   *Fulica americana*

A common to abundant spring and fall migrant and summer resident. It occurs throughout the state, but is most abundant in the Sandhills marshes. Sometimes it overwinters where open water exists. It breeds and migrates throughout the Plains States in suitable habitats.

Migration. Seventy-four initial spring sightings are from February 4 to June 7, with median of March 29. Half of the records fall within the period March 19 to April 24. Eighty-two final fall records are from July 25 to December 31, with a median of November 2. Half of the records fall within the period October 14 to November 21.

Habitats. A wide variety of wetlands, ranging from small ponds or large lakes and reservoirs are used throughout the year, but those that are fairly shallow and rich in submerged aquatic plants are favored. Nesting usually occurs in emergent vegetation.

Comments. Coots have a bad "image" problem; they often are accused of being stupid, and hunters scoff at them as game birds. Back in the 1950s the Fish and Wildlife Service tried to popularize their hunting (and increase the sale of hunting permits) by increasing the daily kill limit and calling them "white-billed ducks," but this did nothing to enhance the coots' popularity. Yet, they are fascinating to watch as they establish and defend their territories, and tend to their odd-looking chicks.

Family Gruidae

Sandhill Crane   *Grus canadensis*

An abundant spring migrant in the Platte Valley from Grand Island to Lewellen, uncommon to rare elsewhere, west at least to the Clear Creek area of Lake McConaughy, and a local breeder. Generally less abundant in the fall. Other than the Platte Valley, the only significant area of concentration is near the Harlan County Reservoir, which the birds have increasingly used in early spring. Elsewhere in the Plains States it is a regular but less common migrant. Since 1996, breeding has occurred in the eastern Rainwater Basin on many occasions (*Nebraska Bird Review* 67:48; 71:113; 75:76; 76:101, 158; 77:54, Brown & Johnsgard, 2013), as well as in Morrill County and Scotts Bluff County (*Nebraska Bird Review* 77:100).

Migration. Fifty-seven initial spring sightings are from January 8 to May 1, with a median of March 1. Half of the records fall within the period February 10-March 20. Thirty final spring sightings are from March 9 to June 1, with a median of April 7. Fifty-five initial fall sightings are from September 2 to November 24, with a median of October 8. Half of the records fall within the period September 28 to October 22. Fifty-three final fall sightings are from October 1 to December 31, with a median of November 5.

Habitats. Slowly flowing rivers, with relatively bare bars and islands for roosting, and adjacent wet meadows and croplands for foraging, are used by this species during migration. The Platte Valley is evidently the optimum spring habitat for this species in the entire Plains region. Spring concentrations there are unequaled anywhere in North America, usually peaking at about 500,000 in late March.

Comments. Sandhill cranes are the perfect harbinger of spring in Nebraska, they arrive with the break in winter weather, and their departure coincides with the leafing out of our flowering trees and shrubs. Breeding Bird Surveys between 1966 and 2011 indicate that the species underwent a significant population increase (4.9% annually) during that period.

Common Crane   *Grus grus*
Extremely rare. Apparently two different individuals were observed in Lincoln County during 1972, and in 1974 one was seen in Kearney County on March 16 and 25. An adult was reported from March 30-31, l996 in Hall County (*Nebraska Bird Review* 64:80-82; Brogie, 1997). Also observed March 6-ca. 14, 1999 in Kearney and Buffalo counties, and a probable male with a sandhill mate and two apparently hybrid offspring were seen in Hall County in mid-March, 2000. Also observed near Lewellen, March 19, 2009, elsewhere (Hershey, North Platte) that same month, and near Hershey March 18 to 24, 2010 (Brown, Dinsmore and Brown, 2012). As of 2011 there were 14 state records (*Nebraska Bird Review* 76:58; 77:54; 78:47; 79:53).

(Hooded Crane)   *Grus monacha*
Hypothetical. Observed (and photographed) in Hall County for 17 days, from March 25 to April 11, 2001. This Asian crane was possibly an escape from captivity (*Nebraska Bird Review* 79:53).

Whooping Crane   *Grus americana*
An occasional spring and fall migrant in Nebraska, more often seen in spring than in fall. It has been observed in at least 26 counties, but most commonly in Buffalo and Kearney counties. It has also been observed at least ten times each in Dawson, Hall, Lincoln and Adams counties. Over 90 percent of the sightings have occurred within 30 miles of the Platte River, and about 80 percent have occurred between Lexington and Grand Island (*Nebraska Bird Review* 45:54-6). There have been many recent sightings, with four confirmed and five probable sightings in the fall of l994 alone (*Nebraska Bird Review* 62:149-150). and 20 during the spring, l996 migration (*Nebraska Bird Review* 64:69). It is also rare to occasional in Oklahoma, Kansas and the Dakotas, extremely rare in Colorado, and accidental in Minnesota.

Migration. A summary of migration records for this species has already been published (*Nebraska Bird Review* 45:54-6), which indicates that the spring migration extends from early March to late May, with a peak during the period April 1-15. The earliest spring record is for February 10, 1995. The fall migration extends from mid-September to early November, with a peak during the period October 11 to 25.

Habitats. While in Nebraska, the Platte Valley is the primary habitat, and a wide and slow-flowing river, with its numerous sand bars and islands, and adjacent wet meadows, grain fields and marshlands, is evidently an important combination of habitat characteristics. The species migrates later in spring than does the sandhill crane, and thus does not normally associate with it. It probably uses marshy areas, "lagoons", and similar wet areas for foraging to a larger degree than does the sandhill crane.

Comments. Whooping cranes have stopped in Nebraska's Platte Valley more often than anywhere else along their entire migration route between wintering and breeding areas. Unlike sandhill cranes flock sizes are quite small, often comprised of single families. In recent years a few cranes have arrived early, with sandhill cranes; presumably these are immature birds.

Family Charadriidae

Black-bellied Plover   *Pluvialis squatarola*

An uncommon spring and fall migrant in eastern Nebraska, becoming rarer westwardly. Less common in fall than during spring, but more common in both seasons than the golden-plover. The migration route includes the entire Plains States region.

Migration. Sixty-six total spring sightings range from April 4 to June 9, with a median of May 16. Half of the records fall within the period May 12-23. Thirteen initial fall sightings are from July 27 to October 2, with a median of August 20. Thirteen final fall sightings are from August 27 to November 12, with a median of October 6.

Habitats. Mudflats, shallow ponds and plowed fields are used by migrating birds.

Comments. In contrast to most shorebirds, ploughed fields are a favorite habitat for migrant black-bellied plovers. In these locations the black and white plumage patterns seem appropriate. This species and the golden-plovers are almost unique among American shorebirds in having darker underparts than backs, which is contrary to the principle of countershading for maximum concealment.

American Golden-Plover   *Pluvialis dominica*

An uncommon to occasional migrant in eastern Nebraska, rarer westwardly. More common in spring than fall, but present both seasons. It migrates throughout the eastern portions of the entire region.

Migration. Forty-nine total spring sightings are from April 6 to May 29, with a median of May 7. Half of the records fall within the period April 25 to May 14. Ten initial fall sightings are from September 2 to October 9, with a median of September 28. Ten final fall sightings are from September 8 to November 20, with a median of October 12.

Habitats. Migrants favor grass stubble, short pasture lands, and newly plowed fields.

Comments. In common with the previous species, the upperpart coloration of adults in breeding plumage is spangled with dark and light markings. When crouched on a nest these patterns merge almost perfectly with the wet tundra (golden-plovers) or dry tundra (black-bellied plover) habitats that are preferred nest sites.

Snowy Plover   *Charadrius nivosus*

Rare summer resident. There are two early specimen records from Lancaster County (*Nebraska Bird Review* 1:31). It was also observed in Antelope County in 1955, in Adams County in 1957, in Lincoln County in 1964, in Lancaster County in 1972, in Phelps County in 1974, and in Keith County in 1977. Also reported in Phelps County in May, 1994 and 1995 (*Nebraska Bird Review* 62:99; 64:71), and in Fillmore and Clay counties in 1996 (Brogie, 1997). A rare nester at Lake McConaughy since 2000 (*Nebraska Bird Review* 73:154-156; Brown, Dinsmore and Brown, 2012).

Migration. Six spring records for this species range from April 6 to May 17, with a mean of April 28. Five fall records are from August 7 to September 7, with a mean of August 21.

Habitats. Migrants are found on mudflats, alkaline flats, sandy shorelines, and in shallow ponds

Comments. Like the piping plover, the pale gray back color of this species matches that of dry sand, and makes the birds almost impossible to see when they are sitting on their eggs. It has been suggested that the black upper breast markings of these birds are examples of disruptive coloration, actually making them harder to see.

Semipalmated Plover   *Charadrius semipalmatus*

An uncommon to occasional spring and fall migrant statewide, but probably more common eastwardly. It also migrates throughout the entire Plains region.

Migration. Eighty-two initial spring sightings are from March 24 to June 6, with a median of May 12. Sixteen initial fall sightings are from July 25 to September 24, with a median of August 11. Sixteen final fall sightings are from July 30 to October 14, with a median of September 18.

Habitats. Migrants favor mudflats, shallow ponds, and the muddy banks of slowly flowing rivers.

Comments. Unlike the snowy and piping plovers, this species is a high-arctic nester, nesting on pebbly tundra sites. Its back is the color of wet sand, which helps to distinguish the species from the two just-mentioned species. Counts in 2006 and 2011 revealed 723 (2006) and 330 birds in the state, many at Lake McConaughy (*Nebraska Bird Review* 79:88).

Piping Plover   *Charadrius melodus*

An occasional to rare spring and fall migrant, and a local rare summer resident. There are numerous older nesting records for the Niobrara, North and South Platte, Loup and Missouri rivers, but most of the recent records are for the Platte (especially from Dawson County eastward), lower Niobrara and upper Missouri, Loup and Middle Loup rivers, and at Lake McConaughy, Keith County. Recent Breeding Bird Surveys indicate that 250-280 pairs breed in the state, most in the central Platte Valley, at Lake McConaughy, and on spoil piles associated with gravel operations. In 2005 202 nests were found at Lake McConaughy, compared with 182 in 2004 and 117 in 2003 (*Nebraska Bird Review* 73:101).

Migration. Sixty-one initial spring sightings are from March 27 to June 1, with a median of May 3. Half of the records fall within the period April 21–May 12. Five final fall sightings are from July 27 to September 5, with a mean of August 19.

Habitats. Breeding birds are usually associated with sparsely vegetated shorelines of shallow lakes and impoundments, especially those having bare sand or salt-encrusted areas of gravel, sand or pebbly mud.

Comments. This is one of the state's breeding species that is considered threatened in Nebraska. Changes in annual river flows of the Missouri and Platte rivers have destroyed much of its historic breeding habitat, although sandpit operations have provided some new opportunities. The total northern Great Plains population comprised about 1,250 pairs in the mid-1990s, of which Nebraska's component represented about 20 percent. In 2006 the Platte Valley population accounted for nearly five percent of the Interior race's population (via Mary B. Brown, cited in Johnsgard, 2012).

Killdeer   *Charadrius vociferus*

A common to abundant spring and fall migrant and summer resident statewide. Overwinters infrequently in the state. Also breeds and migrates throughout the Plains States.

Migration. The range of 86 initial spring sightings is from February 11 to May 27, and with a median of March 13. Half of the records fall within the period March 8-19. The range of 110 final fall records is from August 18 to December 31, with a median of October 19. Half of the records fall within the period September 27 to November 10.

Habitats. This highly adaptable species often occurs on open fields during migration, but typically breeds near wetlands where there is exposed ground nearby. The birds seem to prefer gravely, stony or sandy areas for nesting, but also nest in a wide variety of locations, sometimes even in garden plots and building rooftops.

Comments. This is the most widespread and common plover in North America, often nesting well away from water and close to human population centers. Its conspicuous "*kill-deer*" calls can be heard in Nebraska from mid-March onward, and its defensive "broken-wing" behavior is familiar to every rural schoolchild. Breeding Bird Surveys between 1966 and 2011 indicate that the species underwent a significant population decline (1.1% annually) during that period.

Mountain Plover   *Charadrius montanus*

A rare spring and fall migrant and summer resident in extreme western Nebraska. A record of young seen in Kimball County in 1974 was the first known case of breeding in the state, but it was later found breeding there in 1990 and 1991. Breeding records now exist for at least Kimball, Cheyenne and

Banner counties. In 2005 47 nests were located in Kimball County, and one in Banner County, over 20,000 acres of dry land wheat fields (*Nebraska Bird Review* 73:101). In 2010 109 nests were monitored, which produced 30 broods (*Nebraska Bird Review* 78:93).

Migration. Two initial spring sightings are for May 8 and May 15. There are no available fall records. In Kansas fall records extend to September 16.

Habitats. Migrants or breeders in the Plains States are usually found in short-grass plains habitats, but sometimes also occur on sandy semiarid flats supporting some brush or cactus. Nesting occurs in extremely exposed locations, often on bare ground.

Comments. This characteristic species of the short-grass plains benefits from grazing by bison or cattle, and its population has been seriously declining in recent years. Breeding Bird Surveys between 1966 and 2011 indicate that the species underwent a significant population decline (2.0% annually) during that period.

Family Recurvirostridae

Black-necked Stilt   *Himantopus mexicanus*

A rare spring migrant, with no evidence of nesting within the state until nesting began at Crescent Lake National Wildlife Refuge, Garden County in 1985. Breeding has also occurred near Lakeside, Sheridan County, since at least 1985, in Dawes County in 1994, in Hall County in 1998, at Funk Lagoon in 2003, and at Harvard Lagoon and North Lake Basin (Seward Co.) in 2005. As of 2008 there had been five nestings in the eastern Rainwater Basin (*Nebraska Bird Review* 76:101, 159). There are also scattered non-breeding records from other counties as far east as Antelope County, but no pattern of geographic consistency is evident.

Migration. Eight records extend from April 30 to August 8. Five of the records are for the month of May.

Habitats. Generally associated with alkali ponds and marshes, often those used by avocets.

Comments. This elegant, long-legged shorebird has been slowly increasing in Nebraska, and elsewhere in the Great Plains. It seems to favor shallow, alkaline ponds such as those found in the western parts of Crescent Lake National Wildlife Refuge, where cinnamon teal and Wilson's phalaropes also congregate.

American Avocet   *Recurvirostra americana*

An uncommon spring and fall migrant in eastern and extreme western Nebraska. It is common in central parts of the state, a common summer resident in the Sandhills, and locally also nests in the Rainwater Basin. It is a regular breeder in the western half of the Plains States region, and migrants may appear throughout it.

Migration. Eighty-two initial spring sightings range from April 2 to June 7, with a median of April 28. Half of the records fall within the period April 20 to May 6. Thirty-eight final fall sightings are from July 25 to November 17, with a median of September 4. Half of the records fall within the period August 25-September 2.

Habitats. In Nebraska avocets are associated with shallow ponds or marshes with exposed and sparsely vegetated shorelines, often in association with strongly alkaline waters. Nests are placed in exposed locations on mud flats, sand bars and islands, with little or no surrounding cover.

Comments. The American avocet is one of the most beautiful of American shorebirds, and can be easily seen in the western parts of Crescent Lake National Wildlife Refuge. In the summer of 1995 over 140 avocets were present there at Smith Lake, which was then being drained temporarily.

Family Scolopacidae

Spotted Sandpiper   *Actitis macularia*

A common spring and fall migrant and summer resident statewide. Local nesting occurs throughout the Plains States except in the southern areas, and migrants occur throughout.

Migration. The range of 105 initial spring records is from March 3 to June 5, with a median of May 4. Half of the records fall within the period April 26 to May 3. Sixty-two-final fall records are from July 26 to October 26, with a median of September 9. Half of the records fall within the period August 27-September 22.

Habitats. Throughout its stay in Nebraska, this species is associated with wetlands having exposed or sparsely vegetation shorelines or islands, and ranging from fairly rapidly flowing streams to stillwater habitats. The shoreline features are apparently more important than the characteristics of the water.

Comments. This little sandpiper can be seen along most of Nebraska's waterways, where its teeter to totter behavior and distinctive flight, with strongly down-curved wing actions, make it easily recognizable. It is also the only Nebraska shorebird with spotted underparts, at least in breeding plumage.

Solitary Sandpiper   *Tringa solitaria*

A common to occasional spring and fall migrant statewide, being most abundant eastwardly, and probably least common in the treeless areas. This species' status and distribution in Nebraska has been analyzed in some detail (*Nebraska Bird Review* 10:15-22). The species also migrates throughout the Plains States.

Migration. Eighty-eight initial spring sightings are from March 17 to June 7, with a median of May 4. Half of the records fall within the period April 28 to May 11. Twenty-nine final spring sightings are from May 6 to June 10, with a median of May 13. Thirty-six initial fall sightings are from July 20 to September 9, with a median of August 9. Thirty-five final fall sightings are from August 5 to November 26, with a median of September 1.

Habitats. Wooded ponds, streams and flooded meadows are used by migrants.

Comments. This is indeed a "solitary sandpiper," since it typically forages alone rather than in groups of its own species or even near other shorebirds. Often it can be found along small creeks in the Sandhills that are lined with bushes or trees.

Greater Yellowlegs   *Tringa melanoleuca*

A common spring and fall migrant statewide. It is also a migrant throughout the entire Plains States region.

Migration. The range of 115 initial spring sightings is from March 13 to June 10, with a median of April 13. Half of the records fall within the period April 2-14. The range of 55 final spring sightings is from April 11 to May 30, with a median of May 5. Thirty-eight initial fall sightings are from July 20 to October 16, with a median of August 18. Half of the records fall within the period August 4 to September 3. Thirty-eight final fall sightings are from August 14 to November 16, with a median of October 7.

Habitats. Ponds, marshes, creeks, mud flats and flooded meadows are used by migrants.

Comments. Less common than the lesser yellowlegs, this species has a considerably longer and more robust bill, and when taking flight it usually utters three or four short notes, rather than the two-noted call typical of lesser yellowlegs. The greater yellowlegs is notably less common in Nebraska than is the lesser.

Willet   *Tringa semipalmatus*

An uncommon to locally common spring and fall migrant statewide, and a locally common summer resident in the Sandhills. The Sandhills apparently represent the species southern limits of breeding in the Great Plains. It breeds in both Dakotas, and is a migrant throughout the entire Plains States region.

Migration. The range of 104 initial spring sightings is from March 18 to June 10, with a median of April 27. Half of the records fall within the period April 19 to May 5. Sixteen final fall sights are from August 10 to November 9, with a median of August 24. Half of the records fall within the period August 19 to September 1.

Habitats. A rather wide variety of wetland habitats are used by breeding birds, including streams, ponds, and marshes or shallow lakes, provided that prairie vegetation is located nearby. Less often hayfields or croplands may be used for nesting.

<u>Comments</u>. It is always a surprise to persons unfamiliar with willets when these rather dull-looking birds take flight and suddenly expose their stunning white wing markings; the willet's older generic name *Catoptrophorus* means "bearing a mirror."

Lesser Yellowlegs   *Tringa flavipes*

A common spring and fall migrant statewide, usually somewhat more abundant than the greater yellowlegs. It is also a migrant throughout the entire Plains States region.

<u>Migration</u>. The range of 124 initial spring sightings is from March 13 to May 29, with a median of April 14. Half of the records fall within the period April 10 to June 1, with a median of May 13. Thirty-five initial fall sightings are from July 20 to September 22, with a median of August 15. Half of the records fall within the period August 8 to September 5. Forty-two final fall sightings are from August 20 to November 23, with a median of October 5.

<u>Habitats</u>. Ponds, marshes, creeks, mud flats and flooded meadows are used by migrants. There is no apparent ecological separation of migrating greater and lesser yellowlegs.

<u>Comments</u>. Both species of yellowlegs are tundra nesters, and it is always a shock for persons used to seeing these birds only on wintering or migration sites to find them perching in bushes and low trees in the arctic, where they scan for possible predators or other danger, and utter territorial calls. In eastern Nebraska the lesser yellowlegs is nearly ten times more common than the greater.

Upland Sandpiper   *Bartramia longicauda*

An uncommon spring and fall migrant and local summer resident in natural grasslands nearly statewide, but most common in the Sandhills. Elsewhere it nests in suitable habitats almost throughout the Plains States, and migrants are regular throughout.

<u>Migration</u>. The range of 108 initial spring sightings is from March 9 to May 9th, with a median of May 2. Half of the records fall within the period April 24 to May 10. Seventy-five final fall sightings are from July 21 to October 28, with a median of August 20. Half of the records fall within the period August 10-26.

<u>Habitats</u>. During summer, this species occurs on native prairies, especially mixed-grass and tall grass, on wet meadows, hayfields, retired croplands, and to a limited extent, on fields planted to small grains.

<u>Comments</u>. One of the most typical and beautiful of the Sandhills breeders, the upland sandpiper provides a definition of grace when it lands on a fencepost and momentarily lifts both wings in a ballet-like movement, before inserting them in its flank feathers and coming to rest. Its territorial song-flights are equally memorable. Once called the "upland plover," it is indeed rather plover–like in having a short bill and upland habitat preferences.

Eskimo Curlew   *Numenius borealis*

Extirpated from Nebraska, and nearly extinct if not already extinct. At one time it was a fairly common to abundant spring and fall migrant in the state, but the last definite Nebraska record was on April 8, 1926, near Hastings. The species was once regular through the Plains States from Texas to South Dakota. A Platte River sight record of April 16, 1986 (*Nebraska Bird Review* 55:78) was later withdrawn.

<u>Migration</u>. Ten spring records are from March 22to approximately May 25, with a median of April 12. There are no specific fall records. Some birds possibly migrated through the state in October, although the bulk of the population migrated to the Atlantic Coast and then flew south.

<u>Habitats</u>. While in Nebraska this species would settle in large flocks on newly plowed fields and dry, burnt-off prairies, where they foraged on grasshoppers and other insects. They evidently concentrated in York, Fillmore and Hamilton counties, in flocks of up to several hundred birds. As the native prairies disappeared, they increasingly used wheat fields and tame meadows.

<u>Comments</u>. Some persons believe that a few Eskimo curlews may yet survive, but there have been no verified sightings in the past few decades, and thus that fond wish may be a futile one.

Whimbrel   *Numenius phaeopus*

An extremely rare spring migrant. There seem to have been at least eleven sightings since 1949, with the largest number from Lincoln County, but with other sightings in York, Adams, Webster and Lancaster Counties. There is one fall record (October 17) for Douglas County, and a few other fall records, but it has been reported during fall in Oklahoma. It is also an occasional to rare migrant elsewhere in the Plains States.

Migration. Eleven spring records are from April 12 to May 27, with a median of May 10.

Habitats. Migrating birds favor flooded grasslands, sandbars, and the shorelines of large impoundments.

Comments. There should be more Nebraska records for this species than the summary above would indicate. The birds nest in Canadian tundra directly north of Nebraska, and some birds winter on the Gulf Coast, so a regular movement through Nebraska seems likely.

Long-billed Curlew   *Numenius americanus*

A common migrant and summer resident in western Nebraska, particularly in the Sandhills and High Plains regions. The eastern breeding limits reach at least Garfield and Holt counties, perhaps the eastern edge of the Sandhills. Breeding also occurs in the western Dakotas, Colorado, New Mexico, Texas and Oklahoma.

Migration. Eighty-three initial spring sightings range from March 7 to June 7, with a median of April 11. Half of the records fall within the period April 5-21. Twenty-eight final fall sightings are from July 22 to September 21, with a median of August 18. Half of the records fall within the period August 5-September 1.

Habitats. In Nebraska, this species is associated with Sandhills grasslands, short-grass plains, and other grassy environments offering extensive foraging and nesting opportunities. Nests often occur in prairie vegetation on upland slopes that are close to moist meadows for foraging

Comments. It seems probable that the Nebraska Sandhills represent the last major breeding stronghold of this species in the Great Plains. The author once counted more than 50 curlews in a single wet meadow in Crescent Lake National Wildlife Refuge during July, at a time when flocks were starting to gather prior to fall migration. The Nebraska population has been estimated as about 24,000 (*Nebraska Bird Review* 79:89).

Hudsonian Godwit   *Limosa haemastica*

An uncommon spring migrant in eastern Nebraska, becoming rare or absent in the west. There are no fall records for Nebraska or South Dakota, and very few for Oklahoma and Kansas. It probably regularly migrates through the eastern half of the Plains States.

Migration. Sixty-nine initial spring records are from April 12 to May 27, with a median of May 2. Half of the records fall within the period April 22- May 12. Ten final spring sightings are from May 6 to May 25, with a median of May 15.

Habitats. Associated with marshy ponds, wet grasslands, and flooded fields while on migration.

Comments. This is another beautiful shorebird that breeds in arctic tundra, and that becomes a bush- and tree-perching bird upon arrival at its nesting grounds. Its rich rufous underpart coloration during spring easily separates it from the marbled godwit.

Marbled Godwit   *Limosa fedoa*

An uncommon to locally common migrant throughout Nebraska, but with far fewer sightings in fall than during spring. There are recent state breeding records for the western and northern Sandhills (*Nebraska Bird Review* 76:102), such as in Sheridan County (*Nebraska Bird Review* 73: 102; 76:102). It is a regular breeder in the Dakotas and western Minnesota, and a migrant throughout the Plains States.

Migration. The range of 117 initial spring sightings is from April 5 to May 26, with a median of April 29. Half of the records fall within the period from April 22- May 10. Eleven final spring sightings are from April 19 to May 23, with a median of May 7. Eleven total fall records are from July 20 to October 24, with a median of September 9.

Habitats. Extensive mud flats, wet fields, sand bars and the shorelines of impoundments are commonly used by migrating birds.

Comments. The name "godwit" comes from a traditional English name, meaning "a good thing (to eat)." That may be true, but a godwit is also a very good thing to see and hear; this is the largest of all godwits, and certainly one of the most attractive.

Ruddy Turnstone   *Arenaria interpres*

An occasional to rare spring migrant in eastern Nebraska, very rarely seen as far west as Cherry and Garden counties. The largest number of sightings are for Adams and Lancaster counties, especially the latter. Rarely reported during the fall, with a total of only 12 fall observations (*Nebraska Bird Review 73;140*). Migrants are most common in the eastern portions of the Plains States, especially east of the Missouri River.

Migration. Twenty-three total spring records are from April 19 to May 27, with a mean of May 18; Half of the records fall within the period May 14-25, with a median of May 18. Half the records fall between the period May 14-25. There are two fall records, September 10 & 17 (Rosche, 1982).

Habitats. Mudflats, shallow ponds and plowed fields are used by migrating birds.

Comments. Turnstones get their vernacular name from their tendency to flick rocks and pebbles over with their sharp bills, to find small invertebrates that may be hiding below. Few turnstones occur in Nebraska, but they are exciting finds whenever they can be found.

Red Knot   *Calidris canutus*

An extremely rare spring and fall migrant in eastern Nebraska, not reported west of Sheridan County. Most of the records are for Lancaster and Douglas-Sarpy counties, but there are scattered sightings elsewhere in eastern Nebraska. It is also a rare migrant elsewhere in the Plains States, mainly in the eastern portions.

Migration. A total of six spring records range from May 7 to May 19, with a mean of May 14. Six fall records are from August 27 to October (no date), with a mean of September 12.

Habitats. Mud flats and sand bars are used by migrating birds.

Comments. This is a rather robust little shorebird; its reddish underparts in spring is the basis for its common name "robin snipe" along the Atlantic coast. It is a high-arctic nester, and its short bill would seem better adapted for surface-foraging than for mud-probing.

Sanderling   *Calidris alba*

A rare to occasional spring and fall migrant in Nebraska, mostly in eastern and central parts of the state, becoming rare in the west but observed as far west as Scotts Bluff County. It is a regular migrant throughout the eastern half of the entire Plains States region.

Migration. Fifty-six initial spring sightings are from March 26 to June 2, with a median of May 6. Half of the records fall within the period April 25 to May 15. Thirteen final spring sightings are from April 26 to June 10, with a median of May 13. Seventeen initial fall sightings are from July 27 to October 2, with a median of August 20. Twelve final fall sightings are from August 12 to October 19, with a median of October 4.

Habitats. Migrants are associated with sandy shorelines, sand flats, salt-encrusted flats, and less frequently muddy shorelines.

Comments. When the sanderlings pass through Nebraska they mostly seem to be in the pale winter plumage, during which time their darker anterior wing-coverts become conspicuous field-marks. On their arctic nesting grounds they have a rufous cast on the upperparts.

Semipalmated Sandpiper   *Calidris pusilla*

A common spring and fall migrant, locally abundant or uncommon, the latter typical of western Nebraska. It is a migrant throughout the entire Plains States Region.

Migration. Eighty-nine initial spring sightings are from March 21 to June 10, with a median of April 28. Half of the records fall within the period April 20 to May 10. Thirty-nine final spring sightings are from April 28 to June 1, with a median of May 15. Twenty-three initial fall sightings are from July 20 to September 8, with a median of August 5. Twenty-three final fall sightings are from July 28 to October 16, with a median of September 18.

Habitats. Migrating birds use mud flats, shallow ponds, exposed sand bars, and open shorelines as well, but rarely move onto dry fields with Baird's sandpipers or wet grasslands with least sandpipers.

Comments. Jorgensen (2004) found this species to be the third most abundant spring migrant shorebird in the eastern Rainwater Basin.

Western Sandpiper   *Calidris mauri*

A rare spring and uncommon fall migrant in eastern Nebraska, becoming more common westwardly, but considered rare even at Crescent Lake National Wildlife Refuge, Garden County. The species' status in the state is still only poorly known. It is probably a migrant throughout the entire Plains States region, but more common in western portions and during fall, since the spring migration closely follows the Pacific coastline.

Migration. Forty-one initial spring sightings are from April 7 to June 10, with a median of May 8. Half of the records fall within the period April 28 to May 15. Ten final spring sightings are from May 3 to May 23, with a median of May 13. Fourteen initial fall records are from July 20 to September 19, with a median of August 12. Eleven final fall sightings are from August 26 to October 2, with a median of September 1.

Habitats. Mud flats, shallow ponds and open shorelines are used by migrants, which avoid dry areas and prefer to forage while wading in shallow water, usually forage a slightly greater depth than do semipalmated sandpipers.

Comments. Western sandpipers are much like semipalmated sandpipers in appearance, but are more rufous above (especially in spring) and have a longer bill that droops slightly at the tip.

Least Sandpiper   *Calidris minutilla*

A common spring and fall migrant statewide, but becoming less common westwardly. It is a migrant throughout the entire Plains States region.

Migration. The range of 102 initial spring sightings is from March 8 to May 29, with a median of May 2. Half of the records fall with the period April 20 to May 10. Forty-one final spring sightings are from April 27 to June 2, with a median of May 12. Twenty-three final fall sightings are from July 20 to September 9, with a median of August 2. Twenty-three final fall sightings are from July 28 to November 11, with a median of September 18.

Habitats. Mud flats, shallow ponds, marsh edges and flooded meadows are used by migrants, which frequently gather in small groups foraging in shallow puddles or wet grasslands well away from the larger "peeps".

Comments. This is one of the commonest of the small "peep" sandpipers in Nebraska, and is notable for its olive-yellow legs and small size.

White-rumped Sandpiper   *Calidris fuscicollis*

An abundant spring migrant statewide, but appreciably fewer fall records exist. It is probably somewhat more common in eastern Nebraska than in western areas. It is a migrant throughout the entire Plains States region.

Migration. The range of 100 initial spring sightings is from March 28 to June 1, with a median of April 29. Half of the records fall within the period May 1 to 16. Seventeen final spring sightings are from May 8 to May 25. Eleven total fall sightings are from July 20 to October 4, with a median of August 12.

Habitats. Migrants feed in shallow ponds, flooded pasture lands, flat shorelines, and muddy creeks; often with Baird's sandpipers, but are less likely to forage in dry areas than that species.

Comments. At least in western Nebraska this is a very common spring migrant, which in flight can be easily recognized by its white rump. Jorgensen (2004) found it to be the most abundant spring migrant shorebird in the eastern Rainwater Basin.

Baird's Sandpiper   *Calidris bairdii*

A common spring and fall migrant statewide, and probably the most abundant of the "peeps" in Nebraska, especially in western portions of the state. It is a migrant throughout the entire Plains States region.

Migration. The range of 125 initial spring sightings is from March 12 to May 24, with a median of April 21. Half of the records fall within the period April 6 to May 4. Fifty-four final spring sightings are from April 7 to May 29, with a median of May 13. Thirty-two initial fall sightings are from July 20 to October 1, with median of August 12. Twenty-seven final fall sightings are from August 3 to December 5, with a median of October 6.

Habitats. Migrants use mud flats, shallow ponds, sand bars, and dried areas such as overgrazed pastures, salt plains and similar open habitats while on migration.

Comments. Jorgensen (2004) found this species to be the sixth most abundant spring migrant shorebird in the eastern Rainwater Basin. Baird's sandpipers have a rather distinctive ochre-tinted back pattern that that is more scalloped than linear in appearance.

Pectoral Sandpiper   *Calidris melanotos*

A common to abundant spring and fall migrant almost statewide, but becoming less common to rare westwardly. It is a migrant throughout the entire Plains States region.

Migration. The range of 102 initial spring sightings is from March 4 to June 6, with a median of April 28 and half of the records falling within the period April 15 to May 8. Thirty-nine final spring sightings are from April 5 to May 25, with a median of May 13. Twenty-eight fall sightings are from August 3 to November 20, with a median of October 4.

Habitats. Migrating birds use a variety of habitats, including muddy shorelines, creeks, flooded grasslands and shallow marshy areas where the emergent vegetation is not too thick.

Comments. Larger than the typical "peeps," the pectoral sandpiper often feeds among them, when its greater size and sharply cut-off breast pattern is usually quite apparent. Jorgensen (2004) found this species to be the most abundant fall migrant shorebird in the eastern Rainwater Basin.

Sharp-tailed Sandpiper   *Calidris acuminata*

Accidental, with thee sight records. The first was of a juvenile in Butler County, Oct. 12, 1986 (*Nebraska Bird Review* 54:70), and the second was a bird seen in Sheridan County, September 6, 1996 (*Nebraska Bird Review* 62:114). By 2010 there were four state records (*Nebraska Bird Review* 78:138).

Dunlin   *Calidris alpina*

An occasional spring migrant in eastern Nebraska, rare in western parts of the state. Apparently rare during fall migration in all areas. It has been observed as far west as Cherry and Garden counties, but is extremely rare in these areas. It is a migrant throughout the eastern half of the entire Plains States region.

Migration. Forty-eight spring sightings range from April 6 to June 2, with a median of May 13. Half of the records fall within the period May 9-21. Eleven fall records are from August 15 to November 20, with a median of September 11.

Habitats. Migrants use mud flats, shallow ponds, and open stretches of muddy shorelines, often mingling with other small sandpipers.

Comments. Like the black-bellied plovers and golden-plovers, dunlins in breeding plumage have conspicuous black bellies, a most unexpected feature for a tundra nester. Perhaps this area is displayed during territorial flights, or otherwise has special signal value.

(Curlew Sandpiper)   *Calidris ferruginea*

Accidental. Seen at Funk Lagoon, Phelps County, July 19 and 21, 1997 (*Nebraska Bird Review* 66:3; 154.).

Stilt Sandpiper   *Calidris himantopus*

A common or uncommon spring and fall migrant almost statewide, but becoming less abundant westwardly. It is a regular migrant throughout the entire Plains States region.

Migration. Ninety-nine initial spring sightings are from April 3 to May 29, with a median of May 11. Half of the records fall within the period May 9-19. Sixteen final spring sightings are from May 7 to May 30, with a median of May 17. Eleven initial fall sightings are from July 21 to September 19, with a median of August 11. Nine final fall sightings are from September 3 to October 21, with a median of September 20.

Habitats. Muddy flats, shallow mud-bottom ponds and flooded fields are used by migrants; the birds feed in belly-deep water and are more likely to be in sheltered areas than on exposed shorelines than many other shorebirds

Comments. This is a fairly frequently encountered shorebird in Nebraska, Jorgensen (2004) found this species to be the fifth most abundant spring migrant shorebird in the eastern Rainwater Basin.

Ruff   *Philomachus pugnax*

Extremely rare. Seven records. Observed near Axtell, Kearney County, September, 1991 (*Nebraska Bird Review :*64:31), Phelps County, April 19, 1994 (*Nebraska Bird Review* 62:99), April 10, 1998, Antelope Co. (*Nebraska Bird Review* 66:41), York County September 27, 1998 (Brogie, 1999), Branched Oak, Lancaster County, May 4, 2002 (*Nebraska Bird Review* 70:60), and Clay County, March 26, 2005 (*Nebraska Bird Review* 73:55).

Buff-breasted Sandpiper   *Tryngites subruficollis*

An uncommon spring and fall migrant in eastern Nebraska. This species is highly local, but has been reported several times in York, Seward and Lancaster counties. It is apparently very rare in western Nebraska, but has been reported from Scotts Bluff and Sheridan counties. Jorgensen (2004) found this species to be regular in the eastern Rainwater Basin, especially in Seward County (near Freeman Lake and North Lake Basin) and Fillmore County (Miller's Pond, 2 miles south of Shickley)

Migration. Twelve total spring sightings are from May 1 to May 20, with a median of May 10. Eleven fall sightings are from August 17 to September 26, with a median of September 7.

Habitats. Migrants are usually found on recently plowed fields, mowed or burned grasslands, meadows, heavily grazed pastures and other rather dry habitats. Jorgensen observed use of agricultural fields, hayfields and wetlands, and maximum numbers seen during the second and third weeks of May, and determined that Nebraska is probably the species' most important spring staging area, supporting a large percentage of the world population in May.

Short-billed Dowitcher   *Limnodromus griseus*

Probably a rare migrant and local in eastern Nebraska, becoming rarer westwardly, but identification problems and earlier consideration of the dowitchers as a single species make the distribution impossible to estimate. Studies of the dowitchers in Nebraska (*Nebraska Bird Review* 8:63-74; 64:74-78) suggest that the short-billed dowitcher is fairly rare in the state. Most recent sight records are from eastern counties (e.g., Jorgensen, 2004). The species is probably regular only in the northeastern portions of the Plains States.

Migration. Seven total spring sightings attributed to this species are from April 20 to May 18, with a median of May 14. Fourteen fall sightings are from early August to September 10, with most records between August 19 and September 10.

Habitats. Migrants use muddy flats and mud-bottom ponds probably identical to those of the long-billed dowitcher, at least in Nebraska. They are often seen with black-bellied plovers.

Comments. Rather little is known of this species' occurrence in Nebraska; in spring it is less rufous below than is the long-billed dowitcher, and its usual call is a three-noted whistle.

Long-billed Dowitcher   *Limnodromus scolopaceus*

A common spring and fall migrant statewide. Unless carefully identified, dowitchers in Nebraska should be tentatively assigned to this species. It is a regular migrant throughout the entire Plains States region.

Migration. Thirty-five initial spring sightings range from April 12 to May 23, with a median of May 1. Half of the records fall within the period April 20 to May 11. Thirteen final spring sightings are from May 4 to June 1, with a median of May 11. Eleven initial fall sightings are from July 20 to October 7, with a median of August 8. Thirteen final fall sightings are from August 1 to December 3, with a median of October 14.

Habitats. Associated with muddy flats and mud-bottom ponds in Nebraska; foraging is done by probing in shallow water of ponds or flooded grasslands.

Comments. Nearly all dowitchers seen in Nebraska seem to be of this species, which is distinguished by its rich rufous underparts and usually a single *keek* note upon takeoff. Jorgensen (2004) found this species to be the fourth most abundant spring migrant shorebird in the eastern Rainwater Basin, and the second most abundant during the fall.

Wilson's Snipe   *Gallinago delicata*

A common spring and fall migrant, and a rare or localized summer resident. Stragglers uncommonly overwinter in the state as well. It has bred in Garden, Rock, Cherry, Garfield, Howard and Lancaster counties. It is regular during summer at the Clear Creek marshes, Garden County, and in the Pine Creek drainage north of Smith Lake in Sheridan County, so nesting there is also quite likely, and in Sandhills marshes. Regular nesting probably occurs from North Dakota and Minnesota southward to South Dakota, and migrants occur throughout the Plains States.

Migration. Eighty-one initial spring sightings range from January 1 to May 29, with a median of April 13. Half of the records fall within the period April 4-21. Twenty-three final spring records are from April 12 to May 28, with a median of April 29. Thirty-seven initial fall records are from July 21 to December 21, with a median of September 18. Forth-two final fall records are from July 27 to December 31, with a median of November 12. The data suggest that overwintering is rather rare in this species.

Habitats. Migrating birds are associated with marshes, sloughs and other wetlands that support areas of mudflats or mucky organic soil where foraging by probing is readily performed. Marshes rich in shoreline and emergent vegetation and are preferred over more open ones.

Comments. Snipes are rarely seen until they suddenly take off in a low, twisting flight, usually uttering a raspy *scaip* note. The strange, "winnowing" noises resembling a whirling propeller made by vibrating the tail feathers of territorial birds flying high overhead can be heard in various parts of the state and probably indicate nesting, but very few actual nests or chicks have been found.

American Woodcock   *Scolopax minor*

An uncommon to occasional spring and fall migrant in eastern Nebraska, and an uncommon and local summer resident. Besides some possible early nestings, there is a 1972 breeding record for Sarpy County and a 1978 nesting in Hamilton County (*Nebraska Bird Review* 47:59). During the period 1984-1989 there were confirmed nestings in Holt, Cedar, Stanton, and Burt counties (Mollhoff, 2001) Displaying birds have been regularly observed west to Kearney. It has also been observed west in the Rainwater Basin as far as Clay and Adams Counties. Breeding is regular in Minnesota, and scattered breeding records exist for the areas directly south of Minnesota, as well as for eastern South Dakota west to the Missouri River.

Migration. Thirteen total spring sightings range from March 12 to June 1, with a median of April 10. Thirteen total fall sightings are from September 12 to November 14, with a median of October 15.

Habitats. In Nebraska migrating woodcocks are generally associated with floodplain forests, where the trees are rather scattered and the land is poorly drained, so that earthworms can be readily obtained by probing in the moist soil.

Comments. Seemingly woodcocks have become more frequent nesters in Nebraska recently; or at least there are now many more sightings of displaying territorial males, nests or chicks. The evening song-flight of males is an ethereal experience, and recently has been reported regularly from the hike-bike trail bridge near Fort Kearney, as well as many locations near Lincoln and Omaha. Moist ground and a ready supply of earthworms are major habitat needs.

Wilson's Phalarope   *Phalaropus tricolor*

A common to abundant spring and fall migrant, and a common summer resident, breeding over much of Nebraska, especially in the Sandhills and the Rainwater Basin. Breeding occurs from North Dakota to central Kansas, and migrants appear throughout the region.

Migration. A range of 115 initial spring sightings is from April 6 to June 6, with a median of May 2. Half of the records fall within the period April 25 to May 10. Thirty-eight final fall sightings are from

July 26 to October 20, with a median of September 8. Half of the records fall within the period August 19 to September 12.

Habitats. Breeding occurs in wet meadows near aquatic habitats ranging from flooded ditches to ponds and marshes or shallow lakes, especially somewhat alkaline ones. Migrants forage by swimming in open water, capturing surface invertebrates while swimming in tight circles, which produces a vortex that draws invertebrates up from below.

Comments. Phalaropes are notable in that they exhibit "sex reversal" traits in which females are larger and more colorful. Females also transfer incubation and brood-rearing chores to males, and to varying degrees are polyandrous. This species breeds commonly around Border Lake, a highly alkaline lake at the western edge of Crescent Lake National Wildlife Refuge. Jorgensen (2004) found it to be the second most abundant spring migrant shorebird in the eastern Rainwater Basin; nesting there has occurred several times since 2000 (*Nebraska Bird Review* 75:77). Recent genetic evidence indicates that phalaropes are close relatives of the *Tringa* sandpipers rather than being only peripherally related shorebirds.

Red-necked Phalarope   *Phalaropus lobatus*

An uncommon to rare spring migrant in northern and western Nebraska, less common in southeastern parts of the state. Less common during fall in all areas. Migrants regularly appear in the northern portions of the Great Plains region, and are occasional as far south as the Oklahoma Panhandle.

Migration. Forty-two initial spring sightings range from April 19 to May 27, with a median of May 14. Half of the records fall within the period May 8-19. Seven final spring sightings are from May 9 to May 25, with a mean of May 19. Ten initial fall sightings are from July 20 to September 21, with a median of August 10. Eleven final fall sightings are from August 20 to October 14, with a median of September 27.

Habitats. Migrants use the same habitats as do Wilson's phalaropes, namely open water areas of marshes and shallow lakes, where the invertebrate life is abundant and can be captured by surface foraging.

Comments. Once called the "northern phalarope," this is an arctic-nesting bird that is only seen in Nebraska while on migration. In non-breeding plumage it often closely resembles the Wilson's phalarope, but is somewhat darker dorsally.

Red Phalarope   *Phalaropus fulicarius*

Very rare. The first specimen was collected in Cherry County (*Nebraska Bird Review* 2:38). Since then, there have been nine fall records, mostly of young birds (*Nebraska Bird Review* 70:14).

Family Laridae

Black-legged Kittiwake   *Rissa tridactyla*

Rare. There is a specimen record from Keith County, of an adult found dead on Keystone Lake during late May, 1990 (*Nebraska Bird Review* 58:75). Several sight records exist from Lancaster County (*Nebraska Bird Review* 5:57, 49:42), such as Branched Oak Lake, December 3, 1995. Also observed in Burt and Douglas counties during November, 1995 (Brogie, 1997). Rare or accidental migrant at Lake McConaughy (Brown, Dinsmore and Brown, 2012). As of 2010 there were 19 fall records *(Nebraska Bird Review* 78:139).

Sabine's Gull   *Xema sabini*

A rare vagrant. There are two specimen records from Lancaster and Gage counties for September 1899. It was also seen in Omaha during April of 1928, in Lincoln County in October of 1966, and in Garden County during October of 1978. It was seen at Gavin's Point from October 26 to November 3, 1996. Three more records were obtained September 26-28, 1996, in Lincoln and Keith counties (*Nebraska Bird Review* 65:42-43), and there were three sightings from Lincoln County during September, 1996 (Brogie, 1997). There are thus at least nine records for the species in Nebraska through 1996, but in 1997 about 24–30 or more birds were seen between September 8 and October 12 *(Nebraska Bird Review*

65:167-8). Reported October 3 1998, on or near Gavin's Point Dam, Cedar Co. (Brogie, 1999). There was only one spring record as of 2009 (*Nebraska Bird Review* 77:56).

Habitats. Large rivers, lakes and reservoirs are sometimes used, but most migration occurs coastally.

Comments. Unlike some of the rare gulls of Nebraska, this species can be easily identified by the white triangular patch on its upper wing bounded by all-black wingtips. There is also a yellow tip to its otherwise black bill.

Bonaparte's Gull   *Chroicocephalus philadelphia*

An uncommon spring and fall migrant in eastern Nebraska, becoming rarer westwardly, but reported as far west as Cherry, Lincoln, and Garden counties. Migrants are regular in eastern and northern areas, mainly from the Missouri River eastward.

Migration. Thirty-six total spring sightings are from April 3 to May 27, with a median of April 23. Half of the records fall within the period April 12 to May 9. Twenty fall sightings are from August 18 to November 21, with a median of October 26.

Habitats. Migrants are associated with rivers, lakes and marshes, especially large lakes.

Comments. This is an arctic-nesting gull that, rather surprisingly, often nests on the branches of low conifers rather than on the ground. Its white outer wing patches makes it easily separable from Franklin's gulls, with which it sometimes associates while on migration.

Black-headed Gull   *Chroicocephalus ridibundus*

Accidental. Observed at Walgren Lake, Sheridan County, August 12, 1979 (Rosche, 1982). There are several Kansas records. Recorded December 19 to 21, 2003 at Lake McConaughy (Brown, Dinsmore and Brown, 2012).

Little Gull   *Hydrocoloeus minutus*

Very rare. Observed at Wehrspan Lake on April 26, 1995 (*Nebraska Bird Review* 64:134), and at Pawnee Lake, Lancaster County, October 3, 1996 (Brogie, 1997). Also seen at North Platte National Wildlife Refuge September 6, 1997, and Summit Reservoir on October 19, 1997 (*Nebraska Bird Review* 65:167). Through 2005 there have been 16 records (*Nebraska Bird Review* 73:141). Recorded April to December at Lake McConaughy (Brown, Dinsmore and Brown, 2012).

Ross's Gull   *Rhodostethia rosea*

Accidental. Observed at Sutherland Reservoir, Lincoln County, 17-23 Dec., 1992 (*Nebraska Bird Review*61:88-90) and at Gavins Point Dam and Branched Oak Lake, Nov. & Dec., 2010 (*Nebraska Bird Review*79:13). Also photographed at Branched Oak Lake, December 3, 2010 (*Nebraska Bird Review* 79:104).

Laughing Gull   *Leucophaeus atricilla*

An extremely rare vagrant. Besides two old records from Douglas and Hall counties, it has more recently been reported from Keith County in 1947, 1950, 1952 and 1992, Platte County in 1953, Lancaster County in 1977 and Lincoln County in 1992. By 2011 there were about 20 state records (*Nebraska Bird Review* 78:139; 79:56). Rare late spring and summer migrant at Lake McConaughy (Brown, Dinsmore and Brown, 2012).

Migration. Five spring records are from April 5 to May 21, with a mean of April 22. The species has been observed in June and July, and three fall records are from December 5-22.

Habitats. Normally associated with coastal habitats while wintering and on migration, vagrants are likely to be seen near large impoundments in the interior.

Comments. This rare species closely resembles the common Franklin's gull, but lacks any white near the wingtips. It seems to be increasingly reported in the Midwest.

Franklin's Gull   *Leucophaeus pipixcan*

An abundant spring and fall migrant, and a very rare or accidental summer resident in Nebraska, with the only known breeding records from Garden County (*Nebraska Bird Review* 34:63; 35; 32). Stragglers sometimes are present during the summer in the Sandhills area. Breeding is regular in the Dakotas, and migrants appear throughout the entire region.

Migration. Eighty-nine initial spring sightings range from March 6 to June 8, with a median of April 10. Half of the records fall within the period March 27 to April 21. Fifty-eight final spring sightings are from April 2 to June 2, with a median of May 14. Fifty-two initial fall sightings are from July 20 to October 24, with a median of September 7. Fifty-eight final fall sightings are from August 17 to December 20, with a median of October 17. Half of the records are for the period October 3 to November 2.

Habitats. Migrants are often found on plowed fields, often closely following the moving plow in large flocks. Breeding occurs on large prairie marshes having extensive areas of semi-open emergent vegetation for nesting.

Comments. The Franklin's gull is a "seagull" with a nesting area that is a thousand miles from the sea, and is actually associated with prairie marshes for nesting. During migration it occurs in large flocks, and breeding also is performed in colonies.

Mew Gull   *Larus canus*
Very rare. Numerous sightings from Dec. 1 to May 11, at Lake McConaughy have been reported (*Nebraska Bird Review* 66:42), One to five adults were seen at Branched Oak lake, Lancaster County, December 1-3, 1996. As of 1998 there were at least 11 records, nearly all from Lake McConaughy (Brogie, 1999). By 2010 there were 24 state records (*Nebraska Bird Review 78:139*). Rare winter and spring migrant at Lake McConaughy; reported at Lake McConaughy from December 14 to May 11 (Brown, Dinsmore and Brown, 2012). As of 2011 there were about 20 records, including 14 fall records (*Nebraska Bird Review 78: 139; 79:13*).

Ring-billed Gull   *Larus delawarensis*
A common to abundant spring and fall migrant statewide, with stragglers sometimes remaining through the summer months. Nesting occurs in North Dakota, and locally in South Dakota, and migrants are regular throughout the entire region.

Migration. Eighty initial spring sightings range from January 3 to May 15, with a median of March 16. Half of the records fall within the period March 5-26. Fifty final spring sightings are from March 12 to June 7, with a median of May 12. Forty-eight initial fall sightings are from July 20 to November 15, with a median of September 12. Fifty-seven final fall sightings are from August 25 to December 21, with a median of November 28.

Habitats. A wide variety of lakes, reservoirs, rivers, marshes and other water areas are used by migrants.

Comments. This is the most common white-headed gull in Nebraska. Breeding Bird Surveys between 1966 and 2003 indicate that the species underwent a significant population increase (1.9% annually) during that period.

California Gull   *Larus californicus*
A rare migrant or winter vagrant in most of Nebraska, but apparently regular and uncommon in northwestern Nebraska (Rosche, 1982). Other than in the northern Panhandle, it has been observed in Garden, Lincoln, Lancaster and Douglas counties. The species breeds in North and South Dakota, and migrants are to be expected in western Nebraska from Colorado.

Migration. Seven spring records are from March 19 to April 26, with a mean of March 28. There is at least one June record. Ten late summer and fall records are from July 18 to November 10. Nine winter records extend from December 13 to February 15.

Habitats. Lakes, large marshes and similar habitats are used by migrants.

Comments. California gulls closely resemble herring gulls, but have yellowish green or grayish green legs and are somewhat smaller. When seen beside a herring gull their darker upperparts are also apparent.

Herring Gull   *Larus argentatus*
        An uncommon spring and fall migrant throughout Nebraska, but becoming rarer westwardly. Stragglers are sometimes seen during the summer months. Migrants are regular everywhere in the Grant Plains region.
        Migration. Forty-seven initial spring records range from January 13 to May 13, with a median of March 18. Half of the records fall within the period March 2 to April 1. Twenty-seven final spring sightings are from March 5 to May 28, with a median of April 21. Twenty-four initial fall sightings are from July 21 to November 24, with a median of October 26. Eighteen final fall sightings are from August 29 to December 21, with a median of November 28.
        Habitats. Migrating birds are widely distributed over rivers, lakes, reservoirs and other water areas.
        Comments. This is the largest of Nebraska's gulls, and the state's most common large gull.

Thayer's Gull   *Larus thayeri*
        Rare but regular overwintering migrant. Observed at Lake North, Platte County, December 4, 1981, and at Gavin's Point Dam, November 24-30, 1985 (Bray et al 1986). Also reported from Gavin's Point Dam and Cunningham Lake during November, 1995 (*Nebraska Bird Review* 63:103), at Branched Oak Lake, Lancaster County, on December 1, 1996, and at Sutherland Reservoir on December 26, 1996. As of 1996 there were 22 reports of this species (*Nebraska Bird Review* 64: 53), and there were several additional sightings in December of 1996 (*Nebraska Bird Review* 65:210). Brogie (1997) listed seven probable records for 1995 and 1996. Reported as early as November 24 and as late as April 15, with most sightings from November through January. At least 20 were seen at Lake McConaughy during the winter of 1997-98 (*Nebraska Bird Review* 66:13). A spring, fall and uncommon winter migrant at Lake McConaughy, reported from October 4 to May 2 (Brown, Dinsmore and Brown, 2012).

Iceland Gull   *Larus glaucoides*
        Rare, 22 records to 2009, half in winter (*Nebraska Bird Review* 7:27). There is a Saline County record in January, 1907. Also seen in Keith County, February, 1994 (*Nebraska Bird Review* 64:39), and at Branched Oak Lake, Lancaster County, December 2, 1996. There are two reports from Keith County in February and March of 1996 (Brogie, 1997). Three were reported at Lake McConaughy in February, 1998 (Brogie, 1999). There was also a sighting at Lake Ogallala. Dec, 14, 2000 (*American Birds* 55:319). A spring and rare winter migrant at Lake McConaughy; reported from December 12 to April 29 (Brown, Dinsmore and Brown, 2012).

Lesser Black-backed Gull   *Larus fuscus*
        Rare. About 100 records have been noted for this species through 2011, mostly from February to April (*Nebraska Bird Review* 80:57). First observed at Pawnee Lake, Lancaster County, February 16 & 24, 1992 (*Nebraska Bird Review* 64:32). Also seen twice at Kingsley Dam in February and March, 1994 (*Nebraska Bird Review* 64:39), and at Branched Oak Lake on March 12, 1995 (*Nebraska Bird Review* 64:135). As of 1996 there were at least 11 records (*Nebraska Bird Review* 64: 53), Several were seen at Lake McConaughy during the winter of 1997-98 (*Nebraska Bird Review* 66:14; Brogie, 1999); now a rare spring, fall and winter migrant at Lake McConaughy (Brown, Dinsmore and Brown, 2012).

(Slaty-backed Gull)   *Larus shistasagus*
        Hypothetical. Reported January 22, 2000, at Harlan County Reservoir (*Nebraska Bird Review* 68:19), and in Sarpy County, December 21, 2006 (*Nebraska Bird Review* 75:8).

Glaucous-winged Gull   *Larus glaucescens*
        Accidental. Observed and photographed on April 12, 1995, at Lake McConaughy (*Nebraska Bird Review* 64:3-4.), and a more recent sighting, December 13, 2000 (Brown, Dinsmore and Brown, 2012).

Glaucous Gull   *Larus hyperboreus*
        Rare overwintering migrant, but more regular in the west, especially at Lake McConaughy. In addition to an early specimen obtained in the Omaha area, there are at least four sight records for Lancaster

County, and additional sightings from Douglas, Dawes, Harlan, Keith, Garden, Lincoln and Scotts Bluff Counties. Several were at Lake McConaughy during the winter of 1997-98 (*Nebraska Bird Review* 66:14). There is also a possible sighting from Adams County. It has also been reported from the Dakotas and Kansas, and is regular in Oklahoma during winter. Spring, fall and winter migrant at Lake McConaughy; reported from October 16 to April 6 (Brown, Dinsmore and Brown, 2012).

Migration. Ten total spring records range from January 24 to April 29, with a median of March 24. Five fall records are from December 3 to 27.

Habitats. Rivers, lakes and coastal shorelines are normally used by migrants.

Great Black-backed Gull   *Larus marinus*
Rare. About 30 records have been noted for this species through 2011 (*Nebraska Bird Review* 80:57). There is a record for May of 1871 from the vicinity of Dakota City, Dakota County. Additionally it was sighted in Hamilton County in April, 1952, and seen at Kingsley Dam, Keith County, March 14, l994 (*Nebraska Bird Review* 64:39), and on February 15, 1997 (*N.O.U. Newsletter*, March/April, 1997). Also seen at Wagontrain Lake, Lancaster County, April 3, 1996; as of 1996 there were five records (*Nebraska Bird Review* 64: 53). Five sightings (perhaps of the same bird) occurred at Lake McConaughy between January 20 and August 4, 1996 (Brogie, 1997), and seen at Gavin's Point Dam on Nov. 12, 1997. By 2010 there were 10 fall records (*Nebraska Bird Review* 78:140.) Rare year-around migrant at Lake McConaughy (Brown, Dinsmore and Brown, 2012). As of 2011 there were 11 fall records (*Nebraska Bird Review* 79:14).

Least Tern   *Sternula antillarum*
An uncommon spring and fall migrant in eastern Nebraska, and a highly local and rare summer resident in the state's major valleys, and around the shorelines of Lake McConaughy (*Nebraska Bird Review* 59:133-150;(Brown, Dinsmore and Brown, 2012). It also breeds locally in the other Plains States from North Dakota southward, and a local migrant in these states.

Migration. Eighty-seven initial spring sightings range from March 8 to June 10, with a median of May 23. Half of the records fall within the period May 16-30. Twenty-six final fall sightings are from July 20 to October 6, a median of August 14.

Habitats. Associated with rivers, lakes and impoundments on migration; nesting is mostly on river sand bars or islands, but sometimes also on barren shorelines of large impoundments, gravel beaches, or even newly cleared land. Nesting is typically done in colonies, on a sand or gravel substrate. In 2008 215 nests were found along the Missouri River in Dixon County (*Nebraska Bird Review* 76:103).

Caspian Tern   *Hydroprogne caspia*
An uncommon spring and fall migrant in eastern Nebraska, especially along the Missouri River, but regularly reported as far west as Sheridan, Garden, Keith, and Lincoln Counties. It is a local migrant in eastern and northern areas, mostly along the Missouri River. A few non-breeding birds often summer in the Lake McConaughy area (Brown, Dinsmore and Brown, 2012).

Migration. Twenty-seven total spring sightings are from March 23 to May 28, with a median of May 10. Half of the records fall within the period May 3-17. Twenty-four fall records are from July 20 to October 14, with a median of September 19. Half of the records fall within the period September 4-25.

Habitats. Larger rivers, deep marshes, lakes and reservoirs are used by migrants.

Black Tern   *Chlidonias niger*
An abundant spring and fall migrant statewide, and a common summer resident, primarily in the Sandhills but locally elsewhere as well. Breeds from North Dakota and Minnesota southward to Kansas, and a migrant throughout the entire region.

Migration. The range of 130 initial spring sightings is from April 9 to June 5, with a median of May 12. Half of the records fall within the period May 6-18. Sixty-six final fall sightings are from July 21 to October 5, with a median of September 2. Half of the records fall within the period August 19 to September 11. The more precise nature of this species' migration as compared with the other terns and gulls is no doubt a reflection of its insectivorous diet.

Habitats. Migrants are found over a variety of aquatic habitats, and sometimes also forage well away from water over adjoining grasslands. Breeding occurs on small to large marsh areas having a combination of open water and stands of emergent vegetation.

Comments. Breeding Bird Surveys between 1966 and 2003 indicate that the species underwent a significant population decline (0.4% annually) during that period.

Common Tern   *Sterna hirundo*

An uncommon to rare spring and fall migrant in eastern Nebraska, becoming rarer westwardly. Frequent confusion with the Forster's tern makes the status of this species somewhat uncertain, but it is probably relatively common only in eastern Nebraska. Breeding occurs in the Dakotas and Minnesota, and migrants are most common in the northeastern portions of the Great Plains region.

Migration. Sixty-five initial spring sightings are from March 18 to June 7, with a median of May 5. Half of the records fall within the period April 24 to May 15. Fourteen final spring sightings are from April 25 to June 6, with a median of May 11. Eleven initial fall sightings are from August 9 to October 14, with a median of September 2.

Habitats. Migrants use lakes, reservoirs and rivers, and less often are found near smaller marshes and ponds.

Arctic Tern   *Sterna paradisaea*

Accidental. An adult was found September 20, 2000, at Lake Minatare (*N.B.R* 68:158), and one was seen at Lake Ogallala, December 21, 2003 (*Nebraska Bird Review*72:61; Brown, Dinsmore and Brown, 2012).

Forster's Tern   *Sterna forsteri*

A common spring and fall migrant statewide, and a rather localized summer resident in the Sandhills, especially Garden, Cherry and Grant counties. It probably also breeds in some Sheridan County marshes. Breeding is regular in Minnesota and the Dakotas, and migrants appear throughout the entire Plains States region.

Migration. Fifty-eight initial spring sightings are from April 11 to June 8, with a median of April 28. Half of the records fall within the period April 19 to May 5. Twenty-one final spring sightings are from April 24 to June 6, with a median of May 17. Thirteen initial fall records are from July 21 to September 22, with a median of August 1. Twenty final fall sightings are from August 1 to October 8, with a median of September 11.

Habitats. Associated with lakes, rivers and marshes while on migration. Breeding occurs in large marshes having extensive areas of emergent vegetation or muskrat houses for nesting sites. Small marshes seem to be avoided for nesting.

Royal Tern   *Thalasseus maximus*

Accidental. A single specimen record, North Lake, York County (*Nebraska Bird Review* 75:108; 76:39–45).

Family Stercorariidae

Pomarine Jaeger   *Stercorarius pomarinus*

Very rare but probably the most frequently seen jaeger in Nebraska. There are early records for Dakota County in 1869, Fremont County in 1873, and Lincoln County in 1895 (Bruner, Wolcott and Swenk, 1904). One was observed in Lancaster County in September of 1973. There was a sighting of a single bird at Conestoga Lake, Lancaster County on December 15-17, 1991 (*Nebraska Bird Review* 54:31) and at Lewis and Clark Lake, Knox County, on June 30, 1990 (Brogie, 1997). There was also a sighting at Pawnee Lake, Lancaster County, November 15-19, 1997 (*Nebraska Bird Review* 65:167). Rare summer and fall migrant at Lake McConaughy (Brown, Dinsmore and Brown, 2012). Twelve state records accumulated through 2005 (*Nebraska Bird Review* 73:141), and more have since occurred. .

Parasitic Jaeger   *Stercorarius parasiticus*
         Accidental or very rare. There is a specimen record from Lancaster County in 1898, and a second
bird was obtained in Sheridan County in August of 1968 (*Nebraska Bird Review* 36:76, 37:31). The latter
was first believed a great skua *Catharacta skua* (*Nebraska Bird Review* 36:4). Also reported from Lake
McConaughy on 5 October, 1997 (*Nebraska Bird Review* 65: 167). Rare or accidental fall vagrant at Lake
McConaughy (Brown, Dinsmore and Brown, 2012).

Long-tailed Jaeger   *Stercorarius longicaudus*
         Accidental or very rare. A specimen record from Lancaster County in 1952 (*Nebraska Bird Review*
21: to 3), and three more recent records, mostly of immatures (*Nebraska Bird Review 69:170)*. Rare
summer and fall migrant at Lake McConaughy (Brown, Dinsmore and Brown, 2012). By 2009 there were
five state records (*Nebraska Bird Review* 77:110-111). As of 2010 there were eight reports, most in fall
(*Nebraska Bird Review* 78:139).

Family Alcidae

Ancient Murrelet   *Synthliboramphus antiquus*
         Accidental. There is a single specimen record from Burt County (*Nebraska Bird Review* 1:14).
Not reported from elsewhere in the Plains States, but there are two Colorado specimen records.

Family Columbidae

Rock Pigeon   *Columba livia*
         An introduced and common permanent resident statewide, especially in towns and around farms,
but feral in a few western locations. Also a resident throughout the entire Great Plains.
         Habitats. Mostly associated with human habitations in cities, villages and farms, but also occurring
to a limited extent as feral populations around bluffs and cliffs in western Nebraska.

Band-tailed Pigeon   *Patiogioenas fasciata*
         Accidental. One was reported in Morrill, Scotts Bluff County, October 15, 1996 *(Nebraska Bird
Review* 64:116; Brogie, 1997). Also observed at Ceresco from November 2007 to March, 2008. This was
Nebraska's third record, as there is one other sight record from Scotts Bluff County (*Nebraska Bird Review*
76:7). The nearest breeding is Colorado.

Eurasian Collared-Dove   *Streptopelia decaocto*
         This introduced and increasing species has become common and widespread since first reported in
1997 *(Nebraska Bird Review* 65:168; 66:42). Nesting began in 1998 (*Nebraska Bird Review* 66:43). By
1998 it had been seen at Kearney, Shelton and Superior (*Nebraska Bird Review* 67:95). By 2007 it had
been reported from all of Nebraska's counties. (*Nebraska Bird Review* 75:9). Breeding Bird Surveys
between 1966 and 2011 indicate that the species underwent a significant population increase (18.3%
annually) during that period.

White-winged Dove   *Zenaida asiatica*
         Rare to occasional summer resident. Photographed in Lincoln May 11-l6, l994 (*Nebraska Bird
Review* 64:39), photographed at Malcolm, Lancaster County, May 13, 1994, and seen at Scottsbluff on 15-
21 April, 1995 (*Nebraska Bird Review* 64:135). By 2005 there were at least 40 state records, mostly
between April 15 and October 10 (*Nebraska Bird Review* 73:10, 56, 142), and a probable nesting
(*Nebraska Bird Review* 73:120). In recent years this dove has been reported several times per year, but
breeding records are few, the first reports occurring in 2005 and 2007 (*Nebraska Bird Review* 75:78;
78:95).

Mourning Dove   *Zenaida macroura*

   An abundant spring and fall migrant and summer resident statewide. Overwintering often occurs in mild winters and sheltered locations. Also breeds and migrates throughout the entire Great Plains region.

   Migration. Sixty-two initial spring sightings range from January 1 to May 29, with a median of March 26. Half of the records fall within the period March 9 to April 8. Ninety final fall sightings range from August 30 to December 31, with a median of November 1. The wide spread of fall departure dates suggests that the species frequently overwinters in the state.

   Habitats. A widely adaptable species, occurring in open woods and edge areas, in parks and cities, on grasslands far from trees, and in cultivated fields. Although nests are most often placed in trees, in treeless areas the birds regularly nest on the ground.

   Comments. Mourning doves are among the most abundant of nesting birds in Nebraska, The birds nest repeatedly through the long Nebraska summer, and may raise several broods successfully during that time. Breeding Bird Surveys between 1966 and 2003 indicate that the species underwent a significant population decline (0.4% annually) during that period.

Passenger Pigeon   *Ectopistes migratorius*

   Extinct. Formerly a common migrant and summer resident in eastern parts of Nebraska and elsewhere in the Plains States, with the last records at about the turn of the century.

Inca Dove   *Columbina inca*

   Extremely rare. Birds of this species wintered in Kearney during December and January, 1988, and were seen in Keya Paha County during late November, 1989 (*Nebraska Bird Review* 58:93). Also reportedly observed at a Chadron bird feeder during the early fall of 1996. There are many records of this species for Kansas, usually occurring in late fall or early winter. By 2009 eight records had accumulated, for summer, fall and winter (*Nebraska Bird Review* 77:102).

Common Ground-Dove   *Columbina passerina*

   Accidental. Reportedly seen at Lincoln, Lancaster County , in November 1976 (*American Birds* 31:96), and at DeSoto N.W.R. on November 18, 1979 (*Nebraska Bird Review* 48:22). One was seen November 26, 2004, the second accepted Nebraska record (*Nebraska Bird Review* 73:81).

Family Cuculidae

Yellow-billed Cuckoo   *Coccyzus americanus*

   A spring and fall migrant and summer resident statewide, common in the east but less common westwardly, and becoming rare in the Panhandle. Also breeds throughout the Plains States north to South Dakota and southern Minnesota.

   Migration. The range of 170 initial spring sightings is from April 12 to June 10, with a median of May 23. Half of the records fall within the period May 15-29. The range of 101 final fall sightings is from July 23 to October 14, with a median of September 15. Half of the records fall within the period September 1-27.

   Habitats. Migrating and breeding birds favor moderately dense thickets near watercourses, second-growth woodlands, deserted farmlands overgrown with shrubs and brush, and brushy orchards. Extremely dense woods are avoided.

   Comments. This is the so-called "rain crow" of Nebraska, the birds often calling as the skies darken just prior to rain. Cuckoos are great skulkers, which may predispose them to brood parasitism, although that is rare among our native cuckoo species. Breeding Bird Surveys between 1966 and 2011 indicate that the species underwent a significant population decline (1.5% annually) during that period.

Black-billed Cuckoo   *Coccyzus erythropthalmus*

A spring and fall migrant and summer resident almost statewide, most common in the northeast, rarer in the south and west, and nearly absent from parts of the Panhandle. Also breeds throughout the Plains States from North Dakota and Minnesota south to Oklahoma, and migrates throughout.

Migration. The range of 163 initial spring sightings is from April 1 to June 10, with a median of May 24. Half of the records fall within the period May 16-30. The range of 60 final fall sightings is from July 28 to October 9, with a median of August 30. Half of the records fall within the period August 25 to September 9.

Habitats. Relatively dense wooded habitats are favored by this species, especially those that provide a variety of trees, bushes and vines for possible nesting sites

Comments. This species is considerably less common than the yellow-billed cuckoo in Nebraska, but its call is more like that of a cuckoo-clock. Both species feed largely on hairy caterpillars such as tent caterpillars, and their yearly abundance varies greatly, probably in relation to food supplies. Breeding Bird Surveys between 1966 and 2011 indicate a significant population decline (1.6% annually) during that period.

Groove-billed Ani   *Crotophaga sulcirostris*

Accidental. There have been four sight records, including one seen in Antelope County during September and October 1952, one in Hall County during October of 1975, one in Cuming County in October of 1976 and one seen at Beaver Lake, Cass County (*Nebraska Bird Review* 43:49; 45:13; 53:78). It is accidental in South Dakota and Kansas, and irregular in Oklahoma.

Family Tytonidae

Barn Owl   *Tyto alba*

An uncommon permanent resident statewide, but probably more common in the southern counties. Also breeds throughout the Plains States north to South Dakota.

Habitats. Open to semi-open habitats, where small rodents are abundant and where hollow trees, old buildings, or caves are available to provide roosting and nesting sites are favored by this species. Rats are particularly favored as prey species, but many other rodents are also consumed.

Comments. Barn owls are rodent-catchers without peer, and the presence of a pair at a farm may account for the disappearance of several thousand mice or rats per year. They are thus highly valuable birds, although farmers often seem unaware of their presence or, if so, may actually try to kill them. Near Cedar Point Biological Station in Keith County the nesting birds concentrate on pocket mice and kangaroo rats for prey, but in turn are preyed upon by great horned owls.

Family Strigidae

(Flammulated Owl)   *Otus flammeolus*

Hypothetical. An owl identified as possibly this species on the basis of its calls was heard in Chadron State Park, Dawes County in June of 1978 (*Nebraska Bird Review* 46:70). The nearest known breeding area is in northern Colorado.

Eastern Screech-Owl   *Megascops asio*

A common permanent resident in wooded areas throughout the state, but rare or absent from the treeless areas. Even in eastern Nebraska the rufous plumage morph is rare. There are no Nebraska records of *kennicottii.*

Habitats. This widespread species occurs in a variety of wooded habitats, including farmyards, cities, orchards, and other human-made habitats, as well as in forests and woodlands. It is probably more common in cities than in heavy woodlands, where it is preyed upon by larger owls.

Comments. Screech-owls often go unnoticed in places where they are common, the whinny-like call these birds utter is not very owl-like, and they hide during daylight hours in tree cavities. In eastern Nebraska about 90 percent of the birds are gray morphs, and farther west the rufous type is even rarer.

Breeding Bird Surveys between 1966 and 2011 indicate that the species underwent a significant population decline (1.3% annually) during that period.

Great Horned Owl   *Bubo virginianus*

An uncommon permanent resident statewide, but probably most common in the heavily wooded major river valleys and the Pine Ridge area. Also breeds and migrates throughout the entire Plains States region.

Habitats. This highly adaptable species occurs in a variety of habitat types ranging from dense forests to city parks and farm woodlands, and extends into non-wooded environments in rocky canyons and gullies.

Comments. This is Nebraska's largest and most powerful owl, and it is able and likely to attack skunks, feral cats, and sometimes even very small dogs. It is not safe to climb up to a nest of these birds without protective headgear; their talons are long and the birds have a vise-like grip.

Snowy Owl   *Bubo scandiacus*

An occasional winter visitor, not present every winter, but occurring almost anywhere in the state. Progressively more common to the north of Nebraska during winter.

Migration. This winter visitor shows a range in 18 initial fall sightings from November 6 to December 29, with a median of December 4. Twenty-three final spring sightings are from January 3 to April 30, with a median of February 5.

Habitats. Wintering birds are usually associated with open fields, plains, marshes, and grassy lowlands, often perching on haystacks or other somewhat elevated sites.

Comments. Only during occasional winters do snowy owls enter Nebraska in any numbers; this probably occurs during population crashes of lemmings in the arctic. Over 200 were reported during the invasion of 2011–2012 (*Nebraska Bird Review* 80: 72–76). The birds are highly conspicuous where snow is absent from the landscape, and many snowy owls are shot by ignorant hunters.

Northern Hawk Owl   *Surnia ulula*

Accidental. The only record is a specimen obtained in Lancaster County during November of 1891 (Bruner, Wolcott and Swenk, 1904). Also reported from Sheridan County, 1912.

Burrowing Owl   *Athene cunicularia*

A common to uncommon spring and fall migrant and summer resident in western and central Nebraska, becoming rare eastwardly, and not known to breed east of Lancaster County. Also breeds widely elsewhere in the Plains States, excepting the more easterly portions.

Migration. The range of 119 initial spring sightings is from March 10 to June 10, with a median of April 24. Half of the records fall within the period April 13 to May 9. Forty-three final fall sightings are from July 21 to November 9, with a median of September 16. Half of the records fall within the period August 30 to September 30.

Habitats. This species is normally associated with heavily grazed grasslands, especially those supporting colonies of large rodents such as prairie dogs. Normally colonial, scattered nestings may also occur by individual pairs where suitable excavations are available.

Comments. Partly because of state laws requiring the control of prairie dogs on private lands, the numbers of both prairie dogs and burrowing owls have plummeted in recent decades, and there are few places left where these fascinating little owls can be readily observed. Unlike most owls the birds are daytime-feeders, and they also are mostly insect-eaters, at least while they are in Nebraska. Breeding Bird Surveys between 1966 and 2011 indicate that the species underwent a significant population decline (1.1% annually) during that period.

Barred Owl   *Strix varia*

An uncommon permanent resident in southeastern Nebraska, becoming rarer westwardly, and absent from the western half of the state. The western breeding limits of this species are not known, but it is a rare straggler to eastern Colorado. Also breeds widely through the eastern portions of the Plains States.

Habitats. Throughout the year this species is found in dense river–bottom woods, which in Nebraska are typically of hardwoods. However, coniferous forests are also used when available, and seem to be preferred.

Comments. The dark brown eyes of the barred owl mark it as a highly nocturnal species; those that hunt during the day and in twilight have yellow eyes. It is also one of the most vocal of owls, and can be easily called up by imitation or playback of its calls. Breeding Bird Surveys between 1966 and 2011 indicate that the species underwent a significant population increase (1.9% annually) during that period.

Great Gray Owl   *Strix nebulosa*

Accidental. In addition to a specimen record from Douglas County for December of 1893, a bird was shot during January of 1978 in Dixon County, and a specimen was taken in the vicinity of Long Pine, Brown County in 1977 (*Nebraska Bird Review* 47:63). It was also observed in Douglas County in April 1948, in Lincoln County in January of 1950, The nearest breeding area is in northwestern Wyoming.

Long-eared Owl   *Asio otus*

A permanent resident in wooded areas such as major river valleys throughout the state, uncommon in the east and becoming rarer westwardly. The population is probably supplemented from migrants from farther north during winter. Also breeds and migrates throughout the other Plains States.

Migration. Twenty-four spring sightings range from January 2 to May 14, with a median of March 9th. Nineteen fall sightings are from July 21 to December 31, with a median of November 24. These limited data suggest that the species is a summer resident and a late fall and early spring migrant, with frequent overwintering.

Habitats. Throughout the year this species is associated with wooded areas, including river bottom forests, parks, orchards and woodlots. Both coniferous and hardwood forests are utilized, with the former apparently preferred.

Comments, This attractive owl is mainly a bird of rather dense forests in the east, but two newly fledged young were found perched in low junipers at Cedar Point Biological Station, Keith County, in 1995. Like the barred owl it is quite a vocal bird, but it is hard to find during daytime hours as it hides quietly in dense wood vegetation.

Short-eared Owl   *Asio flammeus*

A permanent resident throughout Nebraska, being more common in the summer in the Sandhills and other natural grasslands. During winter the population is apparently supplemented by migrants from farther north. Probably least common in the Pine Ridge area. Also breeds in the other Plains States south to about Kansas, and occurs farther south during migration.

Migration. Thirty-five spring sightings range from January 8 to June 6, with a median of March 12. Twenty-nine fall sightings are from July 20 to December 31, with a median of November 30. The data are very similar to those of the long-eared owl, suggesting that the species is a summer resident and a late fall and early spring migrant, with frequent overwintering.

Habitats. Throughout the year this species is found in open, grass-dominated environments, and in Nebraska the Sandhills prairie and other natural grasslands are favored habitats. Nesting usually occurs in grassy cover, with several pairs often nesting fairly close to one another in a loose colonial situation.

Comments. Like the northern harrier this is a prairie raptor. Breeding Bird Surveys between 1966 and 2011 indicate that the species underwent a significant population decline (3.5% annually) during that period.

Boreal Owl   *Aegolius funereus*

Accidental. There are two early Lancaster County records for October, 1907 and December, 1892, a Clay County record for 1916, and a more recent record from Webster County in December of 1963 (*Nebraska Bird Review* 32:13). Casual in South Dakota.

Northern Saw-whet Owl   *Aegolius acadicus*

An uncommon to rare winter visitor at least in eastern Nebraska, and perhaps statewide. There is evidence of breeding at Chadron State Park (*Nebraska Bird Review* 77:147). Calling by a territorial male was heard yearly at Fort Robinson for many years during the 1980s, and again in 1997 near Ash Creek Canyon, northeastern Dawes County. A newly fledged juvenile was found as a road kill in Antelope County in late May, 2002 (*Nebraska Bird Review* 70: 63). The species is known to nest in the nearby Black Hills of South Dakota.

Migration. Ten fall records are from July 29 to December 22, with a median of November 8. Seven spring records are from January 1 to May 16, with a median of February 20. These and other limited data suggest that the species is primarily a winter visitor In northwestern Nebraska it is reportedly a rare summer resident, arriving as early as April 18 (Rosche, 1982). Banding by Dan Kim at the Crane Trust, Hall County, captured 40 owls over a several winters (*Nebraska Bird Review* 73:67–70; Brown & Johnsgard, 2013).

Habitats. Although normally associated with rather dense woods, especially cedar groves in Nebraska, this species sometimes appears in unexpected locations during migration. In the Black Hills of South Dakota it breeds in pine and spruce forests, and probably the same is true in the Pine Ridge area.

Comments. Most saw-whet owls in Nebraska are obviously migrants, but there is always the chance that a breeding pair will turn up someday in the Pine Ridge or Niobrara Valley.

Family Caprimulgidae

Common Nighthawk   *Chordeiles minor*
An abundant spring and fall migrant and summer resident statewide, particularly around cities. It is a regular migrant and breeder throughout the entire Plains States region.

Migration. The range of 170 initial spring records is from April 16 to June 7, with a median of May 21. Half of the records fall within the period May 16-28. The range of 137 final fall records is from July 21 to October 24, with a median of September 18. Half of the records fall with the period September 8 to October 2.

Habitats. During its stay in Nebraska, this species occurs widely in open habitats such as grasslands, sparse woods and cities, perhaps being more common near humans than anywhere else, where the tops of flat buildings provide perfect nest locations.

Comments, This is easily the most common of Nebraska's "nightjars", a group of insect-eating and semi-nocturnal birds mostly recognized (and usually named for) their distinctive vocalizations. The common nighthawk's familiar "*beep*" call can be heard over cities and towns from late May onward. Breeding Bird Surveys between 1966 and 2011 indicate that the species had a significant population decline (1.2% annually) during that period; this is perhaps an under-estimate of the rate of this species' decline in the Great Plains..

Common Poorwill   *Phalaenoptilus nuttallii*
A common spring and fall migrant and summer resident in western Nebraska excluding the Sandhills, and generally west of a line from Sheridan to Harlan Counties. There have been scattered sightings of migrants in eastern counties, and a nesting in Lancaster County in 1976 (*Nebraska Bird Review* 39:70; 45:42). It breeds from southwestern North Dakota southward to central Oklahoma.

Migration. Thirty-three initial spring records range from April 25 to June 9, with a median of May 6. Half of the records fall within the period May 1-16. Eighteen final fall records are from July 20 to November 1, with a median of September 4. Half of the records fall within the period August 18 to September 16.

Habitats. Although this species is most common in rather rocky habitats with scrubby cover or dry woodlands, it also locally extends into grasslands. However, the Sandhills area is evidently avoided by breeding birds.

Comments. This rock- and canyon-adapted bird is only rarely seen. Often it is flushed by one's headlights while driving down gravely roads at night in western Nebraska, when it momentarily is visible before disappearing into the darkness. Its "*poor-will*" call is a common sound in much of western Nebraska, but apparently only one nest has ever been located in the state.

Chuck-will's-widow   *Antrostomus carolinensis*
    A highly local but regular spring and fall migrant and presumed summer resident in southeastern Nebraska, reported regularly from the Indian Cave area of Richardson and Nemaha counties north to Douglas County (*Nebraska Bird Review* 35:50) and more recently to Dakota County. It has been heard as far north in the Missouri Valley as the Oahe Dam area in central South Dakota, and as far west in the Platte Valley to Saunders County, and recently even to Kearney.
    Migration. Fourteen spring records range from May 2 to June 9, with a median of June 3. No fall records after August 15 are available.
    Habitats. Heavy woodlands near streams, frequently comprised of mixed oaks and pines, are the favored habitat of this species.
    Comments. This is another caprimulgid that is named for its usual vocalization, and the largest member of its family that occurs in the state. Although its distinctive onomatopoetic call has been heard along the Missouri Valley all the way to South Dakota, only a single nest of this highly elusive species has been located. This was in Saunders County. Breeding Bird Surveys between 1966 and 2011 indicate that the species had a significant population decline (2.1% annually) during that period.

Eastern Whip-poor-will   *Antrostomus vociferus*
    A locally common spring and fall migrant and summer resident along the Missouri's forested valley from South Dakota to the Missouri borders, and probably also in Pawnee County along the Big Nemaha River. Also reported in 2003 from Sioux County (*Nebraska Bird Review* 71:119), apparently the *arizonae* taxon.
    Migration. Thirty-four initial spring records range from April 14 to May 21, with a median of May 2. Half of the records fall within the period April 25 to May 7. Fifteen final fall records range from July 31 to October 1, with a median of September 2. Half of the records fall within the period August 26 to September 7.
    Habitats. During the breeding season this species occupies open hardwood or mixed woodlands, especially younger stands in fairly dry habitats. Woodlands with scattered clearings also seem to be preferentially used.
    Comments. Like the chuck-will's-widow, this species can usually be heard nightly along the forests of the Missouri Valley, but there are only two confirmed nesting records, for Pawnee and Dakota counties.

Family Apodidae

Chimney Swift   *Chaetura pelagica*
    An abundant spring and fall migrant and summer resident throughout most of Nebraska, but becoming less common westwardly, and probably not usually breeding west of a line from Dawes to Hitchcock counties. Western limits now include Gering and Alliance. It breeds almost throughout the entire region of the Plains States, but is rare or absent in extreme western areas.
    Migration. The range of 129 initial spring records is from March 7 to June 6, with a median of April 27. Half of the records fall within the period April 20 to May 4. The range of 111 final fall records is from July 22 to October 14, with a median of October 7. Half of the records fall within the period October 2-14.
    Habitats. Like the common nighthawk, this species occurs in a wide variety of open habitats, but is probably most common in cities, where chimneys and other similar human-made structures provide roosting and nesting sites.
    Comments. Chimney swifts are now almost entirely city birds, depending on chimneys rather than large hollow trees for roosting and nesting. They have been seen circling over Cedar Point Biological Station, but there are no suitable chimneys there, and the birds have moved on. Reportedly chimney swifts mate in flight, and some swifts are believed even to sleep in flight, although this is difficult to imagine.

Their flight speeds have been exaggerated, probably because of their very rapid wing beats. Breeding Bird Surveys between 1966 and 2011 indicate that the species underwent a significant population decline (2.3% annually) during that period.

White-throated Swift   *Aeronautes saxatalis*

A locally common spring and fall migrant and summer resident in the Pine Ridge, the vicinity of Scottsbluff, and in the Wildcat Hills. Vagrants sometimes are seen farther east.

Migration. Twenty-six initial spring sightings range from April 19 to June 10, with a median of May 18. Half of the records fall within the period May 10 to June 1. Ten final fall sightings are from August 1 to September 22, with a median of August 29.

Habitats. Steep cliffs and deep canyons are the ideal habitat of this species, with nesting occurring in the inaccessible cracks and crevices of such locations.

Comments. Nests have been found at West Ash Creek Canyon, Dawes County (*Nebraska Bird Review* 73:17).

Family Trochilidae

Ruby-throated Hummingbird   *Archilochus colubris*

An uncommon to common spring and fall migrant and summer resident in eastern Nebraska, with nesting occurring at least in the Missouri's forested valley and west along the Platte, at least to Keith County (*Nebraska Bird Review* 76:60; 105). Vagrants appear farther west during migration, sometimes as far as Garden, and Scotts Bluff counties. It breeds in the eastern half of the entire Plains States region.

Migration. The range of 160 initial spring sightings is from April 7 to June 10, with a median of May 12. Half of the records fall within the period May 5-17. Sixty-four final fall sightings are from July 30 to October 8, with a median of September 13. Half of the records fall within the period September 2-18.

Habitats. Migrants often appear in city gardens or other areas where nectar-bearing flowers occur, but breeding is done in woodlands, orchards and parks where large trees, as well as flowering herbs and shrubs are available.

Comments. Although seen fairly often in eastern and central Nebraska, the only nesting records for this species are from Douglas and Sarpy counties south to Nemaha County. Hummingbird nests are not easily found, but should be expected in the Missouri Valley of northeastern Nebraska. Breeding Bird Surveys between 1966 and 2011 indicate that the species underwent a significant population increase (1.9% annually) during that period.

Black-chinned Hummingbird   *Archilochus alexandri*

Accidental. An adult female was photographed in Scottsbluff, May 7-8. 2012 (*Nebraska Bird Review* 80:59–60.

Costa's Hummingbird   *Calypte costae*

Accidental. One record, a bird present from about October 5 to November 17, 2001, at a Lexington feeder (*Nebraska Bird Review* 69:175; 71:97).

Broad-tailed Hummingbird   *Selasphorus platycercus*

An occasional migrant in western Nebraska, mostly in fall, but with some summer records. Possible breeding has occurred in Scotts Bluff County (*Nebraska Bird Review* 75:70). Most of the records are for Dawes and Scotts Bluff counties, but it has also been seen in Lincoln, Keith, Adams, and McPherson counties. It is of uncertain breeding status in western South Dakota, is accidental in Kansas, and hypothetical in Oklahoma. It is a common breeder in Wyoming and Colorado.

Migration. Fifteen initial fall records of this autumn migrant range from July 20 to September 13, with a median of August 4. Sixteen final fall records are from August 3 to September 14, with a median of August 14. Half of the total fall records fall within the period July 29 to August 16. There is a single spring sighting in May.

Habitats. Migrants are normally associated with open plains, forest clearings, and mountain parklands, but sometimes appear in gardens or at hummingbird feeders as well.

Comments. Broad-tailed hummingbirds are very common nesters in the mountains of Colorado and Wyoming, and probably the birds seen in western Nebraska are vagrants from there or perhaps migrants from the Black Hills. There were about ten fall records for eastern Nebraska through 2011 (*Nebraska Bird Review* 80:96).

Rufous Hummingbird   *Selasphorus rufus*

An occasional fall migrant in western Nebraska, rare in east. Most of the records are for Scotts Bluff County. As of 2010, there had been more than 20 records for eastern Nebraska (*Nebraska Bird Review* 78:96). It is of probably a regular migrant in western South Dakota, and is occasional to rare in Kansas and Oklahoma. The nearest breeding area is in northwestern Wyoming.

Migration. Sixteen fall sightings of this species range from July 30 to September 14, with a median of August 12. Half of the records fall within a period August 9-17. There are no spring records.

Habitats. Migrants are associated with plains, foothills and urban gardens.

Comments. Rufous hummingbirds have greatly expanded their wintering range in recent years, now commonly overwintering along the Gulf Coastal states. and even occasionally wandering east to the New England states. Probably this has resulted at least in part from the increase in hummingbird feeding activities, and more records of such rare hummingbirds can be expected.

Calliope Hummingbird   *Selasphorus calliope*

Rare, mainly in western Nebraska. There is a specimen record for Lincoln County, obtained in April of 1962 (*Nebraska Bird Review* 30:55), and the species was seen in the same county in August of 1960. A specimen was collected in Sioux County on June 23, 1994 (*Nebraska Bird Review* 64:135). There were 13 records through 2003, mostly for fall (*Nebraska Bird Review* 71:157).

Family Alcedinidae

Belted Kingfisher   *Megacerle alcyon*

A common spring and fall migrant and summer resident statewide in suitable habitats, and an uncommon winter resident where open water persists. It also breeds and migrates throughout the entire Plains States region.

Migration. Forty-three initial spring sightings range from January 2 to May 10, with a median of March 20. Half of the records fall within the period February 14 to April 10. Forty-seven final fall sightings are from July 26 to December 31, with a median of November 15. The concentration of fall records toward the end of the year (nearly half occurring in December) suggest that the species overwinters frequently.

Habitats. Throughout the year this species occurs near water areas supporting populations of fish, amphibians and similar aquatic life. Nests are excavated from nearly vertical earth exposures in bluffs, road cuts, eroded stream banks, and the like.

Comments. The belted kingfisher is Nebraska's only representative of this large and diverse family of mostly fish-eating birds, although the smallest kingfishers are largely insectivorous and the largest ones are omnivorous. Only the female of this species has chestnut underparts, making the sexes easy to identify. Breeding Bird Surveys between 1966 and 2011 indicate that the species underwent a significant population decline (1.5% annually) during that period.

Family Picidae

Lewis' Woodpecker   *Melanerpes lewis*

A vagrant and rare summer resident in the Pine Ridge area. Now an extremely rare breeder, with one Sheridan County record (Mollhoff, 2001) and three Dawes County records (*Nebraska Bird Review* 72: 155, 73:17). During the winter these birds wander, which might account for occasional sightings in

Nebraska. During fall, winter and spring it sometimes occurs in northwestern Nebraska, occasionally reaching as far east as Brown, Buffalo and Adams counties. It has also been reported in Kansas and has bred in Cimarron County, Oklahoma.

Migration. There are too few records to judge this rare species' migration, but 15 records range from January 20 to September 23, with the largest number of sightings in May. Like the red-headed woodpecker, it is somewhat dependent on aerial insects, and is probably relatively migration-prone.

Habitats. The edges of pine forests and streamside cottonwood groves having considerable dead growth are favored Black Hills habitats, and probably similar habitats are used in the Pine Ridge area.

Comments. Burned-over areas of coniferous forest are favorite places for this species, as well as the three-toed and black-backed woodpeckers, since insect-foraging opportunities are probably improved in such situations. Thus the burned sections of the Pine Ridge forests are a good place to look for this unusual woodpecker.

Red-headed Woodpecker   *Melanerpes erythrocephalus*

A common spring and fall migrant and summer resident nearly statewide, but more common eastwardly. It extends west into Colorado along the Platte Valley, and reaches or nearly reaches the Wyoming border in the Pine Ridge area. It is distinctly migratory, and only very infrequently overwinters in the state. Breeding occurs virtually throughout the entire Plains States region.

Migration. Ninety-eight initial spring sightings are from January 2 to June 9, with a median of May 7. Half of the records fall within the period April 28 to May 17. The range of 106 final fall sightings is from August 8 to December 31. Half of the records fall within the period September 8 to October 3. Less than ten percent of the fall records are for December, suggesting that this species only rarely overwinters. Presumably its relatively high dependence on aerial insects accounts for this species' migration tendencies as compared with most other Nebraska woodpeckers.

Habitats. While in Nebraska this species occurs in fairly open forests, woodlots, urban parks, and wooded housing areas. It occupies somewhat more open areas than does the red-bellied woodpecker, and is more widespread than is that species. Breeding Bird Surveys between 1966 and 2011 indicate that the species underwent a significant population decline (2.7% annually) during that period

Comments. This is one of the most migratory of Nebraska's woodpeckers, and it is also one that is very prone to catching insects in flight, as well as probing for them in the ground. At times it will even eat acorns or berries, a trait better developed in its relative the acorn woodpecker. Breeding Bird Surveys between 1966 and 2011 indicate that the species underwent a significant population decline (2.6% annually) during that period.

Acorn Woodpecker   *Melanerpes formicivorous*

Accidental. Seen and photographed at a feeder at Chambers, Holt County, May 18-22, 1996 (*Nebraska Bird Review* 64:55; Brogie, 1997).

Red-bellied Woodpecker   *Melanerpes carolinus*

A common permanent resident in eastern Nebraska, extending westward along the major river systems, at least to the Valentine area of Cherry County in the Niobrara Valley, to Garden County in the Platte Valley, and to Dundy County in the Republican Valley. It breeds from eastern South Dakota and Iowa south to Oklahoma and Texas.

Habitats. Throughout the year this species occupies somewhat open stands of coniferous or hardwood forests, often river bottom forests. It also frequents orchards, gardens and similar urban or suburban areas.

Comments. The name "red-bellied woodpecker" is not very appropriate; "zebra-backed" would have been a much better descriptive choice. In any case, these are highly attractive woodpeckers and welcome sights whenever they are seen. Breeding Bird Surveys between 1966 and 2011 indicate that the species underwent a significant population increase (1.1% annually) during that period, and seem to be increasing in eastern Nebraska.

Williamson's Sapsucker   *Sphyrapicus thyroideus*

Accidental. There are three sight records for the state, including one for Adams County in March of 1939, one for Douglas County in February of 1945, and one for Hall County in May of 1959 (*Nebraska Bird Review* 7:27; 13:61; 27:52). There also is a 1988 State Museum specimen obtained May 13, 1989 in Omaha. It is accidental in South Dakota, Kansas and Oklahoma.

Yellow-bellied Sapsucker   *Sphyrapicus varius*

An uncommon spring and fall migrant in eastern Nebraska, becoming rarer westwardly. An occasional to uncommon winter visitor perhaps statewide. Probably more birds winter in southern Nebraska than in the northern parts of the state, where the species may be entirely migratory. It breeds in eastern North Dakota and Minnesota,

Migration. Thirty-four initial fall sightings are from September 1 to December 30, with a median of October 3. Twenty-five final fall sightings are from October 9 to December 31, with a median of December 18. Sixteen initial springs sightings are from January 1 to May 28, with a median of March 14. Fourteen final spring sightings are from January 9 to May 21, with a median of March 23. These data would suggest that this species is a very late fall migrant, frequently overwintering in the state, and remaining for a rather variable period in spring.

Habitats. While in Nebraska this species is associated with various woodlands, especially those having poplars or aspens, which are favored foraging trees. However, it also drills in birches, maples, cottonwoods, apple trees and junipers, but only infrequently in such hardwoods as oaks and hackberries.

Comments. Yellow-bellied sapsuckers are among the few woodpeckers that would rather drink the sap of trees than capture insects, and they are very efficient at drilling equally spaced holes in poplars and birches to extract such fluids. Sapsucker–drilled trees often attract other species too, such as hummingbirds and flying squirrels. Ay least in eastern Nebraska these birds seem to be increasing.

Red-naped Sapsucker   *Sphyrapicus nuchalis*

A rare fall migrant in the Panhandle. There are three known specimen records for Sioux County (Bray *et al.* 1984). An uncommon resident of the Black Hills, probably straying to northwestern Nebraska occasionally. As of 2008 there were eight documented fall reports, the most easterly of which was from Lake Ogallala, Keith County (*Nebraska Bird Review* 76:146

Downy Woodpecker   *Picoides pubescens*

A common permanent resident statewide, occupying essentially the same habitats as the hairy woodpecker, but probably somewhat more common than that species. It breeds virtually throughout the Plains States region.

Habitats. Throughout the year this species is found in dense or open forests, but also extends into cities to visit parks, gardens, and the like. Besides foraging in smaller trees and the smaller branches of large trees, it also sometimes visits shrubs and tall weeds.

Comments. Downy woodpeckers are perhaps the commonest of Nebraska's woodpeckers, and the nesting holes that they drill provide potential nesting sites for many other cavity-dependent birds, such as bluebirds, tree swallows, chickadees, and nuthatches. In locations where it competes with hairy woodpeckers the downys concentrate their foraging on smaller branches and twigs, or even on shrubs or weeds that are able to support their weight. Woodpeckers probably help protect many tree species from boring beetle infestations, and so fully deserve our protection.

Hairy Woodpecker   *Picoides villosus*

A common permanent resident statewide in suitable wooded habitats.

Habitats. Throughout the year this species prefers fairly extensive areas of coniferous or deciduous forest, or streamside groves of trees. Although sometimes seen in urban areas, the species more commonly remains in mature forests, especially hardwood forests, where it forages on the trunks and larger branches. It breeds virtually throughout the entire Plains States region.

Comments. Hairy woodpeckers have substantially longer and more robust beaks than do downy woodpeckers, so they can drill deeper into wood. They also excavate somewhat larger nest cavities, which eventually get used by other species. Breeding Bird Surveys between 1966 and 2003 indicate that the species underwent a significant population increase (1.8% annually) during that period. Records from the Nebraska breeding bird atlasing project suggest that the hairy woodpecker is less than half as common as the downy woodpecker in Nebraska. (Mollhoff, 2001) Its distribution in the state may be more closely tied to the larger river valleys, where large trees are more abundant. Censuses in eastern Nebraska suggest that the downy woodpecker is about eight times more common than the hairy.

American Three-toed Woodpecker   *Picoides dorsalis*

Accidental in Nebraska, with a single specimen record, from Scotts Bluff County, June 15, 1916, and two additional sightings that are not considered as reliable (Bray *et al.* 1988), plus a 1994 sighting *(Nebraska Bird Review* 62:111). It is a rare permanent resident of the Black Hills.

Black-backed Woodpecker   *Picoides arcticus*

Accidental. There are three early records from Nebraska, including two from Douglas County, and one from Dakota County. Additionally, the species was reported in Custer County in August of 1970 (*Nebraska Bird Review* 25:46). It is an uncommon permanent resident of the Black Hills, but unreported elsewhere in the Plains States. Both this and the preceding species may become more abundant as dead pines are increasingly common in the Pine Ridge.

Northern Flicker   *Colaptes auratus*

A common permanent resident statewide. In eastern Nebraska the population is predominantly of the yellow-shafted race or hybrids, with typical red-shafted types found only in extreme western Nebraska. Probably most of the Nebraska population is influenced by hybridization. Collectively, the species breeds in and migrates through the entire Plains States region.

Habitats. Throughout the year this species occupies diverse habitats, including relatively open woodlands, orchards, woodlots, and urban environments. Dense forests are apparently avoided, and much foraging is done by probing in the ground.

Comments. To a greater degree than other Nebraska woodpecker this is an ant-eating species, and because of that flickers often forage in fields well away from woodlands. Although essentially sedentary, some movement out of the state may occur in most winters. Breeding Bird Surveys between 1966 and 2011 indicate that the species underwent a significant population decline (1.4% annually) during that period.

Pileated Woodpecker   *Dryocopus pileatus*

Very rare local resident. Previously an uncommon permanent resident in extreme eastern counties, but probably eliminated prior to 1900. There have been recent sightings in Washington, Richardson, Otoe, Franklin, Sarpy and Douglas counties, indicating a re-invasion of southeastern Nebraska. A pair was seen tending a nest hole during April and May 1999, in Fontenelle Forest, and has since bred there most years since. As many as two active nests have been found at Fontenelle Forest in some years, and has bred in Indian Cave State Park in recent years (*Nebraska Bird Review* 75:79). There have been some recent sightings elsewhere (*Nebraska Bird Review* 80:60).

Habitats. This species is generally limited to mature forests, often river bottom forests, having a mixture of tall living trees and dead stubs. Trees that are at least 15 inches in diameter are required for nesting birds.

Comments. It is unfortunate that Nebraska now lacks a breeding population of pileated woodpeckers, for they are the largest and most spectacular of America's woodpeckers. Breeding Bird Surveys between 1966 and 2011 indicate that the species underwent a significant population increase (1.4% annually) during that period.

Family Falconidae

Crested Caracara   *Caracara cheriway*

Accidental. Reported from Seward County, August 20 to 21, 2011 (*Nebraska Bird Review* 79:125). In the spring of 2013 an adult was found near Genoa that was emaciated and blind in one eye. It was brought to the Nebraska Raptor Recovery Center in Lincoln for rehabilitation, and later sent to Texas for release. (*Fly Free*, 30(1):1, 2013).

American Kestrel   *Falco sparverius*

Common permanent resident statewide. Less common in winter (mainly males), and more abundant during spring and fall, so substantial migration must occur. The species occurs throughout the Plains states as a migrant or breeder.

Migration. Twenty-nine spring records and 22 fall records are widely scattered, suggesting that the species is largely residential in Nebraska.

Habitats, Open country with elevated perching sites such as telephone lines or scattered trees are used throughout the year, and nesting is usually done in tree hollows (nest boxes are also often used) near large areas of grasslands or croplands.

Comments. The American kestrel, once called the "sparrow hawk," is one of the most attractive of all our raptors. The smaller males are bright rufous with bluish gray wings and a rusty tail, whereas the female is nearly all barred or striped with rufous and brown. They are hole-nesters, often choosing old woodpecker cavities, but also nest in artificial cavities. During summer they feed largely on grasshoppers and other large insects, but turn to small mammals and other prey in cold weather. Breeding Bird Surveys between 1966 and 2011 indicate that the species underwent a significant population decline (1.5% annually) during that period.

Merlin   *Falco columbarius*

An uncommon migrant and winter visitor statewide, and an extremely rare summer resident in the Pine Ridge area. There are nesting records for Sioux County in 1975 and 1978 (*Nebraska Bird Review* 47:39), and one during the atlasing period (Mollhoff, 2001). Nesting occurs in western South Dakota, Minnesota and rarely in North Dakota, and migrants may appear anywhere in the Plains States.

Migration. Ninety-nine initial spring sightings range from January 1 to June 6, with a median of March 19. Half of the records fall within the two periods January 1-20 and March 30 to April 24, suggesting that the species is primarily a winter visitor and spring migrant. Forth-eight fall records extend from August 16 to December 31, with a median of October 23. The largest number (21) of fall records are for December, followed by September (15) and October (7).

Habitats. Open country with elevated perches such as telephone lines or scattered trees are used throughout the year, and nesting is typically in scattered trees or groves near large areas of grasslands, croplands or badlands.

Comments. This little falcon is slightly larger than the American kestrel, and is largely a hunter of small birds. The males are mostly bluish gray above, whereas females are various tones of brown and buffy. It is likely that nesting occurs more frequently in Nebraska than the few available records suggest. Breeding Bird Surveys between 1966 and 2011 indicate that the species underwent a significant population increase (2.8% annually) during that period.

Gyrfalcon   *Falco rusticolus*

A rare winter visitor. A single specimen was obtained in Johnson County in 1885, and another was captured in Kearney County in 1974. Additionally there are sight records from Cuming County (1880's), Keith County (1947), Dawes County (1965), Lincoln County (1975), Kearney County (1977), Garden County (1979), Adams County (1980) and Buffalo County (2011). Falconers have captured several during winter in the Sandhills in recent years, such as two in Cherry County in 1983 (Brogie, 1997). One was near Keystone Dam, Keith County, January 1, 2001 (*Nebraska Bird Review* 71:98). Rare or accidental winter migrant in the Lake McConaughy region (Brown, Dinsmore and Brown, 2012).

Migration. Eight total records for this species range from November 27 to March 3. There are three records for January, two for December, and one each for November, February and March.

Habitats. Open plains and prairies are used during migration and while wintering.

Comments. This is the bird most prized by falconers for their sport; gyrfalcons have been trained to kill birds as large as bustards, and will readily attack pheasants or large waterfowl. The species exhibits an array of color morphs, ranging from nearly pure white to dusky gray. The lighter–colored birds are typically nesters of high-arctic latitudes.

Peregrine Falcon   *Falco peregrinus*

A rare to occasional migrant and winter visitor statewide, and a local breeder. It apparently once bred in the Panhandle (Bruner, Wolcott and Swenk, 1904), and a recovery program in Omaha and Lincoln has produced several successful nestings in both locations in recent years.

Migration. A total of 97 initial spring sightings range from January 1 to May 17, with a median of March 20. Half of the records fall within the two periods January 1-20 and April 21–May 11, suggesting that the species is a winter visitor and spring migrant. Twenty total fall records extend from July 26 to December 26, with a median of September 22. The largest number of fall records (8) is for September, but the sample is too small to suggest a peak period.

Habitats. During migration this species is most likely to be found in open, grassland habitats, but sometimes enters cities while hunting pigeons.

Comments. Until the successful release program undertaken in Omaha, peregrines were believed to have been extirpated from the state as breeders. However, thanks to this and other similar programs, the sight of peregrines is no longer a rarity, and a few unsuccessful attempts at nesting have occurred near the dome of the state capitol building. These city-adapted birds have even learned to hunt by night, using the lights that illuminate the capitol to capture night-flying prey such as nighthawks.

Prairie Falcon   *Falco mexicanus*

An occasional to rare permanent resident in western Nebraska, and a rare migrant and winter visitor in eastern Nebraska. It is a rare and local breeder in the western Panhandle, with nesting records for Dawes, Sheridan, Sioux counties, Scotts Bluff and Banner counties, mainly in the Pine Ridge and also the Wildcat Hills. It also breeds in the western parts of the Dakotas, eastern Colorado, northeastern New Mexico and adjacent Oklahoma.

Migration. A total of 135 initial spring sightings range from January 1 to May 22, with a median of January 30. Half of the records fall within the period January 1–30, suggesting that the species is primarily a resident and winter visitor, with no obvious secondary peak of spring migration. Forty-five fall records extend from July 21 to December 31, with a median of November 13 and no obvious fall peak in records. There is a progressively smaller number of monthly records from December backwards to July.

Habitats. This species is associated with large expanses of open grasslands or sagebrush scrub, with nearby cliffs, bluffs or rocky outcrops for nesting.

Comments. The prairie falcon resembles a paler version of the peregrine, and is a species more likely to specialize on prairie-dogs and ground squirrels than on birds. It attacks such prey at high speed and from nearly ground-level altitudes, rather than from high-altitude stooping dives, but is equally deadly. Like the peregrine it prefers to nest on steep cliffs, and seeing a female diving on birds such as ravens that stray too close to the nest is a lesson in high-speed acrobatics.

Family Psittacidae

(Monk Parakeet)   *Myopsitta monarchus*

Hypothetical. Individuals of this species were observed in the Omaha area in 1972 and 1973, in Kearney in 1975, and in Lincoln in 1975 and 1976. It was seen again in Omaha in 1998. It is possible that they represent escaped cage birds rather than ones from the feral population in the eastern United States. The species has also been reported in Oklahoma.

Carolina Parakeet   *Conuropsis carolinensis*

Extinct. Formerly a common resident in the Missouri Valley of Nebraska (*Nebraska Bird Review* 2:55-59) and elsewhere in the Plains States.

Family Tyrannidae

Olive-sided Flycatcher   *Contopus cooperi*

    An uncommon to occasional spring and fall migrant in eastern Nebraska, at least west to Lancaster County. Farther west the species is less common, but it probably migrates statewide. It breeds in northern Minnesota, and migrates throughout the Plains States region.

    Migration. Sixty-eight initial spring sightings range from April 3 to June 4, with a median of May 18. Half of the records fall within the period May 10-26. Sixteen final spring sightings are from May 10 to June 8, with a median of May 24. Thirteen initial fall sightings are from August 24 to September 9, with a median of September 2. Twelve final fall sightings are from September 1 to September 29, with a median of September 20.

    Habitats. Migrants are found in wooded areas in which there are trees having prominent dead upper branches, and sometimes also perch on telephone wires in open country.

    Comments. This flycatcher is rather easily identified by its olive-gray flanks, which remind one of an unbuttoned vest. Its song is an easily remembered "Quick, three beers" or "Look, three deer." The birds somewhat resemble oversized wood-pewees, and are only slightly smaller than kingbirds. Breeding Bird Surveys between 1966 and 2003 indicate that the species underwent a significant population decline (3.3% annually) during that period.

Western Wood-pewee   *Contopus sordidulus*

    A common spring and fall migrant and summer resident in western and northwestern Nebraska; the breeding range including Sioux, Dawes and Scotts Bluff counties, and probably extending east at least to Garden County. Hybridization with *virens* possibly occurs in areas of contact with *cooperi*. Singing has been heard east to Brown and Keya Paha counties in the Niobrara Valley (*Nebraska Bird Review* 71:119), and both species occur in Keith County in the North Platte Valley (*Nebraska Bird Review* 76:105), and the central Niobrara Valley (*Nebraska Bird Review* 76:195).

    Migration. Sixty-four initial spring sightings range from March 20 to June 10, with a median of May 21. Half of the records fall within the period May 13-26. Thirty-three final fall sightings are from July 8 to October 9, with a median of September 4. Half of the records fall within the period August 22-September 12.

    Habitats. In the Black Hills, and probably in the Pine Ridge area, this species is mostly associated with open, mature pine forests. Generally the birds use habitats dominated by conifers, but also use mixed woodlands, and generally occupy drier areas than do eastern wood-pewees.

    Comments. Although the two wood-pewees differ in the color of their lower mandibles, and slightly darker plumage it is probably easier to recognize this species by its more raspy "*pee-err*" vocalization. Breeding Bird Surveys between 1966 and 2011 indicate that the species underwent a significant population decline (1.6% annually) during that period.

Eastern Wood-pewee   *Contopus virens*

    A common spring and fall migrant and summer resident in eastern Nebraska, extending west locally at least as far as Dawes, Cherry, Keith, Deuel and Dundy counties along river systems. Breeding in the Sandhills in apparently infrequent. It breeds widely through the eastern portions of the Plains States, and occurs almost throughout as a migrant.

    Migration. Seventy-seven initial spring sightings range from March 20 to June 10, with a median of May 10. Half of the records fall within the period May 3-21. Sixty-one final fall sightings are from July 29 to October 12, with a median of September 10. Half of the records fall within the period August 31–September 18.

    Habitats. While in Nebraska this species is generally associated with deciduous forests, including floodplain and river–bluff forests, but also occurs in woodlots, orchards and suburban areas with tree plantings.

    Comments. Over most of Nebraska the wood-pewees seen are most likely to be the eastern species, whose song is a distinctive "*pee-a-wee*". However, in the Panhandle and western Niobrara Valley one should be on the alert for possible western wood-pewees. Breeding Bird Surveys between 1966 and 2011 indicate that the species underwent a significant population decline (1.3% annually) during that period.

Yellow-bellied Flycatcher   *Empidonax flaviventris*

An uncommon spring and fall migrant in eastern Nebraska, rarely occurring as far west as Cherry County. There were possible nestings of this species in Sarpy County and Lancaster County in 1978, records that have subsequently been questioned (*Nebraska Bird Review* 46:86; 72:155). It also regularly migrates through the eastern portions of the other Plains States.

Migration. Twenty-six total spring sightings range from April 16 to June 7, with a median of May 16. Half of the records fall within the period May 10-20. Fifteen total fall sightings range from August 8 to October 5, with a median of September 4. Half of the records fall within the period September 1–14.

Habitats. Associated with second-growth woodlands while on migration, and normally limited to alder and willow thickets in boreal forest during the breeding season.

Comments. This eastern species of *Empidonax* is distinctly yellowish below, and its song is a "che-lek" that is more liquid-sounding than the least flycatcher's distinctly enunciated "*che-bek.*"

Acadian Flycatcher   *Empidonax virescens*

An uncommon spring and fall migrant in eastern Nebraska, and a probable summer resident in the forested valley of the Missouri River (*Nebraska Bird Review* 62:11; 63:77; 80:61). It also breeds in western Iowa and southward through eastern Kansas and Oklahoma.

Migration. Fifty-five initial spring sightings range from April 17 to June 9, with a median of May 15. Half of the records fall within the period May 8-21. Fourteen final fall sightings range from July 28 to October 1, with a median of August 28.

Habitats. During the summer, this species is found in shady and humid river bottom forests, forested swamps, and wooded uplands.

Comments. One of the many difficult empidonaces (the generic name means "king of the flies"), this species is rather greenish-toned and has a sharp "*peet-sa*" song,

Alder Flycatcher   *Empidonax alnorum*

Apparently a regular but migrant in Nebraska, at least in spring. The small proportion of sightings attributed to this species since it was separated from *traillii* suggest that it must be quite infrequent by comparison. However, it has been reported to possibly breed in southeastern South Dakota, so should be looked for in Nebraska. It probably is a regular migrant through the eastern portions of all the Plains States, with banding indicating that some Nebraska migrants may migrate as far as north-central Alaska.

Migration. Eight initial spring sightings attributed to this species range from May 8 to May 29, with a mean of May 21. Six final spring sightings are from May 24 to June 18, with a mean of June 7. Six fall sightings range from July 20 to September 16, with a mean of August 19.

Habitats. Migrants probably use the same habitats as does the willow flycatcher, namely shrubbery and small trees near openings of grassland or water. While breeding it generally occupies the more northerly and easterly forested areas, compared with the more open and arid habitats of the willow flycatcher.

Comments, This little flycatcher is seemingly too little known in Nebraska to say much about it. However, 92 of 203 "Traill's flycatchers" banded in the Platte Valley by Dr. William Scharf were identified as alders. Thus, the species may be a much more regular migrant through Nebraska than is now appreciated. Breeding Bird Surveys between 1966 and 2011 indicate that alder/willow flycatchers underwent a significant population decline (1.2% annually) during that period.

Willow Flycatcher   *Empidonax traillii*

A common spring and fall migrant and uncommon to rare summer resident in eastern Nebraska. Breeding extends west at least to Cherry, Thomas and Keith counties in the Sandhills, and to Sheridan County in the Panhandle. It also breeds in the other Plains States from North Dakota to Oklahoma. Only four confirmed Nebraska breedings occurred during the years 1984-1989 (Mollhoff, 2001).

Migration. Seventy-eight initial spring sightings range from April 17 to June 10, with a median of May 15. Half of the records fall within the period May 9-25. Sixteen final fall sightings range from July 26 to September 21, with a median of September 2. Half of the records fall within the period August 29 to September 7.

Habitats. In Nebraska this species inhabits edge habitats such as thickets or groves of small trees and shrubs surrounded by grasslands, and the edges of gallery forests along rivers.

Comments. Probably this is the most common and widespread of Nebraska's empidonaces, although in appearance it is extremely similar to the last-named species. Breeding Bird Surveys between 1966 and 2011 indicate that alder/willow flycatchers underwent a significant population decline (1.2% annually) during that period.

Least Flycatcher   *Empidonax minimus*

A common spring and fall migrant statewide, and apparently an extremely rare summer resident. Besides some early reports of breeding in Douglas and Dakota counties, territorial birds have also been reported in Brown and Dawes Counties. Thus northern Nebraska apparently constitutes part of the breeding range, but there were no confirmed or possible breedings during the atlasing years 1984-1989 (Mollhoff, 2001).

Migration. The range of 100 initial spring sightings is from April 7 to June 9, with a median of May 8. Half of the records fall within the period May 3-11. Sixteen final spring sightings are from May 3, to June 3, with a median of May 14. Twenty-four fall sightings range from July 29 to October 1, with a median of September 5. Half of the records fall within the period August 30 to September 12.

Habitats. While in Nebraska this species occupies floodplain forests in grassland areas, scattered grovelands, shelterbelts, and urban parks or gardens.

Comments. This is the smallest of the *Empidonax* species, but in the field this difference is not apparent. Breeding Bird Surveys between 1966 and 2011 indicate that the species underwent a significant population decline (1.8% annually) during that period.

Hammond's Flycatcher   *Empidonax hammondii*

Very rare but probably regular migrant in western Nebraska. A specimen identified as this species was collected in Dawes County in 1911. Observed and photographed more recently in Adams County on September 2, 1995 (*Nebraska Bird Review* 64:135). By 2003, 21 fall records had accumulated (*Nebraska Bird Review* 71:158).

Gray Flycatcher   *Empidonax wrightii*

Accidental. A few sight record for Oliver Reservoir, including May 17, 1999, and several August & September sightings in 2002 (*Nebraska Bird Review* 70:152).

Dusky Flycatcher   *Empidonax oberholseri*

Very rare. By 2003 at least 20 fall records had accumulated for this elusive western species. (*Nebraska Bird Review* 68:118, 162; 71:158).

Cordilleran Flycatcher   *Empidonax occidentalis*

An occasional or local migrant and summer resident in Nebraska, long thought to have a nesting area, in Sioux County (*Nebraska Bird Review* 43:18) in Sowbelly Canyon and in nearby Monroe Canyon. Now known to extend eastward into Dawes County (*Nebraska Bird Review* 76:106). Also observed in Scotts Bluff, Garden, and McPherson counties, with a 2003 nesting in the Wildcat Hills (*Nebraska Bird Review* 71:120).

Migration. Five fall records are all in the period August 9 to September 10 (*Nebraska Bird Review* 65:167).

Habitats. While breeding this species is associated with forested canyons and mountain slopes, but on migration it may occur in deciduous trees along streambeds, in oak-lined gullies, and other wooded habitats.

Comments. This species has one of the most localized breeding ranges of any of Nebraska's birds, being largely limited to a few small canyons in northwestern Nebraska. It used to be called the "western flycatcher," but has been "split" into a Pacific coastal form and this interior-breeding species.

Eastern Phoebe   *Sayornis phoebe*
       A common spring and fall migrant and summer resident in woodlands of eastern Nebraska, and extending west locally to Sioux, Thomas, Lincoln, Garden, and Dundee counties along the major river valleys. It also breeds throughout the eastern portions of the other Plains States, west to eastern Colorado and northeastern New Mexico.
       Migration. The range of 169 initial spring sightings is from March 20 to June 10, with a median of April 16. Half of the records fall within the period March 28 to April 29. Sixty-seven final fall sightings range from August 4 to October 25, with a median of September 26. Half of the records fall within the period September 5 to October 6.
       Habitats. During summer, this species is usually found near water in woodlands or partially wooded areas, including farmsteads. Farm buildings, bridges, and other locations providing artificial or natural ledges protected from above are used for nest sites.
       Comments. Eastern phoebes are the earliest of the flycatchers to arrive in eastern Nebraska, where they soon take up residence under bridges and in farm outbuildings. They typically return to the same nest site each year. One site on a window sill of the author's Minnesota lake cabin was used every year for five years, even though it had to be temporarily moved one summer to allow for repainting of the sills while the birds were still tending nestlings.

Say's Phoebe   *Sayornis saya*
       A common spring and fall migrant and summer resident in western Nebraska, extending east locally to at least Cedar, Wayne, Cuming. York and Clay counties. Vagrants may be seen all the way to the Missouri River. It also breeds throughout the western portions of the other Plains States, from North Dakota to Texas.
       Migration. The range of 129 initial spring sightings is from March 20 to June 10, with a median of April 16. Half of the records fall within the period April 5-24. Fifty-two final fall sightings range from July 29 to October 29, with a median of September 14. Half of the records fall within the period September 8-20.
       Habitats. In Nebraska this species is found in fairly open and dry habitats, including rocky canyons, badlands, and ranchlands. The species is independent of surface water, but in common with the eastern phoebe, it often nests under bridges or on the horizontal ledges of other manmade structures.
       Comments. In Keith County near Cedar Point Biological Station both the eastern and Say's phoebes occur, but they do not appear to interact, and rarely nest in the same immediate area. Breeding Bird Surveys between 1966 and 2011 indicate that the species underwent a significant population increase (1.1% annually) during that period.

Vermilion Flycatcher   *Pyrocephalus rubinus*
       An accidental vagrant in Nebraska, with a sight record for Douglas County in November 1954, a specimen from Lincoln County in December of 1954, and a carcass probably of this species found in Lincoln County in November of 1960 (*Nebraska Bird Review* 23:28; 29:23). Observed and photographed in Lancaster County on May 16, 1995 (*Nebraska Bird Review* 64 :135). There was also a sight record for Lincoln County in May of 1976 (*American Birds* 30:861).
       Habitats. During the summer this species is usually found in trees or shrubs along roadsides, or in open forested river bottoms.
       Comments. This amazingly bright-plumaged species is a distinct change from the many dull-plumaged flycatchers, and one can only wonder what sorts of selective pressures drove the species to evolving such a brilliant male plumage.

Ash-throated Flycatcher)   *Myiarchus cinerascens*

Very rare summer resident, found breeding in Kimball County on 2007 (*Nebraska Bird Review* 75:40; 76:43-37, 161). Also observed there in 2009, and in Scotts Bluff County in July, 2009 (*Nebraska Bird Review* 77:105), There is also a 1957 sight record for Dawes County (Bray *et al.* l988), and another for Sowbelly Canyon July 20, 2000 (*Nebraska Bird Review* 68:118).

Great Crested Flycatcher   *Myiarchus crinitus*
     A common spring and fall migrant and summer resident in eastern Nebraska, mainly along the larger river valleys, but extending west locally to Sioux County in the north, Garden, Keith and Deuel counties along the North Platte and South Platte, and Dundy County in the Republican Valley.
     Migration. The range of 130 initial spring sightings is from March 30 to June 9, with a median of April 30. Half of the records fall within the period May 2-15. Sixty-six final fall sightings are from July 22 to October 3, with a median of September 6. Half of the records fall within the period August 30 to September 12.
     Habitats. During the breeding season this species occurs in rather extensive hardwood forests, including river bottom forests, and especially those with fairly open canopies. Unlike most flycatchers, nesting is in cavities such as woodpecker holes.
     Comments. This eastern deciduous forest species is notable for its rufous wing and tail markings, and its loud "*wheep*" calls.

Cassin's Kingbird   *Tyrannus vociferans*
     A spring and fall migrant and regular summer resident of the western Panhandle, ranging from rare to uncommon. The species breeds locally in Nebraska, at least in the southwestern Panhandle, in the Wildcat Hills, and also from about Crawford westward in the north (Mollhoff, 2001). It is regularly seen south of Reddington, but there were no proven breedings there until 2003.
     Migration. Eight initial spring sightings range from April 27 to May 30, with a mean of May 2. Twelve last fall sightings range from August 22 to September 28, with a median of September 17.
     Habitats. To a greater degree than the western kingbird this species is associated with dry, open country such as plains and semi deserts, with only scattered tall trees. However, it overlaps widely with this species, and probably competes locally with it.
     Comments. Few breeding records have been obtained in Nebraska for this western kingbird look-alike. Nests have been found in a canyon south of Reddington, Morrill County (*Nebraska Bird Review* 73:18) This species lacks the white outer tail feather markings of the western, as well as having a more conspicuous dark ear-patch. Its usual call is a loud "*chi-bek.*"

Western Kingbird   *Tyrannus verticalis*
     A common spring and fall migrant and summer resident almost statewide, becoming less common eastwardly. Approximately equally common with the eastern kingbird in much of western Nebraska. It is a breeder and migrant throughout the entire Plains States region.
     Migration. The range of 117 initial spring sightings is from April 30 to May 26, with a median of May 5. Half of the records fall within the period May 1–10. The range of 125 final fall sightings is from July 26 to October 10, with a median of September 3. Half of the records fall within the period August 24 to September 10.
     Habitats. While in Nebraska this species seems to occupy the same habitats as does the eastern kingbird, including a variety of edge habitats such as shelterbelts, orchards, woodland margins, and tree-lined residential districts.
     Comments. In western Nebraska around Cedar Point Biological Station these noisy birds nest almost anywhere medium-to-tall trees occur near open foraging areas. There they often outnumber eastern kingbirds, and seem to be adapted to somewhat drier habitats.

Eastern Kingbird   *Tyrannus tyrannus*
     A common spring and fall migrant and summer resident statewide, generally considerably more common that the western kingbird in eastern Nebraska, becoming relatively less common westwardly. It is a breeder and migrant throughout the entire Plains States region.

<u>Migration</u>. Seventy-three initial spring sightings range from March 24 to May 29, with a median of May 3. Half of the records fall within the period May 1–7. The range of 126 final fall sightings is from August 4 to October 14, with a median of September 9. Half of the records fall within the period September 1–16.

<u>Habitats</u>. While in Nebraska this species occupies open areas having scattered trees or tall shrubs, and forest edges or hedgerows. It frequently occurs in cities, foraging out over streets or intersections, and perching on favored vantage points such as street lights or telephone lines.

<u>Comments</u>. The kingbirds are named for their rather imperial behavior, and the generic name *Tyrannus* is a further indication of their tyrannical nature. The birds also have hidden golden–reddish crown patches, although these are exposed only rarely. Breeding Bird Surveys between 1966 and 2011 indicate that the species underwent a significant population decline (1.2% annually) during that period.

Scissor-tailed Flycatcher   *Tyrannus forficatus*

A rare spring and fall migrant and summer resident in extreme southern Nebraska, with definite breeding records by 2005 from Adams, Lancaster, Logan, Gage, Cass and Clay counties. By 2008 there had been at least 15 state nesting records (*Nebraska Bird Review* 76:106) It is a regular breeder from Kansas and extreme southeastern Colorado southward. Vagrants have been seen elsewhere in the state, and rarely have been seen in South Dakota as well. It is a regular breeder from Kansas southward, and is casual in South Dakota.

<u>Migration</u>. Seventeen initial spring sightings range from April 19 to June 10, with a median of May 2. Half of the records fall within the period April 29 to May 3. Eight final fall sightings are from July 23 to October 5, with a mean of September 14.

<u>Habitats</u>. During the summer this species is found in open to semi open habitats with a scattering of trees or other elevated perching sites, and in woodlands with edges or openings for foraging. Nesting usually is in isolated trees or tall structures such as utility poles or windmills rather than in groves or heavy cover.

<u>Comments</u>. Although this beautiful species is fairly common in southern Kansas, it only occasionally reaches Nebraska. However, its Kansas range is slowly advancing northward, so perhaps in the future it will become a regular breeder in southern Nebraska. Breeding Bird Surveys between 1966 and 2011 indicate that the species underwent a significant population decline (0.8% annually) during that period.

Family Laniidae

Loggerhead Shrike   *Lanius ludovicianus*

A common spring and fall migrant and summer resident statewide. A few birds overwinter in some years, but apparently the population is essentially migratory. Breeding occurs throughout the Plains States in suitable habitats.

<u>Migration</u>. The range of 95 initial spring sightings is from January 2 to May 28, with a median of April 4. Half of the records fall within the period March 17 to April 21. Ninety-eight final fall sightings are from July 26 to December 30, with a median of September 19. Half of the records occur August 26 to October 1.

<u>Habitats</u>. Outside the breeding season these birds occupy the same open country that northern shrikes utilize, and during the nesting period they are also associated with open habitat with scattered or clustered shrubs or small trees.

<u>Comments</u>. The Nebraska Sandhills seem to represent perfect habitat for these birds; scattered Russian olive trees are favorite nesting sites, and the open country provides for excellent viewing of the surroundings. Shrikes are often called "butcher birds," as they frequently impale their prey on barbed wire or the thorns of trees to store them temporarily. Breeding Bird Surveys between 1966 and 2011 indicate that the species underwent a significant population decline (3.2% annually) during that period. Nebraska Sandhills populations now seem to be part of that decline.

Northern Shrike   *Lanius excubitor*

An uncommon to locally common winter resident statewide, but perhaps more common in the western areas than in the east. It also occurs throughout the other Plains States as a migrant or winter visitor.

Migration. The range of 44 initial fall sightings is from August 28 to December 26, with a median of November 9. Half of the records fall within the period October 23 to November 28. Twenty-four final spring sightings range from January 7 to April 24, with a median of March 11. Half of the records fall within the period February 23 to March 25.

Habitats. Migrants and wintering birds are found on open plains or prairies having scattered trees or telephone posts for perches.

Comments. The larger size, somewhat barred breast, and more contrasting black ear-stripe all help to identify this species, and it rarely overlaps in seasonal occurrence with the loggerhead shrike. Both are surprisingly effective predators, sometimes killing birds as large as warblers and sparrows.

Family Vireonidae

White-eyed Vireo   *Vireo griseus*

An uncommon to occasional spring and fall migrant in eastern Nebraska, and a local summer resident in the lower part of the Missouri's forested valley, with a northern limit at least as far as Sarpy County. Reported west to Keith and Sioux counties. Breeding also occurs from eastern Kansas south through eastern Oklahoma to Texas. Casual in South Dakota.

Migration. Forty-four initial spring sightings range from April 19 to June 5, with a median of May 10. Half of the records fall within the period May 3-15. Fourteen final fall sightings are from August 2 to September 22, with a median of September 6.

Habitats. During the breeding season this species occupies the dense understory of wooded bottomlands, and thickets near streams.

Comments. White-eyed vireos are well named; they are the only native vireos with pale white eyes, which are exaggerated by a white eye-ring. Breeding Bird Surveys between 1966 and 2003 indicate that the species had a significant population increase (0.4% annually) during that period.

Bell's Vireo   *Vireo bellii*

A common spring and fall migrant and summer resident in eastern Nebraska, becoming rarer westwardly, and breeding locally to Dawes County in the Pine Ridge, Cherry County in the Niobrara Valley, Garden County and probably Scotts Bluff County in the North Platte River Valley, and the Colorado border in the valleys of the South Platte and Republican rivers. Breeding also occurs north to western North Dakota and south to Oklahoma and the Texas Panhandle.

Migration. The range of 114 initial spring sightings is from March 30 to June 10, with a median of May 13. Half of the records fall within the period May 6-20. Sixty-four final fall sightings range from July 24 to October 20, with a median of September 8. Half of the records fall within the period August 25 to September 17.

Habitats. In Nebraska this prairie-adapted vireo is widespread in thickets near streams or rivers, and in second-growth scrub, forest edges, and brush patches.

Comments. Like many vireos, this species is more easily heard than seen; it often sings from heavy brush near ground.

Black-capped Vireo   *Vireo atricapilla*

Extirpated. There are two definite early records; a sight record for Sarpy County in 1894, and a specimen from Sarpy County in 1921. Oklahoma is the nearest area of current breeding.

Yellow-throated Vireo   *Vireo flavifrons*

An uncommon spring and fall migrant in eastern counties, and an uncommon summer resident in the forested valley of the Missouri River from South Dakota to Kansas, and west along various tributaries to at least Garfield and Hall counties. Breeding also occurs widely in the eastern parts of the Plains States, from central North Dakota southward through eastern Oklahoma, and migrants are somewhat more widespread.

Migration. Eighty initial spring sightings range from March 24 to June 3, with a median of May 7. Half of the records fall within the period April 30 to May 13. Twenty-seven final fall sightings range from July 21 to October 26, with a median of September 9. Half of the records fall within the period August 30 to September 16.

Habitats. Migrants and breeding birds are associated with mature, moist deciduous forests, especially river–bottom forests and shady slopes, and infrequently extends to wooded residential areas.

Comments. There were only three confirmed breedings of this species during the atlasing years, and all were along the Missouri River in Dakota, Sarpy and Otoe counties (Mollhoff, 2001). Breeding Bird Surveys between 1966 and 2011 indicate that the species had a significant population increase (1.0% annually) in that period.

Plumbeous Vireo   *Vireo plumbeus*

A rare fall migrant in the Pine Ridge, especially in the westernmost canyons of Sioux, Dawes and Sheridan County. Breeding also occurs in the Black Hills. The range map for the includes the breeding distribution of the related eastern species (blue-headed vireo), which breeds in Minnesota, whereas the plumbeous breeds from eastern Montana and western South Dakota south to western Texas.

Migration. No good migration data for this rather recently recognized species (see *Condor* 97:903-19) exists. The few available fall dates are for September.

Habitats. While breeding, pine forests and scrubby oak woodlands are favored habitats in the Black Hills and Colorado.

Cassin's Vireo   *Vireo cassinii*

A regular fall migrant, in western Nebraska. Until the taxonomic splitting of this form from the following species there was little information on this species in Nebraska. Besides two specimen records, there have been many fall sightings in the Panhandle between August 24 and September 21. Perhaps this represents a somewhat earlier migration than that typical of the blue-headed vireo (*Nebraska Bird Review* 65:173). Also reported 16-17 May, 1998. Many of the records are from Oliver Reservoir.

Blue-headed Vireo   *Vireo solitarius*

An uncommon spring and fall migrant in eastern Nebraska. Breeds in Minnesota, and migrants occur throughout the Plains States region.

Migration. Seventy-seven initial spring sightings (for the originally constituted Solitary Vireo) range from April 18 to June 10, with a median of May 9. Half of the records fall within the period May 3-16. Fourteen final spring sightings range from May 7 to June 7, with a median of May 18. Eighteen initial fall sightings range from July 22 to October 6, with a median of September 11. Half of the records fall within the period September 3-16. Twenty final fall sightings are from September 22 to November 3, with a median of October 1. It is possible that this form migrates through Nebraska somewhat later in fall than does the plumbeous vireo (*Nebraska Bird Review* 65:173).

Habitats. Migrating birds occupy river–bottom cottonwood forests and other deciduous wooded habitats, where the birds usually forage among the larger branches. It breeds in swampy coniferous forests.

Comments. The solitary vireo is notable for its very conspicuous white eye-ring; like the Swainson's thrush I like to think it needs large eyeglasses as a result of too much solitary reading. Its song consists of repeated two to six-noted phrases. Breeding Bird Surveys between 1966 and 2011 indicate that the species had a significant population increase (4.7% annually) during that period.

Warbling Vireo   *Vireo gilvus*

A common spring and fall migrant statewide, and a common summer resident almost throughout the state, extending west to the Pine Ridge, throughout the Sandhills in suitable habitats, and to the Colorado border in Deuel and Dundy counties. Breeding occurs widely in the Plains States region, west to Colorado and the Texas panhandle.

The range of 112 initial spring sightings is from April 30 to June 10, with a median of May 8. Half of the records fall within the period May 1–14. Seventy-nine final fall sightings range from July 26 to October 4, with a median of September 9. Half of the records fall within the period August 30 to September 16.

Habitats. During the summer this species occurs in open stands of deciduous trees, including streamside vegetation, groves, scrubby hillsides, and residential areas. Tall streamside trees such as cottonwoods are favored nesting sites.

Comments. Usually foraging high in the treetop canopies of tall hardwood trees, my students hated to try identify this species until I told them that its song is easily learned if they simply remember that it is saying in a syncopated manner, "Lets go down to the corner and buy us a beer!" From then on they rarely mis-identify the species. Breeding Bird Surveys between 1966 and 2011 indicate that the species underwent a significant population increase (0.8% annually) during that period.

Philadelphia Vireo   *Vireo philadelphicus*

An uncommon spring and fall migrant in eastern Nebraska, west to at least Garden County. Breeding occurs in northern Minnesota and adjacent North Dakota, and migrants are widespread in the eastern half of the Plains States region.

Migration. Fifty-two initial spring sightings range from April 23 to June 4, with a median of May 13. Half of the records fall within the period May 5-19. Eleven final spring sightings are from May 10 to June 10, with a median of May 24. Thirteen initial fall sightings range from July 30 to September 25, with a median of August 25. Twelve final fall sightings are from September 1 to October 21, with a median of September 21.

Habitats. Migrants are associated with open second-growth woodlands, old burned-over wooded areas and clearings, and with streamside or lakeside thickets.

Comments. Like the red-eyed vireo this species lacks wing-bars and has a striped head. Its song is also similar; both species sing extended songs consisting of short phrases separated by brief pauses.

Red-eyed Vireo   *Vireo olivaceus*

A common spring and fall migrant statewide, and a common summer resident in wooded areas of eastern Nebraska, locally extending north to Sioux (White River), Cherry (Niobrara River), Thomas (Nebraska National Forest), Scott's Bluff (North Platte River), Deuel (South Platte River), and Dundy (Republican River) counties. Breeding occurs widely throughout the eastern portions of the Plains States region, locally west to Wyoming and Colorado.

Migration. The range of 129 initial spring sightings is from March 20 to June 10, with a median of May 14. Half of the records fall within the period May 9-22. Eighty final fall sightings range from July 23 to October 20, with a median of September 7. Half of the records fall within the period August 25 to September 5.

Habitats. While in Nebraska these birds are usually found in deciduous forests, especially those with rather open canopies and fairly large trees.

Comments. This is one of the commonest breeding vireos in eastern Nebraska. Like many vireos its song consists of many short phrases that alternately end on ascending and descending notes, as if the bird were asking a question and then immediately answering it, as in, "Do you have any eggs? I don't have any eggs." Breeding Bird Surveys between 1966 and 2011 indicate that the species underwent a significant population increase (0.8% annually) during that period.

Family Corvidae

Gray Jay   *Perisoreus canadensis*

An extremely rare winter visitor or vagrant. There are early records from Belmont (presumably Dawes County) and Monroe Canyon (Dawes County). It has also been reported from Sioux , Cuming, and Douglas counties, usually during winter and spring months. These birds presumably originate from the Black Hills, where the species is known to breed commonly.

Migration. This species has been observed from November 12 to April (no date), but almost no specific dates are available.

Habitats. Associated throughout the year with coniferous or mixed forests.

Comments. Like other jays this is an inquisitive and bold bird, often acting as a "camp robber" in protected sites such as parks, stealing bits of food that it is able to carry off and perhaps cache for later consumption.

Pinyon Jay   *Gymnorhinus cyanocephalus*

An uncommon to rare permanent resident of the Pine Ridge area (Sioux, Scotts Bluff and probably Sheridan and Morrill counties). Vagrants may appear elsewhere in the state (Lincoln, Dawson, and Webster counties) during winter months. Breeding was not documented in the state (Pine Ridge region) until 1999.

Migration. Probably a permanent resident in northwestern Nebraska. Vagrants sometimes appear in other parts of the state during late winter or spring.

Habitats. In the Black Hills, and probably also in the Pine Ridge, this species is found in pine forests where the soil is fairly dry and the trees are small and scattered.

Comments. This is another of the attractive members of the corvid family, with similar raucous notes and tendencies to cache food that are common to many species. Breeding Bird Surveys between 1966 and 2003 indicate that the species underwent a significant population decline (3.8% annually) during that period.

Steller's Jay   *Cyanocitta stelleri*

An extremely rare vagrant. More often seen in western parts of the state, but in addition to sightings in Scotts Bluff and Sioux counties, it has been seen in Keith, Lincoln, Logan, and Lancaster counties. It is also a vagrant in South Dakota, Oklahoma, and Kansas. As of 2009 there were about 30 state records (*Nebraska Bird Review* 776:60).

Migration. This species has been observed from October 6 to April 30, with two records each for November, December, January, and April.

Habitats. Throughout most of the year this species is associated with montane coniferous or mixed forests and woodlands, but sometimes flocks or individuals move to city edges and feeding stations during the fall and winter.

Comments. Steller's jays are bold and brassy birds of the American west. In a few areas they overlap with blue jays, and have been known to hybridize with them rarely.

Blue Jay   *Cyanocitta cristata*

A common permanent resident statewide, perhaps somewhat less common in western Nebraska than in eastern parts of the state. It is also a resident almost throughout the Plains States, excepting the extreme southwestern portions.

Habitats. Throughout the year this species is widely distributed in forests, parks suburbs, cities, and almost anywhere a combination of trees and grasslands occur. It is somewhat more adapted to city life than is the Steller's jay.

Comments. This familiar bird of cities and countryside is a noisy and sometimes annoying bird, as it will often steal eggs from the nests of smaller songbirds. However, its "*thief*" call warns all within range of possible danger, and it sometimes effectively mimics the alarm calls of red-shouldered and red-tailed hawks. Breeding Bird Surveys between 1966 and 2011 indicate that the species underwent a significant population decline (0.7% annually) during that period.

(Western Scrub -Jay)   *Aphelocoma californica*

Hypothetical. There are some early questionable references to this species in western Nebraska, but these have been generally discounted. There is a report of seeing this species in Bull Canyon, Banner County, very close to the Wyoming border (*Nebraska Bird Review* 48:89). This species is resident in eastern Colorado, New Mexico, and adjacent Oklahoma, and has wandered to central Kansas.

Clark's Nutcracker   *Nucifraga columbiana*

An extremely rare species in Nebraska, with most records from the Pine Ridge area, but reported as far east as Douglas and Cass counties. Possibly bred near Harrison in 1987; the only probable or confirmed breedings during early atlasing years were in Sioux County (Mollhoff, 2001).

Migration. Probably an irregular vagrant. Records extend from September 4 to November 9 in the fall, and from March 2 to June 25 in the spring, with the largest number of records for September.

Habitats. Throughout the year this species is normally associated with montane coniferous forests, but winter vagrants may appear almost anywhere.

Comments. The memories of these birds, which often cache hundreds or even thousands of seeds for months, and then are able to locate them accurately, is simply amazing. Although rare in Nebraska, they are typical birds in the high mountains of Colorado, where they are often very tame and depend on the cached seeds of limber and whitebark pines for winter survival. Breeding Bird Surveys between 1966 and 2003 indicate that the species underwent a significant population increase (1.2% annually) during that period. By 2005 there were three state breeding records (*Nebraska Bird Review* 73:58).

Black-billed Magpie   *Pica hudsonia*

A common permanent resident in western Nebraska, becoming rarer eastwardly, but present virtually statewide during winter months, when vagrants wander eastward. It breeds widely in the Plains States, from North Dakota south to Kansas and extreme northern New Mexico.

Habitats. Throughout the year the species normally frequents wooded canyons and river–bottom forests and forest edges, but ranges out into more arid environments wherever there are thickets of shrubs or small trees that provide nest sites.

Comments. Magpies are widespread and highly adaptable birds that seem to have their eastern breeding limits in the state rather rigidly limited to areas west of Grand Island. Their large stick nests, usually placed in low trees, are a certain indicator of breeding pairs in the area. Breeding Bird Surveys between 1966 and 2003 indicate that the species underwent a significant population decline (0.6% annually) during that period.

American Crow   *Corvus brachyrhynchos*

A common to abundant spring and fall migrant statewide, and a common summer resident. Numbers are greatly increased in winter by migrants from farther north, so the species is present throughout the year. Breeding occurs over most of the Plains States region excepting the southwestern portions, and the species is a migrant throughout.

Habitats. Throughout the year this species occurs in a wide variety of forests, wooded river bottoms, suburban areas, orchards, parks and woodlots.

Comments. The familiar crow has become more of a city-adapted bird in recent decades, where is gains some safety from great horned owls and perhaps some large hawks. Breeding Bird Surveys between 1966 and 2011 indicate that the species underwent a significant population increase (0.2% annually) during that period.

Fish Crow   *Corvus ossifragus*

Accidental. Observed on several occasions, from May 29 to August 8, 2009, along the lower Platte and Missouri rivers (*Nebraska Bird Review* 77: 60, 155-159).

Chihuahuan Raven   *Corvus cryptoleucus*

Previously an uncommon or local resident in Adams and Kearney counties; at present perhaps a rare and irregular breeder in the state, with a recent nesting record for Dundy County (*Nebraska Bird Review* 45:16) and a possible nest of this species (or perhaps an American crow) in the Grand Island area (*Nebraska Bird Review* 44:38-39). There are scattered sightings of vagrants elsewhere in the state, but the status of this species in the state remains very questionable. Regular breeding occurs from western Kansas and eastern Colorado southward.

Migration. Too few dates are available for an analysis. Six initial spring sightings range from January 1 to June 6, with no obvious clustering of dates. No fall departure dates are available.

Habitats. The usual breeding habitat consists of open and arid grasslands, with scattered trees, telephone poles, or windmills for nest sites. It is generally not associated with river valleys or heavily forested areas.

Comments. This species once was called the "white-necked raven," but the white bases of the neck feathers are rarely visible. It is only slightly larger than the American crow, and has a slightly higher–pitched voice.

Common Raven   *Corvus corax*

Extirpated or nearly so from Nebraska. Previously occurred and probably bred in western parts of the state, but extirpated by 1900. Recent sightings attributed to this species include two for Scotts Bluff County and one each for Adams and Douglas counties, all between March 31 and May 26. Similarities to the Chihuahuan raven make such sightings suspect, but the species does occur in the eastern plains of Colorado during winter months. Other recent sightings have been made in the Sandhills region (*Nebraska Bird Review* 75:111).

Habitats. This species is associated with open plains, canyons and forests throughout the year.

Comments. Perhaps the common raven will one day return to western Nebraska, but the egg- and chick-eating tendencies of these birds make them a threat to many other species, and so its absence is not a great loss. Breeding Bird Surveys between 1966 and 2011 indicate that the species underwent a significant population increase (2.4% annually) during that period.

Family Alaudidae

Horned Lark   *Eremophila alpestris*

A common to abundant spring and fall migrant and summer resident statewide, and a common winter visitor as well. Several subspecies are present in the state at various times of the year. It breeds in or migrates through the entire Plains States region.

Habitats. A variety of low-stature open habitats are used by this species throughout the year, but in Nebraska it is mostly found in natural grasslands and cultivated fields. The sparse grasslands of the Sandhills are probably a nearly optimum habitat.

Comments. Probably few if any other species of songbirds are as common as the horned lark in the Nebraska Sandhills, although the coloration of the birds matches their substrate so well that they are usually overlooked until they fly, when their mostly black tails become apparent. Breeding Bird Surveys between 1966 and 2011 indicate that the species underwent a significant population decline (2.4% annually) during that period.

Family Hirundinidae

Purple Martin   *Progne subis*

A common spring and fall migrant and summer resident throughout most of Nebraska, with the western limits generally east of a line from eastern Cherry County through Dundy County. The range may still be expanding west, but presently Ogallala, Lewellen and Crescent Lake represent the approximate western limits. It breeds in the eastern parts of the Plains States, from North Dakota south to Texas.

Migration. The range of 143 initial spring sightings is from March 8 to June 5, with a median of April 10. Half of the records fall within the period March 27 to April 15. The range of 101 final fall sightings is from July 22 to October 15, with a median of August 30. Half of the records fall within the period August 20 to September 15.

Habitats. Widespread in urban, suburban and rural habitats, usually fairly near water and always where suitable nesting cavities are available. Typically these are in birdhouses, but the birds sometimes also nest in clusters of gourds or even in unused woodpecker holes or crevices in old buildings.

Comments. Purple martins are sociable nesters that readily accept martin houses, although it is necessary to keep house sparrows from confiscating such locations before the martins arrive in mid-April. The houses must also be place fairly high, in obstacle-free locations, if they are to be used by the birds.

Tree Swallow   *Tachycineta bicolor*
    A common spring and fall migrant in eastern Nebraska, becoming infrequent farther west, and uncommon to rare summer resident in the forested valley of the Missouri, extending locally westward as far as Cherry County (probably to Dawes County) in the Niobrara Valley and Garden County in the Platte Valley. It also breeds in the Dakotas, Minnesota, Iowa, and Missouri, and migrates throughout the Plains States.
    Migration. The range of 86 initial spring sightings is from March 20 to June 8, with a median of April 29. Half of the records fall within the period April 14 to May 11. Twenty-eight final fall sightings are from July 25 to October 27, with a median of September 17. Half of the records fall within the period August 26 to October 7.
    Habitats. During summer this species occurs in open woodlands, usually fairly close to water. Woodpecker holes in dead trees, especially aspens and willows, are favorite nesting sites.
    Comments. Tree swallows have benefited from the bluebird nest-box program in Nebraska and elsewhere, and have expanded their breeding range in the state accordingly. There nests are always feather–lined, unlike those of bluebirds, and they are as much of a delight to have on one's property as are bluebirds. Breeding Bird Surveys between 1966 and 2003 indicate that the species underwent a significant population decline (1.1% annually) during that period.

Violet-green Swallow   *Tachycineta thalassina*
    A local but common spring and fall migrant and summer resident in western Nebraska, including the Pine Ridge area, the Wildcat Hills, and the Scottsbluff area, with confirmed breedings during the atlasing years only in Scotts Bluff County (Mollhoff, 2001). Vagrants have appeared east to Perkins and Cuming counties during migration. It also breeds in western South Dakota, migrates through eastern Colorado, and has bred once in western Kansas.
    Migration. Thirty-eight initial spring sightings range from April 17 to June 10, with a median of May 13. Half of the records fall within the period May 5-19. Four final fall sightings are from August 20 to September 5, with a mean of August 27.
    Habitats. During summer, this species is found in open forests such as ponderosa pine forests or poplar woodlands, but sometimes also extends into urban areas, occasionally nesting in birdhouses. Old woodpecker holes are the usual nesting sites in forested areas.
    Comments. Violet-green swallows are close relatives of tree swallows, but perhaps are even more attractive. The "racing stripe" white markings on their upper tail-coverts seem to be a perfect decorative touch to their plumage, and allow for easy identification.

Northern Rough-winged Swallow   *Stelgidopteryx serripennis*
    A common spring and fall migrant and summer resident throughout Nebraska. It breeds in and migrates through virtually the entire Plains States.
    Migration. The range of 136 initial spring sightings is from March 2 to May 29, with a median of April 28. Half of the records fall within the period April 18 to May 6. Seventy-two final fall sightings are from July 21 to October 15, with a median of September 3. Half of the records fall within the period August 23 to September 15.
    Habitats. This is an open-country species, often found near rivers or creeks having exposed vertical banks of clay or other materials that can be excavated to provide nest sites. Unlike the colonial bank swallow, this species is a solitary nester.
    Comments. Rough-winged swallows are among the most common swallows in eastern Nebraska, especially near streams having steep-sided mud banks. They also nest in natural cavities of rocky outcrops, although perhaps less frequently. They have even been found to accept horizontally installed drainpipes as nesting cavities.

Bank Swallow   *Riparia riparia*

A common spring and fall migrant in eastern Nebraska, becoming less common westwardly, and a summer resident almost statewide, but less frequent in western areas. It also breeds throughout most of the Plains States, south to northeastern Kansas, and is a regular migrant farther south.

Migration. The range of 104 initial spring sightings is from March 20 to June 8, with a median of May 6. Half of the records fall within the period April 28 to May 6. Sixty-five final fall sightings range from July 31 to October 29, with a median of September 8. Half of the records fall within the period August 23 to September 15.

Habitats. While in Nebraska this species occurs in a variety of open habitats, especially grasslands and croplands, but is typically found near water and is dependent on suitable potential nest sites in the form of vertical banks of clay, sand or gravel that can be excavated by the birds.

Comments. Bank swallows are local nesters in the state, requiring rather large areas of barren road-cuts to support a breeding colony. The nearly vertical clay-like banks of loess that are common beside roads along the Missouri Valley provide a perfect nesting situation for these birds. Breeding Bird Surveys between 1966 and 2003 indicate that the species underwent a significant population decline (4.6% annually) during that period.

Cliff Swallow   *Petrochelidon pyrrhonota*

A common spring and fall migrant and summer resident statewide. It also breeds in or migrates through the entire Plains States region.

Migration. The range of 125 initial spring sightings is from March 22 to June 10, with a median of April 28. Half of the records fall within the period April 29 to May 18. The range of 101 final fall sightings is from July 22 to October 30, with a median of September 4. Half of the records fall within the period August 20 to September 15.

Habitats. This species occurs over open areas of farmlands, towns, near cliffs, around bridges, and in other areas where mud supplies and potential nest sites exist on vertical and overhanging surfaces. Highly colonial, and often nesting in the same locations year after year.

Comments. There are few if any locations in America that support larger numbers of cliff swallows than the bridges, culverts, and similar structures in the central and western Platte Valley. Breeding colonies supporting up to several thousand nests are present in some locations, and the numbers of mosquitoes, midges and similar aerial insects that are consumed in a summer must be astronomical.

Cave Swallow   *Petrochelidon fulva*

Accidental; four records through 2012. Two birds were caught and banded in Keith County, on May 31, 1991 and June 26, 1995; also reported July 1 1988, and July 8, 2003 (Brown *et al.* 1996; Brown, Dinsmore and Brown, 2012).

Barn Swallow   *Hirundo rustica*

A common spring and fall migrant and summer resident statewide. Judging from migration records, the most common of the swallows in Nebraska. It breeds in and migrates through the entire Plains States region.

Migration. The range of 155 initial spring sightings is from March 9 to June 10, with a median of April 23. Half of the records fall within the period April 18-30. The range of 119 final fall sightings is from August 5 to October 6, with a median of September 30. Half of the records fall between September 19 and October 6.

Habitats. Extremely widespread during the summer, this species occupies open forests, farmlands, suburbs, and rural areas, usually nesting on or inside buildings that have horizontal beams available for nesting sites. Typically colonial and sometimes nesting near or among cliff swallows.

Comments. This is one of the most familiar of our swallows, and few farms in the state lack at least one pair of these graceful birds. At times they will also nest in urban areas, often choosing porch eaves or carports for nest sites. Breeding Bird Surveys between 1966 and 2011 indicate that the species had a significant population decline (1.2% annually) during that period.

Family Paridae

(Carolina Chickadee)   *Poecile carolinensis*

Hypothetical. Specimens were captured in Fontenelle Forest, Sarpy County, in July of 1974, after the species was first heard in the forest in the winter of 1969 (*Nebraska Bird Review* 42:57). These records were not accepted by the NOU Records Committee (1997).

Black-capped Chickadee   *Poecile atricapillus*

A common permanent resident statewide. The population increases during winter months with the arrival of migrants from further north. Also breeds widely in the Plains States south to southern Kansas, and occurs as a migrant slightly farther south.

Habitats. Throughout the year this species is found in deciduous and coniferous forests, as well as orchards and woodlots. Nesting often occurs in edge situations or open areas of forests, but during the winter period the birds frequently appear at residential feeding stations, especially where suet is available.

Comments. Nearly everybody knows the chickadee by both voice and appearance, and it is a regular visitor at feeding stations where suet is available. It is a very hardy little bird, surviving sub-zero temperatures for long periods. Its song is lower–pitched and slower than that of the very similar Carolina chickadee. Breeding Bird Surveys between 1966 and 2003 indicate that the species underwent a significant population increase (0.7% annually) during that period.

Mountain Chickadee   *Poecile gambeli*

An extremely rare winter visitor in western Nebraska. It has been reported at least eleven times in Scotts Bluff County, and one or more times in Lincoln, Dawson and Sioux counties. It has also been observed in western South Dakota, southwestern Kansas, and northwestern Oklahoma.

Migration. Records for this rare winter vagrant extent from October 5 to May 23. The largest number of records are for October (5), November (4) and December (4), followed by February and April, with two each.

Habitats. Normally associated with montane coniferous forests throughout the year, but winter vagrants may appear at residential feeding stations.

Comments. This species tends to replace the black-capped in coniferous forests, but they are very similar in size and behavior. Its whistled "*fee-bee*" call is extended to three or four notes that descend in pitch.

(Boreal Chickadee)   *Poecile hudsonicus*

Hypothetical. A single individual was observed during the winter of 1972-73 in Lancaster County (*Nebraska Bird Review* 41:43). It has also been reported a few times in South Dakota and North Dakota, and breeds in northern Minnesota.

Tufted Titmouse   *Baeolophus bicolor*

A common permanent resident in eastern Nebraska, with breeding largely limited to the Missouri's forested valley, north perhaps to the South Dakota border and west in southern Nebraska at least as far as Saline and Thayer counties. During the atlasing years no birds were reported north of Washington County. It breeds from Iowa southward through Missouri and eastern Kansas to Oklahoma and Texas.

Habitats. Throughout most of its range this species is generally found in coniferous or deciduous forests, orchards, woodlots and suburban areas. At the edge of its range in Nebraska it is confined to bottomland deciduous forest.

Comments. The loud "*Peter, Peter, Peter*" call of this species is a certain indication of the presence of tufted titmice in an area, long before the bird is usually visible. Near Lincoln it is mostly limited to the mature forests of Wilderness Park, but it is more common along the Missouri Valley. Breeding Bird Surveys between 1966 and 2011 indicate that the species had a significant population increase (1.1% annually) during that period.

Family Sittidae

Red-breasted Nuthatch   *Sitta canadensis*

A common winter visitor in eastern Nebraska and the Pine Ridge; generally uncommon elsewhere in the state. There is a 1980 nesting record, for Nebraska National Forest, Cherry County. During the atlasing years confirmed nestings were reported from Sioux, Cherry, Boyd and Scotts Bluff counties (Mollhoff, 2001). It breeds in the Black Hills and occurs as a migrant throughout the Plains States.

Migration. Seventy-two initial fall sightings range from August 10 to December 31, with a median of October 9. Half of the records fall within the period September 18 to October 17. Thirty-nine final spring sightings are from January 4 to June 8, with a median of April 3. Half of the records fall within the period March 3 to April 23.

Habitats. Except for the northern Panhandle, where the species probably breeds in coniferous forests, this bird is likely to be found in conifer plantations, mixed woodlands, and sometimes also appears at feeding stations during winter.

Comments. Over most of Nebraska this species is a winter visitor, especially around coniferous plantings. Its voice is similar to that of the white-breasted nuthatch, but is more rapid and higher–pitched.

White-breasted Nuthatch   *Sitta carolinensis*

An uncommon permanent resident in eastern Nebraska, breeding in wooded habitats locally as far west as the Pine Ridge area in the Niobrara Valley and to at least Hall County in the Platte Valley. It also breeds widely in the other Plains States, mainly in eastern portions, but west locally to the Black Hills.

Habitats. In Nebraska this species is generally associated with fairly mature floodplain forests during the breeding season, while during the rest of the year it is more widespread and often visits residential feeding stations, especially where suet is provided.

Comments. The long, sharp beak of nuthatches adapts them to probing in the crevices of tree bark, feeding on some of the same insects that woodpeckers consume. The distinctive voice of this species reminds one of a toy trumpet or the bleating of a miniature sheep. Breeding Bird Surveys between 1966 and 2011 indicate that the species underwent a significant population increase (1.6% annually) during that period.

Pygmy Nuthatch   *Sitta pygmaea*

Probably a local but regular permanent resident of the Pine Ridge and Scotts Bluff area. A single nesting record had existed for Sioux County (*Nebraska Bird Review* 40:70) until studies proved its nesting in Dawes, Sioux and Sheridan counties (*Nebraska Bird Review* 65:150-8). It also probably nests in Banner County (*American Birds* 50:296-300), the Wildcat Hills, Scotts Bluff County (first fully documented in 1996), and McKelvie National Forest, Cherry County. Vagrants sometimes appear east to Lancaster County. It is a permanent resident of the Black Hills.

Habitats. Throughout the year this species is generally associated with ponderosa pines, especially those growing in open, park-like situations. In the winter, vagrants may appear along cottonwood-lined rivers, often in small flocks.

Comments. Pygmy nuthatches are tiny nuthatches that feed in the same manner as the larger species, and they have a voice that is even higher pitched and the notes more rapid than in the red-breasted nuthatch. There are only a few definite nest records for the state so far, which are for Sioux County, plus some possible single records for Dawes and Douglas counties.

Brown-headed Nuthatch   *Sitta pusilla*

Accidental. Two adults were seen and photographed at Holmes Lake Park, Lincoln, during November 8, 2010 through mid-January, 2011 (*Nebraska Bird Review* 79:16; 136–138).

Family Certhiidae

Brown Creeper   *Certhia americana*

A common winter visitor in eastern Nebraska and the Pine Ridge, less frequent elsewhere in the state. There are several early nesting records, but more recent ones were for 1975 and 1977 in Sarpy County (*Nebraska Bird Review* 43:80; 46:14). Nesting also has been recently observed in the Pine Ridge near Crawford, Dawes County (*Nebraska Bird Review* 72:157). It breeds in the Black Hills and northern Minnesota, and occurs throughout the Plains States as a migrant or winter visitor.

Migration. Ninety-two initial fall sightings range from August 5 to December 30, with a median of October 17. Half of the records fall within the period September 17 to October 17. Forty-four final spring sightings are from January 8 to May 29, with a median of March 22. Half of the records fall within the period March 3 to April 23. In a few areas the species breeds and must be considered a permanent resident.

Habitats. While breeding, these birds are associated with fairly mature deciduous or coniferous forests, but in the winter the birds move to wooded streams, wooded parks, suburbs, and the like.

Comments. This small and inconspicuous bark-hugging species virtually blends into its background when it is not moving. The nests are hidden behind loose bark, and very difficult to locate, which accounts for the scanty nesting records.

Family Troglodytidae

Rock Wren   *Salpinctes obsoletus*
A common spring and fall migrant in western Nebraska, becoming rare eastwardly, and a common summer resident in western areas, generally exclusive of the Sandhills, with local breeding as far east as Cherry, Custer, Lincoln and Red Willow counties. It breeds from the western Parts of North Dakota southward through western Kansas and western Oklahoma.

Migration. Eighty-three initial spring sightings range from April 2 to June 9, with a median of May 2. Half of the records fall within the period April 22-May 13. Thirty-three final fall sightings are from August 18 to October 29, with a median of October 27. Half of the records fall within the period September 17 to October 6.

Habitats. In Nebraska this species occurs on eroded slopes and badlands, rocky outcrops, cliff walls, talus slopes and similar generally arid environments.

Comments. Rock wrens make their presence known by their loud trilling songs, which echo up and down the steep canyons they usually inhabit. The nests are well hidden in rock crevices, but their entrance is often lined with tiny pebbles.

Canyon Wren   *Catherpes mexicanus*
Accidental. Individuals have been seen on two occasions in Dawes County in recent years (*Nebraska Bird Review* 42:16, 78). Also seen in Sioux and Knox counties. The species is an uncommon permanent resident in the Black Hills, and vagrants in Nebraska might be expected. It is also a resident in western Oklahoma, but not reported from Kansas.

House Wren   *Troglodytes aedon*
A common spring and fall migrant and summer resident throughout Nebraska, becoming abundant in the Platte and Missouri Valley forests. It breeds widely in the Plains States, from North Dakota and Minnesota south to northern Oklahoma and northeastern New Mexico, and occurs farther south as a migrant.

Migration. The range of 136 initial spring sightings is from March 10 to May 24, with a median of April 24. Half of the records fall within the period April 19 to May 2. The range of 131 final fall sightings is from July 24 to October 22, with a median of September 26. Half of the records fall within the period September 10 to October 7.

Habitats. Originally associated with deciduous forests and open woods, this species now is also city-adapted, and frequently nests in birdhouses. However, it is also abundant in river–bottom forests, cottonwood groves, and wooded hillsides or canyons.

Comments. One of the worst mistakes bird-lovers can do is to put up nest boxes for house wrens in their back yard. The presence of house wrens is likely to cause losses of all other cavity-nesting birds such as chickadees, tree swallows and bluebirds owing to the predatory nature of house wren males on the eggs and chicks of other hole-nesting birds. Breeding Bird Surveys between 1966 and 2011 indicate that the species underwent a significant population increase (0.5% annually) during that period.

Winter Wren   *Troglodytes troglodytes*

A spring and fall migrant and winter resident, ranging from uncommon in eastern Nebraska to rare in western areas. It breeds in northern Minnesota and occurs throughout the Plains States as a migrant or winter visitor.

Migration. The range of 38 initial fall sightings is from August 30 to December 26, with a median of October 16. Half of the records fall within January 21 to May 29, with a median of April 13. Half of the records fall within the period April 5-23.

Habitats. While in Nebraska this inconspicuous species is usually found among dense ravine thickets along streams, but sometimes also occurs in suburban gardens, parks and other habitats.

Comments This tiny but very beautiful wren is too rarely seen in Nebraska, and its wonderfully loud and lilting song is probably never uttered here. In spite of its tiny size this wren has found its way to Asia and Europe, and has a larger breeding range than other single wren species. A western species of winter wren, the Pacific wren,. *T. pacificus*, has recently been described, but so far has not been proven to occur in Nebraska *(Nebraska Bird Review* 78:144).

Sedge Wren   *Cistothorus platensis*

An uncommon spring and fall migrant in eastern Nebraska, and an occasional summer resident in the eastern third of the state, mostly east of a line from Knox to Gage counties, but west to at least Hall County and perhaps to Lincoln County (Mollhoff, 2001). Elsewhere in the Plains States it breeds from North Dakota and Minnesota southward to eastern Kansas, and migrates through most of the region.

Migration. Twenty-five initial spring sightings range from April 16 to June 3, with a median of May 8. Half of the records fall within the period May 1–12. Seventeen final fall sightings are from July 29 to October 22, with a median of September 28. Half of the records fall within the period September 11 to October 9. Many birds seem to arrive in mid-summer and begin nesting at that time.

Habitats. In Nebraska and the northern plains these birds breed in wet meadows, typically those dominated by sedges and tall grasses, and less often breed in the emergent vegetation of marshes as well as retired croplands and hayfields.

Comments, Sedge wrens are common breeders in southeastern Nebraska, where they arrive and begin to sing in early May. Then, in July or August a new song cycle begins, leading some to speculate that these are late arriving birds, perhaps from farther north, where they may have been unsuccessful breeders. A similar summer migration might occur in marsh wrens *(Nebraska Bird Review* 76: 107*)*.

Marsh Wren   *Cistothorus palustris*

A common spring and fall migrant statewide and locally common summer resident north of the Platte River, with local or infrequent breeding south of the Platte *(Nebraska Bird Review* 39:47). It breeds from North Dakota and Minnesota south to Nebraska, with local breeding in Colorado and occurs elsewhere as a migrant in the Plains States. Both eastern and western song types occur in the state, the dividing line passes southeast through O'Neill, approximately along the Elkhorn Valley *(Nebraska Bird Review* 64:99), or along the eastern edge of the Sandhills (Mollhoff, 2001).

Migration. Seventy-eight initial spring sightings range from March 13 to June 9, with a median of May 5. Half of the records fall within the period April 26 to May 15. Thirty-two final fall sightings are from August 9 to November 22, with a median of October 2. Half of the records fall within the period September 8 to October 10.

Habitats. During the breeding season these birds are primarily found in freshwater marshes having extensive tall emergent vegetation, such as bulrushes and cattails. They also nest along the banks of slowly flowing brackish tidal marshes.

Comments. The marsh wrens of Nebraska pose a problem in evolution, with two distinct song types occurring in the state, as noted above. Perhaps the two types represent "sibling species" that seem to differ only in their vocalizations, but act biologically as distinct species. Breeding Bird Surveys between 1966 and 2011 indicate that the species underwent a significant population increase (2.0% annually) during that period.

Carolina Wren   *Thryothorus ludovicianus*
        An uncommon permanent resident in eastern Nebraska, extending locally or periodically to Dakota, Lancaster, Cuming and Nuckolls counties, and west along most of the Republican River Valley (*Nebraska Bird Review* 76:64). A remarkable confirmed nesting occurred in Cherry County during the atlasing years (Mollhoff, 2001) Fall vagrants have been seen west in the Platte Valley at least to Gibbon. It is also resident in eastern Kansas, Oklahoma, and northern Texas.
        Migration. Seventy-two initial spring sightings range from January 1 to June 4, with a median of March 1. Nearly half occur in the month of January. Seven final fall sightings range from August 29 to December 31, with a mean of October 21. The data suggest that the species is primarily a permanent resident within its limited Nebraska breeding range, and is a vagrant elsewhere.
        Habitats. During the breeding season and probably also the rest of the year this species occupies river bottom forests, forest edges, cutover forests, and cultivated areas with brush heaps, and suburban parks and gardens. It is more closely associated with bottomland forests in Nebraska than is the Bewick's wren or house wren. The three species all overlap in their ecological distributions.
        Comments. The attractive Carolina wren reaches its distributional limit in southeastern Nebraska, where it periodically seems to extend northward for a few years. Its usual song consists of repeated *"teakettle"* phrases, Breeding Bird Surveys between 1966 and 2011 indicate that the species had a significant population increase (1.0% annually) during that period.

Bewick's Wren   *Thryomanes bewickii*
        A rare spring and fall migrant and summer resident in southern Nebraska. Breeding may be regular west to Gage County, and exceptionally as far west as Buffalo County, but an early report of breeding in Lincoln County seems very questionable. Elsewhere it breeds in eastern Kansas, southeastern Colorado and south tone Mexico and Texas. It is accidental in South Dakota.
        Migration. Forty-four initial spring sightings range from March 26 to May 28, with a median of April 24. Half of the records fall within the period April 9 to May 8. Nine final fall sightings range from August 11 to October 3, with a mean of September 20.
        Habitats. Habitats used during the breeding season include open woodlands, brushy habitats, farmsteads, and towns. In Colorado they are mostly associated with dry canyons and scrubby forests, but farther east they overlap with the house wren in their habitats.
        Comments. Just as the Carolina wren reaches its range limits in eastern Nebraska, the Bewick's wren has its terminus in southern Nebraska. Its possible status in southwestern Nebraska is dubious, but it was reported there on Breeding Bird Breeding Bird surveys, although no breeding records exist for this area or for adjacent northwestern Kansas or northeastern Colorado. There have been few Nebraska records of this species in recent years; apparently its range has retracted. It has also become quite rare in the eastern states, perhaps because of undesirable interactions with house wrens.

Family Polioptilidae

Blue-gray Gnatcatcher   *Polioptila caerulea*
        A common spring and fall migrant and summer resident in most of Nebraska excepting the Sandhills, with historic breeding limited to the Missouri River's forested valley in the southeast, west to about Lancaster and Jefferson counties. However, breeding (of *P. c. amoenissima*) now also occurs in the Wildcat Hills, and increasingly elsewhere over much of western Nebraska excepting the Sandhills (*Nebraska Bird Review* 77: 107 78:144).

Migration. Eighty-five initial spring sightings range from March 30 to June 6, with a median of May 2. Half of the records fall within the period April 23 to May 10. Seven fall sightings are from July 26 to September 22; a mean of September 1.

Habitats. Breeding occurs in deciduous bottomland forests of eastern Nebraska. The western race *amoenissima* often uses scrubby woodlands for breeding.

Comments. This tiny sprite of a bird is usually seen high in the tree canopy, industriously searching for tiny insects. Breeding Bird Surveys between 1966 and 2011 indicate that the species underwent a significant population increase (0.6% annually) during that period.

Family Cinclidae

American Dipper   *Cinclus mexicanus*

An extremely rare vagrant. Individuals have been reported once each from Sioux, Dawes, Cherry, Holt, Chase and Adams counties. There have been at least four records since 1960, the most recent one from Cherry County (*Nebraska Bird Review* 45:52). It is a permanent resident in the Black Hills, but not reported from elsewhere in the Plains States.

Migration. Probably an irregular vagrant. Records exist for May, June, October and December.

Habitats. Throughout the year this species is normally associated with rapidly flowing mountain streams in wooded areas, but in winter the birds sometimes move to open water at lower elevations.

Comments. American dippers are sometimes called "water ouzels," and they are the only American songbirds that regularly dive into the water and search for food at the bottom of fast-moving steams. It seems possible that some of the branch streams of the Niobrara River might support breeding pairs of these fascinating birds.

Family Regulidae

Golden-crowned Kinglet   *Regulus satrapa*

A common to uncommon spring and fall migrant, and an uncommon winter resident statewide, perhaps less common in western than eastern areas. Breeding occurs in the Black Hills and northern Minnesota but the species is widespread through the Plains States as a migrant.

Migration. Seventy-five initial fall sightings range from August 13 to December 30, with a median of October 19. Half of the records fall within the period October 10-29. Fifty-nine final fall sightings are from November 6 to December 31, with a median of December 26, suggesting that the species should be normally considered a winter resident. Fifty-three final spring records are from January 9 to May 29, with a median of April 10. Half of the records fall within the period April 3-26.

Habitats. While in Nebraska this species occupies a wide variety of woodlands, forests and scrubby habitats, including both coniferous and hardwoods but especially the former.

Comments. Kinglets are named for their brilliant golden or ruby-colored crown markings, although only in this species are these markings always exposed. The birds are tiny, and their voices are so high-pitched that older birders are likely to miss hearing them altogether.

Ruby-crowned Kinglet   *Regulus calendula*

A common to uncommon spring and fall migrant statewide, and a rare and local winter resident. Breeding in the Plains States is restricted to the Black Hills and probably northern Minnesota, but the species is found throughout the region on migration.

Migration. Seventy-four initial spring sightings range from January 12 to May 28, with a median of April 13. Half of the records fall within the period April 1-22. Forty-nine final spring sightings are from April 7 to May 22, with a median of May 10. Seventy-five initial fall sightings are from August 7 to December 10, with a median of September 23. Half of the records fall within the period September 10 to October 7. Sixty-nine final fall records are from August 16 to December 31, with a median of October 28. Less than a fourth of the final fall records are for December, suggesting that the species only rather rarely overwinters in Nebraska.

Habitats. While in Nebraska this species occurs in a wide variety of forested and shrubby habitats, including gardens and parks. It occurs in both deciduous and coniferous vegetation, showing no apparent preference for the latter.

Comments. This is the more common of the two kinglets, and it often pays little attention to humans as it clambers about on twigs and branches.

Family Turdidae

(Northern Wheatear)   *Oenanthe oenanthe*

Hypothetical. In addition to an early sight record for Dawes County by John T. Zimmer, the species was reported in Gage County in January of 1970 (*Nebraska Bird Review* 39:18). It is considered hypothetical in South Dakota, but there are no specimen records from the Plains States.

Eastern Bluebird   *Sialia sialis*

A spring and fall migrant statewide, most common in the east, but uncommon even there, and rare in the extreme west. An uncommon to occasional summer resident in eastern areas, locally breeding as far west as Dawes County in the White River drainage, Brown or Cherry County in the Niobrara Valley and the Colorado border in the South Platte and Republican valleys. There is also local breeding in the eastern Sandhills where wooded habitats exist. Local overwintering sometimes occurs. Breeding occurs widely in the eastern portions of the Plains States, locally west to Colorado and Wyoming, and migrants occur throughout the area.

Migration. The range of 123 initial spring sightings is from January 1 to June 8, with a median of March 23. Half of the records fall within the period March 1 to April 25, and over ten percent of the records are for January. Seventy-four final fall sightings are from August 14 to December 31, with a median of November 5. Half of the records are within the period October 8-27, and nearly a third are for December. The data suggest that this species occasionally overwinters in Nebraska.

Habitats. During summer this species frequents open hardwood forests, especially those adjacent to grasslands. Forest edges, shelterbelts, city parks, farmsteads, and similar habitats are also used by breeding birds and migrants.

Comments. After the disastrous decline of bluebirds and other songbirds in the 1960s, it has taken several decades for bluebirds to regain their original numbers as breeding birds. Bluebird nest-box programs have contributed greatly to this resurgence, although boxes used by bluebirds are often attacked by house wrens, which may destroy bluebird eggs, and may kill their nestlings. In recent years erection of bluebird boxes has greatly improved the Nebraska population. Breeding Bird Surveys between 1966 and 2011 indicate that the species had a significant population increase (1.8% annually) in that period.

Western Bluebird   *Sialia mexicana*

An extremely rare vagrant. Individuals have been observed during fall and spring in Dawes, Scotts Bluff, Webster and Knox counties at least on five occasions. Considered hypothetical in Kansas and reported twice in Oklahoma. The nearest breeding occurs in Colorado.

Migration. Five records of this rare migrant range from April 11 to October 16. There are two records for August and October, and one for April.

Habitats. Migrants are associated with open plains and foothills, or similar habitats to those used by mountain bluebirds.

Comments. This is by far the rarest bluebird species in Nebraska, although it might be searched-for in the counties bordering Colorado.

Mountain Bluebird   *Sialia currucoides*

A common spring and fall migrant in western Nebraska, sometimes observed east to Douglas and Lancaster counties, and a common summer resident in the Panhandle, particularly the Pine Ridge and Wildcat Hills area. Overwintering in the state sometimes occurs. Breeding also occurs in western portions of the Dakotas, and migrants are fairly widespread in the western half of the region.

Migration. Eighty-four initial spring sightings are from January 1 to May 25, with a median of March 11. Half of the records fall within the period February 28 to March 2. Thirty-five final fall sightings are from July 21 to December 31, with a median of October 16. Half of the records fall within the period October 8-27.

Habitats. During the breeding season this species occupies open woodlands, especially open pine forest stands, burned or cutover areas, and aspen clumps. While on migration it often occurs in flocks in open country, perching on roadside fences or telephone wires.

Comments. Although perhaps not quite so attractive as the eastern bluebird, a flock of migrating mountain bluebirds making their way over the plains is a sight that will be long-remembered. The birds seem to be more gregarious than eastern bluebirds, which generally migrate in very small groups or even singly.

Townsend's Solitaire   *Myadestes townsendi*

An uncommon to locally common spring and fall migrant in western Nebraska, and a locally common winter resident in juniper–rich habitats of western and central Nebraska. There are two early reports of breeding in Sioux County, as well as a 1980s record (Mollhoff, 2001), but it is uncertain if the species still nests in the Pine Ridge. Presumably the source of Nebraska's wintering population is the Black Hills of South Dakota. Vagrants may be seen east to the Missouri River in the winter. Breeding is limited to the Black Hills region, but migrants are widespread in the western parts of the region.

Migration. Fifty initial fall sightings are from August 23 to December 5, with a median of September 26. Half of the records fall within the period September 17 to October 1. Forty-five final spring sightings are from January 10 to May 25, with a median of March 20. Half of the records fall within the period February 9 to April 7. The species is sometimes seen during summer in northwestern Nebraska and perhaps rarely breeds there, but essentially must be considered a winter visitor in Nebraska.

Habitats. Breeding habitats of this species are rather dense coniferous forests in mountainous areas. During migration the birds are often found in wooded slopes rich in juniper berries.

Comments. On first seeing a Townsend's solitaire a birder may be confused, since it bears little similarity to thrushes, bluebirds or robins, Its slim body and rufous wing markings may remind one of a thrasher or some other related bird, and the oddly spotted juveniles are even more puzzling. However, its song is a lovely thrush-like warble, and its eggs are similarly often pale bluish, with darker spotting.

Veery   *Catharus fuscescens*

A spring and fall migrant statewide, generally occasional to rare throughout, but probably more common in eastern woodlands. It breeds in North Dakota and Minnesota, and occurs elsewhere through the Plains States region as a migrant.

Migration. The range of 108 initial spring sightings is from March 10 to June 4, with a median of May 15. Half of the records fall within the period May 10-21. Eighteen final spring sightings are from May 9 to May 29, with a median of May 18. Seven fall sightings range from August 28 to September 23, with a mean of September 13.

Habitats. Migrating birds are found in dense and damp bottomland deciduous forests close to flowing water.

Comments. This elusive thrush is more often heard than seen; its song reminds one of a coin rolling down a large funnel. It is generally rusty-colored above, but not as bright on the tail as a hermit thrush, or as spotted on the breast as a wood thrush. Breeding Bird Surveys between 1966 and 2011 indicate that the species underwent a significant population decline (0.9% annually) during that period.

Gray-cheeked Thrush   *Catharus minimus*

A spring and fall migrant statewide, ranging from common in the east to uncommon or rare in the western areas. It occurs as a migrant throughout the entire Plains States region.

Migration. The range of 100 initial spring sightings is from March 20 to June 6, with a median of May 9. Half of the records fall within the period May 4-13. Forty-one final spring sightings are from May 6 to June 5, with a median of May 17. Five initial fall sightings are from September 2 to October 22, with a mean of October 1.

Habitats. While on migration through Nebraska, this species occupies the same forested habitats as does the Swainson's thrush, namely heavy shrubbery and shady deciduous woodlands, often near creeks or rivers.

Comments. This thrush arrives in Nebraska at the same time as the Swainson's thrush during spring, and occupies the same woodland habitats, but is less common. Both are secretive species that only infrequently sing while migrating.

Swainson's Thrush   *Catharus ustulatus*

A common spring and fall migrant statewide, and a very rare summer resident in the Pine Ridge, with breeding records only known for Dawes County (*Nebraska Bird Review* 42:17; 73:19). It breeds in the Black Hills and in Minnesota, and occurs elsewhere through the Plains States as a regular migrant.

Migration. The range of 141 initial spring sightings is from April 9 to May 30, with a median of May 6. Half of the records fall within the period May 1-11. Seventy-four final spring sightings are from April 20 to June 9, with a median of May 27. Fifty-one initial fall sightings are from July 29 to October 14, with a median of September 8. Half of the records fall within the period September 3-16. Fifty-one final fall sightings are from September 11 to December 1, with a median of September 28.

Habitats. While on migration this species occupies river bottom forests, shelterbelts, and parks or shade trees in towns. In the Black Hills and probably also in the Pine Ridge area it is limited to cool and dense coniferous forests having a fairly open understory allowing for easy ground foraging.

Comments. Although somewhat similar in plumage pattern to the gray-cheeked thrush, this species is more olive-toned (an older and more descriptive name was "olive-backed thrush"), and has conspicuous a buffy ring around its eye, which the gray-cheeked thrush lacks.

Hermit Thrush   *Catharus guttatus*

An uncommon spring and fall migrant in eastern Nebraska, becoming rarer to the west, and apparently quite rare in extreme western Nebraska. It has bred in the Black Hills, breeds in Minnesota, and occurs as a migrant throughout the Plains States.

Migration. Except for one January record, the range of 94 initial spring sightings is from March 9 to June 3, with a median of April 20. Half of the records fall within the period April 10 to May 2. Twenty-six final spring sightings are from April 10 to May 26, with a median of April 26. Fourteen initial fall sightings are from September 4 to December 31, with a median of October 6. Twelve final fall sightings are from September 11 to December 14 with a median of October 16.

Habitats. Migrants are found in dense to semi-open areas of woodland, shrubbery, and vine-draped tangles, but occasionally moving into more open areas. Fairly heavy deciduous woodlands are the favored habitat in eastern Nebraska.

Comments. It is unfortunate that Nebraskans never have a chance to hear the song of the hermit thrush while it is in Nebraska; the song begins with a single fluty note that is followed by a cascade of ascending and descending phrases. The rufous tail and fairly heavily spotted breast of this forest thrush provide the best field marks.

Wood Thrush   *Hylocichla mustelina*

A common to uncommon spring and fall migrant in eastern Nebraska, and a local summer resident in wooded eastern areas, extending west locally to Cherry (possibly to Sioux), Lincoln and Thomas counties. It breeds widely in the eastern parts of the region, from Minnesota south to eastern Kansas and eastern Oklahoma.

Migration. The range of 120 initial spring sightings is from April 1 to June 10, with a median of May 10. Half of the records fall within the period May 5-19. Thirty-one final fall sightings are from July 23 to October 6, with a median of September 10. Half of the records fall within the period September 5-23.

Habitats. Migrants and breeding birds are associated with mature, shady forests, especially deciduous woods, and also with wooded parks and gardens. The birds prefer breeding habitats with a dense understory, running water nearby, and tall trees for singing perches.

Comments. Wood thrushes somewhat resemble improperly plumaged robins; they are of about the same size, and they have a distinctly robin-like profile and behavior, and lay eggs that are robin-egg blue, like those of the veery and hermit thrush. Breeding Bird Surveys between 1966 and 2011 indicate that the species underwent a significant population decline (2.2% annually) during that period.

American Robin   *Turdus migratorius*

An abundant spring and fall migrant and common summer resident statewide. Overwintering is frequent in some years and localities. Breeding occurs nearly throughout the Plains States, except for the extreme southwestern areas, where it is only a migrant.

Migration. Forty-five initial spring sightings are from January 1 to May 26, with a median of February 20. Half of the records fall within the period February 2 to March 4. Fifty-four final fall sightings are from September 1 to December 31, with a median of November 19. Half of the records fall within the period October 20 to December 14. Over a third of the records are for December, indicating that the species commonly overwinters in Nebraska.

Habitats. Although this species was originally associated with open woodlands, it is probably most common in cities, suburbs, parks and gardens, and farmlands.

Comments. Everybody recognizes this familiar bird; it is tamer than any of the other thrushes, and is completely at home close to humans. Its cheery song is one of the hallmarks of spring in Nebraska, and it is one of the last birds to leave in the autumn. Breeding Bird Surveys between 1966 and 2011 indicate that the species underwent a significant population increase (0.2% annually) during that period.

Varied Thrush   *Ixoreus naevius*

A rare vagrant. Individuals have been observed in at least five counties, mostly during fall and spring months, but without any obvious geographical pattern. There were 32 state records through 2003 It has also been reported in the Dakotas, Kansas, Colorado and Oklahoma.

Migration. Four fall records for this rare vagrant are from October 1 to December 4, and three spring records are for February 18 to April 10.

Habitats. Normally associated with coniferous montane forests, but migrants move into more open woodlands on migration and during winter, sometimes wandering widely.

Comments. This is one of the most colorful of our typical thrushes; its striking pattern and musical song always comes as a surprise to persons not familiar with the species.

Family Mimidae

Gray Catbird   *Dumetella carolinensis*

A common spring and fall migrant and summer resident over most of Nebraska, but becoming rarer northwestwardly, and now apparently declining in the Pine Ridge area, where habitat is decreasing. It breeds nearly throughout the Plains States, except in the driest and nearly treeless southwestern areas.

Migration. The range of 134 initial spring sightings is from March 20 to June 5, with a median of May 11. Half of the records fall within the period May 5-17. The range of 128 final fall sightings is from July 22 to December 11, with a median of September 24. Half of the records fall within the period September 16 to October 2.

Habitats. Breeding habitats include thickets, woodland edges, shrubby marsh borders, orchards, parks and similar brushy habitats.

Comments. The dull gray plumage and cat-like "*meow*" call makes this an easy species to identify; it is a poorer mimic of other species' songs than the mockingbird or brown thrasher.

Northern Mockingbird   *Mimus polyglottos*

An uncommon spring and fall migrant and summer resident in southern and eastern parts of Nebraska, becoming rarer to the west and north, but rarely breeding as far northwest as Sioux County. It breeds widely from Kansas and eastern Colorado southward to Texas, and rarely north to South Dakota.

Migration. The range of 132 initial spring sightings is from January 1 to June 10, with a median of May 2. Half of the records fall within the period April 21 to May 13, and about six percent of the records are for January. Sixty-one final fall sightings are from July 22 to December 31, with a median of

September 11. Half of the records fall within the period August 15 to October 13, and nearly ten percent of the records are for December. The data suggests that the species overwinters occasionally.

Habitats. A variety of habitats, ranging from open woodlands, forest edges, and farmlands, to parks and cities are utilized, but treeless plains and heavy forests are avoided.

Comments. This famous mimic is one of Nebraska's less common breeding songbirds, but one that is notable for its loud songs, whose phrases are usually repeated several times, and the flashing white wing and tail markings that are apparent during flight. Breeding Bird Surveys between 1966 and 2011 indicate that the species underwent a significant population decline (0.6% annually) during that period.

Sage Thrasher   *Oreoscoptes montanus*

An uncommon spring and fall migrant, especially the latter, in the Wildcat Hills of western Nebraska, and a locally rare summer resident in Sioux County (Rosche, 1982). Vagrants have also been observed in Lincoln, Logan, and Garden counties. It breeds in western South Dakota, and is a migrant in eastern Colorado, eastern New Mexico, and adjacent areas.

Migration. Three initial spring sightings are from March 23 to April 21, with a mean of April 17. Seven final fall sightings are from August 24 to October 12, with a mean of September 16.

Habitats. During the breeding season this species is closely associated with sage-dominated grasslands and similar shrubby arid lands. On migration it has a broader distribution, occurring in open prairies and also in ponderosa pine woodlands.

Comments. Like the sage sparrow, this bird is rarely found far from sagebrush, and so is of very restricted range in Nebraska. It is smaller and darker–colored than the brown thrasher, and its song is a more continuous outpouring of notes.

Brown Thrasher   *Toxostoma rufum*

A common spring and fall migrant and summer resident virtually statewide, but becoming rarer in extreme western Nebraska south of the North Platte River. Breeding occurs nearly throughout the Plains States, excepting the nearly treeless southwestern areas.

Migration. The range of 134 initial spring sightings is from January 1 to June 2, with a median of April 26. Half of the records fall within the period April 19 to May 4. The range of 164 final fall records is from July 22 to December 31, with a median of September 28. Half of the records fall within the period September 13 to October 11. Over ten percent of the records are for December, suggesting that the species overwinters occasionally.

Habitats. During summer this species frequents open brushy woods, scattered patches of brush and small trees in open environments, shelterbelts, woodlands and shrubby residential areas.

Comments. This fox-colored, long-tailed member of the mimic thrush family resembles an elongated thrush in shape, but has a slightly curved bill. Its song consists of a series of short phrases that are each repeated once, followed by a brief pause, and the start of a new phrase. Breeding Bird Surveys between 1966 and 2011 indicate that the species underwent a significant population decline (1.1% annually) during that period.

Curve-billed Thrasher   *Toxostoma curvirostre*

Extremely rare. There is a specimen from Lincoln County obtained in 1936 from a group of several birds, and another dead bird was found in Sioux County in 1962. Another individual that tentatively was identified as this species was obtained at Halsey, Blaine County, in 1970. One was observed in Red Willow County in early 1969, and in June of 1965 in southwestern Nebraska *(Nebraska Bird Review* 38:93; 39:73). A 1996 sighting occurred in Scotts Bluff County on July 2 (Brogie, 1997). As of 2002 there have been eight reports, five of them documented (*Nebraska Bird Review* 70:158). A male that appeared at a Sioux County ranch in 2002 finally disappeared in 2008 (*Nebraska Bird Review* 76:65).

Family Sturnidae

European Starling   *Sturnus vulgaris*

An introduced and common to abundant permanent resident throughout Nebraska, with numbers supplemented during fall and winter by migrants. The species now breeds throughout the entire Plains States region.

Habitats. Found virtually everywhere throughout the year, but especially associated with human habitations such as cities, suburbs and farms, and with mature woodlands having woodpecker holes or other tree cavities for nest sites.

Comments. Starlings arrived in eastern Nebraska in 1939, and since then have become abundant nesters, displacing bluebirds and other cavity-nesting birds that once were common here. They have adapted well to city life, and their flocks in late fall are among the least welcome of our avian visitors. Breeding Bird Surveys between 1966 and 2011 indicate that the species underwent a significant population decline (1.3% annually) during that period.

Family Motacillidae

American Pipit   *Anthus rubescens*

A common spring and fall migrant statewide, and a rare winter resident. Apparently more abundant and much more conspicuous than the Sprague's pipit. It occurs widely throughout the Plains States while on migration.

Migration. The range of 125 initial spring sightings is from January 1 to May 21, with a median of April 23. Half of the records fall within the period April 13 to May 5. Eleven final spring sightings are from April 17 to May 23, with a median of April 28. Eighteen initial fall sightings are from August 24 to October 29, with a median of October 2. Sixteen final fall sightings are from September 14 to December 31, with a median of October 26. Probably overwintering is quite rare, judging from the limited number of late fall records.

Habitats. Migrating birds are found in open plains, fields, and bare shorelines, generally favoring moist to wet environments over dry ones.

Comments. Previously called the "water pipit," this species is rarely found far from water, whereas the Sprague's pipit is more adapted to upland habitats. Pipits are long-tailed and long-legged birds that nervously pump their tails up and down as they move about.

Sprague's Pipit   *Anthus spragueii*

A seemingly rare spring and fall migrant, probably occurring statewide, but with few records for the extreme western and eastern portions, and most observations for central Nebraska (especially Webster and Adams counties). Breeding occurs in North Dakota and northern South Dakota, but migrants occur throughout the Plains States.

Migration. The range of 41 initial spring sightings is from March 17 to May 21, with a median of April 20. Half of the records fall within the period April 8-27. Five final spring sightings are from April 5 to May 23, with a mean of April 21. Seventeen initial fall sightings are from September 14 to October 19, with a median of September 26. Eleven final fall sightings are from October 2 to November 8, with a median of October 23.

Habitats. Associated with dense, grassy vegetation of plains and prairies, and unlike the American pipit this species is not often found in bare areas close to water. It also differs from that species in not usually moving in flocks, and is thus more often overlooked.

Comments. This is one of Nebraska's least-seen regular migrants. Like other pipits its territorial song is uttered in flight, and in this species the song is a high-pitched bell-like whistling. Nationally the species has declined 75 percent since 1966, based on annual Breeding Bird Breeding Bird survey data. Breeding Bird Surveys between 1966 and 2011 indicate that the species had a significant population decline (3.2% annually) during that period.

Family Bombycillidae

Bohemian Waxwing   *Bombycilla garrulus*

A rare winter visitor in Nebraska, irregular in geographic and yearly occurrence. It occurs widely throughout the northern parts of the Plains States, but is very rarely encountered south of Nebraska.

Migration. The range of 11 initial fall sightings is from September 25 to December 27, with a median of November 20. Nineteen final spring sightings range from January 2 to May 22, with a median of February 28.

Habitats. Migrants are associated with fruit-bearing trees in woodlands, shelterbelts, and urban parks or gardens, often in association with cedar waxwings.

Comments. Only during unusually cold winters do Bohemian waxwings usually visit Nebraska. They are somewhat larger birds, and have rufous under tail-coverts and yellow wing-edgings, so they can be easily recognized.

Cedar Waxwing   *Bombycilla cedrorum*

A common spring and fall migrant statewide, a local breeder over much of the state, and an uncommon winter resident. It is erratic in timing of arrival and departure, and probably moves primarily in relation to available food supplies. It breeds from North Dakota and Minnesota south locally to northern Missouri, but occurs throughout the Plains States as migrant.

Migration. The range of 54 initial spring sightings is from January 2 to May 20, with a median of February 24. Half of the records fall within the period February 1 to April 23. Forty-five initial fall sightings are form July 20 to December 28, with a median of October 4. Fifty-eight final fall sightings are in December, suggesting that the species rather frequently overwinters in the state.

Habitats. Outside the breeding season this species occurs in flocks that concentrate in fruit-bearing trees, such as hackberries, mountain ash, and tall shrubs such as pyracantha, junipers, and sumac. Breeding usually occurs in semi-open deciduous woodlands, including floodplain forests, upland woodlands, and sometimes parks, farmsteads or residential areas.

Comments. Few birds are more aesthetically appealing than waxwings; their soft colors remind one of an oriental watercolor, and their gregarious nature is marked by a notable absence of aggressive interactions. The possible social functions of the seemingly decorative wax-like tips on their secondaries are apparently unstudied.

Family Ptilogonatidae

Phainopepla   *Phainopepla nitens*

Accidental. Photographed at Alliance, Box Butte County, between January 1 and February 13, 1983 *(Nebraska Bird Review*: 51 :18).

Family Calcariidae

Lapland Longspur   *Calcarius lapponicus*

A locally common migrant and winter visitor statewide, probably the commonest of the longspurs in Nebraska during winter. The species occurs as a migrant or winter visitor nearly throughout the Plains region, but is rarer southwardly.

Migration. Fifty-six initial fall sightings are from September 25 to December 31, with a median of November 12. Half of the records fall within the period October 25 to November 21. Forty-four final spring records are from January 3 to May 10, with a median of February 27. Half of the records fall within the period February 24 to March 23.

Habitats. Migrants and wintering birds occur in open, grassy plains, stubble fields, overgrazed pastures, and similar grassy or low-stature habitats.

Comments. One should look for Lapland longspurs in open fields that are at least partly snow-free, or along the sides of gravel roads that also are free of snow. There flocks of longspurs may mingle with horned larks, trying to find small seeds on which to survive.

Chestnut-collared Longspur   *Calcarius ornatus*

A migrant and winter visitor over most of Nebraska, ranging from common in the north to occasional in the eastern part of the state, and a summer resident in the northwestern corner of the state, from southern Sioux and Box Butte counties northeastwardly to Sheridan County and perhaps northern Cherry County; also western Kimball County. It also breeds in the Dakotas and western Minnesota and occurs throughout the region as a migrant or winter visitor.

Migration. Thirty initial spring sightings in northwestern Nebraska are from March 18 to June 3, with a median of April 12. Sixteen final fall sightings are from September 22 to October 22, with a median of October 8. Like the McCown's longspur, the migration pattern of this species is extremely difficult to estimate in Nebraska, since in various areas it may be a summer resident, a spring and fall migrant, or a winter visitor.

Habitats. Migrants and wintering birds occur on open plains and grassy fields, including airports. Breeding usually occurs on short-grass or cut mixed-grass prairies, and less frequently in the low meadow zones around ponds, and disturbed grasslands such as grazed pasture lands.

Comments. Although it breeds in some of the same areas as the chestnut-collared longspur, this species is predominantly white-colored on its underparts, and displaying males have a much different visual aspect when displaying overhead. Its song is an extended rattle, and quite different from the chestnut-collared double-syllable *"kettle"* note. Breeding Bird Surveys between 1966 and 2011 indicate that the species underwent a significant population decline (4.1% annually) during that period.

Smith's Longspur   *Calcarius pictus*

A rare to occasional migrant and winter visitor, mainly in east to central Nebraska, with the largest number of records from Adams and Webster counties. It has been reported east to Lancaster County and west to Sioux and Scotts Bluff counties. It is also a local migrant or winter resident in the Dakotas, Kansas, and Oklahoma, but is rare or absent from Colorado and New Mexico.

Migration. Ten fall sightings range from September 18 to December 17, with a median of November 5. Six spring records are from February 5 to May 22, with a mean of April 8.

Habitats. Migrants are associated with open grassy plains and pastures, preferring those covered by thick, short grass, including airports.

Comments. This is another wintering longspur, which is more uniformly brown than the others, at least during the season that these birds are present in Nebraska.

McCown's Longspur   *Rhynchophanes mccownii*

A migrant and winter visitor over most of Nebraska, common to uncommon in the west, becoming rarer eastwardly but occasionally seen in extreme eastern counties. A summer resident in the Panhandle, from central Sioux County west to the Wyoming line and south to western Kimball County. Has bred in South Dakota. Breeding also occurs in western North Dakota and eastern Colorado, and migrants are regular in western portions of the entire region.

Migration. Twenty-six initial spring sightings in northwestern Nebraska are from March 16 to May 21, with a median of April 3. Six final fall sightings are from September 5 to November 26, with a mean of October 1. Elsewhere in the state this species is a spring and fall migrant, and sometimes a winter visitor, so its migration status statewide is impossible to summarize easily.

Habitats. Migrants inhabit short-grass plains, pasture lands, and plowed fields. Breeding occurs in short-grass and mixed grass prairies, stubble fields, and newly sprouted grain fields.

Comments. This is one of Nebraska's two breeding longspur species. Both have distinctive white tail markings that are evident only during flight, and both have song-flight displays performed above the male's breeding territory. In this species the dark underparts are highly visible during such aerial display; the birds resemble giant blackish butterflies as they hover above the ground in full song. Breeding Bird Surveys between 1966 and 20033 indicate that the species underwent a significant population decrease (4.0% annually) during that period.

Snow Bunting   *Plectrophenax nivalis*

A rare winter visitor to Nebraska, appearing only very irregularly and probably mainly in northern counties. It is a regular winter visitor in the Dakotas, but is rare or absent south of Nebraska.

Migration. Eleven initial fall sightings are from October 19 to December 24, with a median of November 16. Thirty-one final spring sightings are from January 1 to March 23, with a median of February 10.

Habitats. Migrants and wintering birds are associated with open plains and snow-covered fields.

Comments. This mostly white sparrow is appropriately colored for the arctic, but tends to be conspicuous on bare plowed fields. It only infrequently migrates south of the winter snow-line.

Family Parulidae

Ovenbird   *Seiurus aurocapilla*

An uncommon to common spring and fall migrant statewide, and a locally common summer resident, mainly in the Missouri's forested valley, the Niobrara Valley west at least to Cherry County, and the Pine Ridge area. Breeding occurs widely in eastern and northern parts of the region, and migrants appear throughout the region.

Migration. The range of 140 initial spring sightings is from April 21 to June 2, with a median of May 13. Half of the records fall within the period May 7-18. Forty final fall records are from July 25–October 11, with a median of September 11. Half of the records fall within the period September 3-18.

Habitats. In the summer these birds are mostly limited to well-drained bottomland deciduous forests, and to mature and shaded upland forests.

Comments. The loud, *"teacher, teacher, teacher"* song of this woodland warbler is a sure sign of its presence. The song rises in volume, unlike the repeated *"Peter"* notes of the tufted titmouse.

Worm-eating Warbler   *Helmitheros vermivorum*

An extremely rare migrant or vagrant, mostly in eastern counties. Originally believed to be a summer resident in southern Nebraska, this now seems an unproved assumption. It has been most often reported in Lancaster and Douglas-Sarpy counties, but has been reported west as far as Box Butte County. The species nests in Oklahoma, is a rare migrant in Kansas and has been observed several times in South Dakota. It has also wandered west to Colorado.

Migration. The range of 17 spring sightings is from April 21 to May 25, with a median of May 8. Half of the records fall within the period May 4-13. Three fall records are from September 3 to October 8, with a mean of September 15.

Habitats. Normally this species is associated with dense river–bottom woodlands, or second-growth medium-sized woodlands on hillsides, with a shrubby undercover.

Comments. This is a ground-foraging warbler of dense undergrowth, and so is only rarely reported in the state.

Louisiana Waterthrush   *Parkesia motacilla*

A rare to uncommon spring and fall migrant in southeastern Nebraska, becoming rarer to the west and north, and reported from as far west as Lincoln and Garden counties. Confirmed breeding during the atlasing years was limited to Washington and Richardson counties (Mollhoff, 2001) and breeding has been suggested or confirmed for Fontenelle Forest, Neale Woods and Platte River State Park. Singing birds have been reported west to Dakota County. Breeding is regular in eastern Kansas and the eastern half of Oklahoma.

Migration. Seventy-six initial spring sightings range from March 30 to May 29, with a median of May 8. Half of the records fall within the period May 2-14. Ten final spring sightings are from April 29 to May 29, with a median of May 15. Ten fall sightings are from July 29 to September 24, with a median of August 29.

Habitats. This species is closely associated with forested hills and ravines near fairly swift streams, the birds foraging in moist areas.

Comments. This waterthrush may be expanding its range in eastern Nebraska; at least it is being reported during summer more frequently in recent years.

Northern Waterthrush   *Parkesia noveboracensis*

An uncommon spring and fall migrant statewide, perhaps becoming rarer westwardly, and considerably less common that the ovenbird. Breeding occurs in Minnesota and northern North Dakota, and migrants may appear anywhere in the Plains States region.

Migration. The range of 135 initial spring sightings is from April 10 to May 27, with a median of May 7. Half of the records fall within the period May 2 to 11. Twenty-six final spring sightings are from May 3 to May 21, with a median of May 14. Eight initial fall sightings are from August 10 to September 10, with a mean of August 29. Seven final fall sightings range from September 9 to October 12, with a mean of September 22.

Habitats. While in Nebraska this species is associated with deciduous forests or woodlands near streams; the birds often foraging on or near the ground.

Comments. The song of this species somewhat resembles the loud song of the ovenbird, but does not rise in pitch and volume, but rather drops toward the end. Like the ovenbird, waterthrushes feed on the ground, often in damp locations.

Golden-winged Warbler   *Vermivora chrysoptera*

An extremely rare spring and fall migrant in eastern counties, with vagrants reaching Logan and Keith counties. It is considered a rare migrant in South Dakota, but is common in North Dakota. There are a few sight records for eastern Colorado. The only known area of breeding in the Plains region is in northern Minnesota.

Migration. Eight spring sightings range from May 5 to May 25, with a mean of May 15. There are fall records for September 6 and 7.

Habitats. Migrating and breeding birds are usually found in second growth woodlands or scrubby thickets, and overgrown pastures.

Comments. Males of this well-named species have large golden wing-coverts, and also a golden crown.

Blue-winged Warbler   *Vermivora cyanoptera*

A rare spring and fall migrant in eastern Nebraska. Once erroneously believed to be a summer resident in south to central Nebraska. It has been observed several times in Custer County, and as far west as Cherry County. It is considered a casual migrant in South Dakota, and is accidental in North Dakota. The only known area of breeding in the region is in eastern Oklahoma.

Migration. Twenty-two spring sightings range from August 25 to June 1, with a median of May 12. Half of the records fall within the period May 5-14. There are four fall sightings from July 6 to September 16, with a mean of August 15.

Habitats. Migrating and breeding birds are usually found in woodland edges, abandoned fields, pastures and tickets, often in slightly wetter habitats than the golden-winged warbler.

Comments. Although none has been reported in Nebraska, hybrids between the blue-winged and golden-winged warblers are not rare, and two of the typical hybrid variants have mistakenly been named as distinct species.

Black-and-white Warbler   *Mniotilta varia*

A common spring and fall migrant statewide, and a local and uncommon summer resident in the forested valleys of the Missouri and Niobrara rivers, probably reaching Cherry County in the Niobrara Valley, and also nesting in the Pine Ridge. Breeding occurs locally from North Dakota southward to eastern Oklahoma, and migrants occur throughout the Plains States region.

Migration. Ninety-two initial spring sightings range from March 25 to June 10, with a median of May 4. Half of the records fall within the period April 25-May 9. Forty final fall sightings are from August 21 to October 6, with a median of September 12. Half of the records fall within the period September 4-20.

Habitats. On migration this species occurs in deciduous woodlands along rivers and streams, and in parks and residential areas. Nesting usually is in semi open upland stands of deciduous or coniferous forest, especially those having immature or scrubby trees and in hillside or ravine groves with thin understories. Foraging is done in a creeper–like fashion on the trunk and larger branches.

Comments. The simple but attractive black and white plumage pattern of this species proves that bright coloration is not necessary to produce beauty among the warblers. The high-pitched song of this species consists of a series of "*we-see*" notes.

Prothonotary Warbler   *Protonotaria citrea*

An uncommon or occasional spring and fall migrant in southeastern Nebraska, and a local summer resident as far north as Sarpy County (*Nebraska Bird Review* 47:57). Vagrants sometimes appear farther west in the state, rarely to Dawes County, and more rarely to eastern Colorado. Breeding also occurs in eastern Kansas and the eastern half of Oklahoma, and it may have nested in South Dakota.

Migration. Thirty-six initial spring sightings range from April 19 to May 24, with a median of May 12. Half of the records fall within the period May 5-17. Four final fall sightings range from July 26 to October 4, with a mean of September 11.

Habitats. This species is restricted during summer to moist bottomland forests and wooded swamps or periodically flooded woodlands, in the vicinity of running water or pools. During migration vagrant birds may appear in other wooded areas.

Comments. This is another species that occurs locally in the mature riparian forests of Fontenelle Forest and regularly nests there. There is also an early breeding record for Otoe County.

Swainson's Warbler   *Limnothlypis swainsonii*

Accidental. There is an early specimen record for Buffalo County of April of 1905, and the species was also reported in Lancaster County in May of 1977 (*Nebraska Bird Review* 45:46). The species breeds in Oklahoma, is a rare migrant in Kansas, and is unreported for the Dakotas.

Tennessee Warbler   *Oreothlypis peregrina*

A common spring and fall migrant in eastern Nebraska, becoming uncommon in western parts of the state. Breeding occurs in northern Minnesota, and migrants may appear throughout the entire region.

Migration. Ninety-five initial spring sightings range from April 1 to June 4, with a median of May 8. Half of the records fall within the period May 4-14. Forty-seven final spring sightings are from April 30 to June 9, with a median of May 23. Thirty-one initial fall sightings are from August 19 to October 22, with a median of September 8. Half of the records fall within the period August 28 to September 15. Twenty-seven final fall sightings range from September 9 to October 27, with a median of October 5.

Habitats. Migrants are associated with deciduous woodlands and forests, usually foraging in the upper portions of rather tall trees.

Comments. This is one of the very common warblers in Nebraska, arriving a few days later on average than the yellow-rumped, and foraging in similar locations, such as around budding trees or emerging catkins.

Orange-crowned Warbler   *Oreothlypis celata*

A common spring and fall migrant throughout Nebraska. The species is also a migrant throughout the entire Plains States region.

Migration. The range of 112 initial spring sightings is from April 8 to May 30, with a median of April 30. Half of the records fall within the period April 25 to May 5. Seventy-four final spring sightings are from April 25 to May 30, with a median of May 13. Sixty-one initial fall sightings are from August 11 to October 12, with a median of September 19. Half of the records fall within the period September 14-28. Sixty final fall sightings are from September 11 to November 6, with a median of October 15.

Habitats. Migrants are associated with deciduous forests, woodlands and brushy thickets. They also forage in stands of tall sunflowers and ragweeds and shrubs, often fairly close to the ground.

Comments, Orange-crowned warblers are notable in that they are almost devoid of field marks; like Sherlock Holmes' dog that didn't bark, they can be identified by the field marks that are lacking. The so-called orange crown is scarcely visible even when the bird is being handled, and is invisible under most field conditions.

Nashville Warbler   *Oreothlypis ruficapilla*

A common spring and fall migrant almost statewide, but perhaps becoming less common westwardly. Originally wrongly believed to nest in the Missouri Valley area (in Otoe and Webster counties) Breeding does occur in northern Minnesota, and migrants appear almost throughout the region, becoming quite rare in western areas.

Migration. Eighty-one initial spring sightings range from March 29 to June 3, with a median of May 7. Half of the records fall within the period May 1-13. Thirty-four final spring sightings are from April 30 to June 2, with a median of May 14. Forty-one initial fall sightings are from July 28 to September 27, with a median of September 10. Half of the records fall within the period September 3-15. Forty final fall records are from September 13 to October 30 (median October 8).

Habitats. Migrants are associated with second-growth woodlands having a brushy undercover. Foraging occurs in tall weeds as well as shrubs and low trees.

Comments. This is a rather dull-plumaged warbler, whose favored nesting habitat of spruce bogs is lacking in Nebraska.

Virginia's Warbler   *Oreothlypis virginiae*

Extremely rare. In addition to an early sight record from Hitchcock County, the species was observed by several persons during April of 1964 in North Platte, Lincoln County (*Nebraska Bird Review* 32:67). Also observed in Scotts Bluff County on May 22, 1995 (*Nebraska Bird Review* 64:136), and at Bushnell on April 17, 1998 (*Nebraska Bird Review* 66:48). It is an uncommon migrant in western Kansas and extreme northwestern Oklahoma. It breeds in Wyoming and locally in the southwestern Black Hills of South Dakota, so it should be a regular if rare migrant in western Nebraska. There have been at least eight state records.

Connecticut Warbler   *Oporornis agilis*

A rare to occasional spring and fall migrant in eastern Nebraska, rarely occurring as far west as Cherry, Lincoln, and McPherson counties. Stragglers have been reported in Colorado. In contrast to the situation in South Dakota, there are more fall than spring records, and the species' exact status in Nebraska is quite unclear.

Migration. Twenty spring records range from April 25 to June 6, with a median of May 18. Half of the records fall within the period May 10-19. Ten initial fall sightings are from September 1 to October 11, with a median of September 30. This is one of the few warblers that seems to be more common in fall than during spring.

Habitats. Generally associated with low woodlands having brushy tangles, the birds foraging on or near the ground.

Comments. One of several gray-headed and yellow-bellied warblers in Nebraska, this species has a conspicuous white eye-ring in both sexes.

MacGillivray's Warbler   *Geothlypis tolmiei*

A rare spring and fall migrant in western Nebraska, with most records from the Panhandle, but at least five each for McPherson and Adams counties, and reported as far east as Platte and Lancaster counties. Breeding occurs in the Black Hills, so migration through the Panhandle should be regular. The species is known to migrate through eastern Colorado.

Migration. Twenty-eight spring sightings range from May 5 to June 2, with a median of May 15. Half of the records fall within the period May 10-17. Thirteen fall records range from August 21 to October 10, with a median of September 6. Half of the records fall within the period August 29 to September 16.

Habitats. This species is usually associated with dense undergrowth near streams, but migrants also are found on hillside brush and in dense stands of weeds such as thistle and sunflowers.

Comments. In contrast to the two preceding gray-headed and yellow-bellied warblers, the MacGillivray's warbler has an incomplete eye-ring that is developed only above and below each eye.

Mourning Warbler   *Geothlypis philadelphia*

An uncommon spring and fall migrant in eastern Nebraska, becoming rarer westwardly, but reported west to Lincoln, Sheridan and Scotts Bluff counties. Reportedly formerly bred in southeastern Nebraska (Bruner, Wolcott and Swenk, 1904), but there is no current evidence of breeding in the state. Breeding does occur in Minnesota and North Dakota, and migrants appear widely throughout the region.

Migration. Eighty-seven initial spring sightings range from March 20 to May 30, with a median of May 19. Half of the records fall within the period May 15-23. Nineteen final spring sightings are from May 18 to June 10, with a median of May 28. Eighteen initial fall sightings are from September 1 to October 20, with a median of September 8. Eighteen final fall sightings are from September 26 to October 24, with a median of October 7.

Habitats. Breeding birds are usually found in dense undergrowth along streams, but during migration the birds often inhabit various thickets and tall weedy areas, usually foraging rather close to the ground.

Comments. The mourning warbler closely resembles the Connecticut warbler, but lacks white around the eyes. It tends to hop while foraging on the ground, whereas Connecticut warblers instead walk.

Kentucky Warbler   *Geothlypis formosa*

A rare to uncommon spring and fall migrant in southeastern Nebraska, and a summer resident in the lower part of the Missouri's forested valley, west to at least Sarpy County. It has nested at Platte River State Park, and as of 2012 there were six state nesting records (*Nebraska Bird Review* 80:66). It is considered a casual visitor in South Dakota, and is unreported in North Dakota. It breeds in eastern Kansas and the eastern half of Oklahoma.

Migration. Forty-six initial spring sightings range from April 30 to June 2, with a median of May 10. Half of the records fall within the period May 5-14. Twelve fall records range from July 21 to October 7, with a median of August 29.

Habitats. During the breeding season this species is found in shrubby moist ravines and bottomlands.

Comments. This very attractive warbler is very dark above and bright yellow below, with yellow eyebrows and a dark ear-patch. It has a surprisingly loud, wren-like song. Breeding Bird Surveys between 1966 and 2003 indicate that the species underwent a significant population decline (0.8% annually) during that period.

Common Yellowthroat   *Geothlypis trichas*

A common to abundant spring and fall migrant and summer resident statewide. It also breeds or migrates throughout the Plains States region.

Migration. The range of 107 initial spring sightings is from April 5 to June 10, with a median of May 7. Half of the records fall within the period May 2-13. The range of 114 final fall sightings is from July 20 to October 29, with a median of September 13. Half of the records fall within the period August 30 to October 3.

Habitats. While in Nebraska this species is found near moist or aquatic sites, especially the tall grasses, emergent vegetation, and shrubs or trees along shorelines. Occasionally it also extends to upland shrub thickets, retired croplands, weedy residential areas, and overgrown orchards.

Comments. This is another favorite for students taking ornithology field quizzes; its repeated "*whichity*" notes emanate from weedy or shrubby thickets and reveal the species' identity long before the bird itself is generally seen. Breeding Bird Surveys between 1966 and 2011 indicate that the species had a significant population decline (0.9% annually) in that period.

Hooded Warbler   *Setophaga citrina*

A rare spring and fall migrant in eastern Nebraska, reported west to Cherry and Dawes counties. The largest number of sightings are from the Douglas-Sarpy counties, but it has also been observed more than once in several other eastern counties, especially Lancaster and Adams. About 50 state records had accumulated through 2003. Vagrants have reached eastern Colorado. Regular breeding is limited to eastern Oklahoma and southeastern Kansas.

Migration. Twenty-four spring sightings range from April 21 to May 27, with a median of May 11. Half of the records fall within the period May 7-15. Five fall records are from August 7 to September 12, with a mean of August 20.

Habitats. Although breeding birds are associated with moist, mature forests having considerable undergrowth, or wooded swamps, migrants are sometimes found in planted woodlands, city parks, and sometimes residential areas.

Comments. This is a stunning warbler, the males having a black "executioner's" hood over their head and neck, except for a golden opening that extends back across the forehead and past the eyes to the ears. It is usually seen at ground level in wet locations.

American Redstart   *Setophaga ruticilla*

A common spring and fall migrant throughout Nebraska, and a common summer resident in eastern counties, with breeding throughout the Missouri's forested valley, the Pine Ridge, probably the entire Niobrara Valley, perhaps locally in the Sandhills (Bessey Division of Nebraska National Forest), and sporadically in the Platte Valley west to Adams or perhaps Phelps counties. Breeding is widespread in the eastern portions of the region, west to the Black Hills and Montana border.

Migration. The range of 131 initial spring sightings is from April 10 to June 3, with a median of May 12. Half of the reports fall within the period May 7-16. Ninety final fall sightings range from August 11 to October 19, with a median of September 10. Half of the records fall within the period September 3-17.

Habitats. Breeding usually occurs in moist bottomland woods, usually deciduous and especially young or second-growth stands, and near the margins of openings in mature forests.

Comments. Probably the breeding range of this species in Nebraska is slowly expanding, as riparian forests along the Platte and other rivers gradually mature. Redstarts resembles little flaming candles as they flit about high in tree canopies; their variable song is louder than those of most other brilliantly colored species.

Cape May Warbler   *Setophaga tigrina*

An uncommon to occasional spring and fall migrant in eastern Nebraska, rarely observed west to Buffalo, Webster and Hall Counties. Breeding occurs in northern Minnesota, and migrants are most common east of the Missouri River.

Migration. Fourteen spring records range from April 29 to May 24, with a median of May 12. Five fall records range from September 28 to October 4, with a mean of September 30.

Habitats. Migrating birds occupy a variety of habitats, ranging from coniferous or deciduous forests to parks and suburban gardens.

Comments. Another beautiful warbler that visits Nebraska in mid-May, the male Cape May has a chestnut ear-patch and both sexes have heavily striped underparts.

Cerulean Warbler   *Setophaga cerulea*

An uncommon spring and fall migrant in eastern Nebraska, and a rare, local summer resident along the Missouri River in southeastern Nebraska. It has regularly nested at Fontenelle Forest, Sarpy County (*Nebraska Bird Review* 46:86) and has also nested in Dakota County. Recent evidence indicates a very small breeding population (*Nebraska Bird Review* 73:124-130). Breeding also occurs in Kansas and Oklahoma.

Migration. Thirty-eight initial spring sightings range from April 26 to June 10, with a median of May 14. Half of the records fall within the period May 5-18. Eight fall sightings range from July 21 to September 3, with a mean of August 15.

Habitats. During the summer this species occurs in moist deciduous bottomland forests, as well as mature upland woods. Rather open forests, with large trees and rather sparse undergrowth, seem to be preferred breeding habitats.

Comments. Males of the well-named cerulean warbler have a deep blue back color much like that of the black-throated blue warbler, but the cerulean has a white throat. It is a species of high conservation concern in Nebraska.

Northern Parula   *Setophaga americana*

An uncommon spring and fall migrant in eastern Nebraska, and a possible uncommon summer resident in the immediate Missouri Valley area near Omaha. Considered a local summer resident in Sarpy County; this species has consistently been observed during summer months in Fontenelle Forest, and an adult was once seen carrying food. Rosche (1994) also reported a possible but distinctly extralimital breeding in the Pine Ridge region, and migrants occur west to Garden and Sheridan counties. Breeds in northern Minnesota and eastern Kansas and Oklahoma.

Migration. Thirty-four spring sightings are from April 2 to May 27, with a median of May 5. Half of the records fall within the period April 20 to May 14. Nine fall records are from August 24 to October 2, with a mean of September 12.

Habitats. During summer this species is restricted to swampy woods, especially those rich in Spanish moss or *Usnea* lichens. On migration they also occur in parks, orchards, and along roadsides.

Comments. Although typical breeding habitat is lacking in Nebraska, this warbler is easily identified and its regular summer occurrence at Fontenelle Forest deserves further study to better understand its breeding status there.

Magnolia Warbler   *Setophaga magnolia*

An uncommon spring and fall migrant in eastern Nebraska, becoming rarer westwardly. Breeding occurs in northern Minnesota, and migrants appear nearly throughout the Plains States region, becoming quite rare in western areas.

Migration. The range of 121 initial spring sightings is from April 20 to June 4, with a median of May 15. Half of the records fall within the period May 10-19. Fifteen final spring sightings are from May 14 to June 4, with a median of May 19. Thirteen initial fall sightings range from August 25 to October 5, with a median of September 9. Twelve final fall sightings are from September 9 to October 24, with a median of October 1.

Habitats. Migrant birds are associated with a wide array of deciduous and coniferous habitats, but they are often in rather thick woods, foraging 20-30 feet above ground.

Comments. This is only one of the many attractive spring migrants that are seen all too rarely, usually during the middle part of May. The birds resemble yellow-rumped warblers, but have gray crowns and yellow underparts.

Bay-breasted Warbler   *Setophaga castanea*

An uncommon spring and fall migrant in eastern Nebraska, becoming rarer westwardly, but observed as far west as Scotts Bluff County. It has also wandered several times to Colorado. Breeding occurs in northern Minnesota, and migrants occur through the eastern half of the region.

Migration. Forty-one initial spring sightings range from April 29 to May 27, with a median of May 17. Half of the records fall within the period May 11-19. Eleven final spring sightings are from May 12 to May 28, with a median of May 19. Seven initial fall sightings are from September 4 to September 20, with a mean of September 14. Seven final fall sightings are from September 17 to October 14, with a mean of September 22.

Habitats. During migration this species occurs in diverse coniferous and deciduous forest types, favoring conifers, but is also found around residential plantings and shrubbery, usually foraging well above the ground.

Comments. The chestnut or bay-colored breast and flank markings of males in this species are its best field marks, and both sexes also have yellowish patches behind the darker ears.

Blackburnian Warbler   *Setophaga fusca*

An uncommon spring and fall migrant in eastern Nebraska, becoming rare to the west. It has been reported as far west as Dawes and Scotts Bluff counties. Breeding occurs in northern Minnesota, and migrants are regular in the eastern half of the region.

Migration. Seventy-six initial spring sightings range from April 5 to June 4, with a median of May 14. Half of the records fall within the period May 10-20. Sixteen final spring sightings are from May 8 to June 8, with a median of May 17. Ten initial fall sightings range from August 20 to September 30, with a median of September 3. Ten final fall sightings are from September 1 to October 9, with a median of October 3.

Habitats. Migrating birds are usually found in tall trees, foraging near their tops, and in either hardwood or coniferous forests.

Comments. Probably most people remember vividly the first Blackburnian warbler of their life; the male's intense golden-orange throat and its black-and-gold facial markings makes it a sight to remember with fondness.

Yellow Warbler   *Setophaga petechia*

A common spring and fall migrant and summer resident statewide. The species occurs throughout the entire Plains States region as a breeder or migrant. In westerly areas it is limited to rivers or moist wooded areas.

Migration. The range of 126 initial spring sightings is from March 20 to May 30, with a median of May 7. Half of the records fall within the period May 1-11. The range of 120 final fall sightings is from July 23 to November 6, with a median of September 3. Half of the records fall within the period August 21 to September 16.

Habitats. During the breeding season these birds prefer rather wet habitats, such as brushy edges of swamps, marshes or creeks, but they also nest commonly in roadside thickets, hedgerows, orchards, and forest edges, avoiding both heavy forests and grassy environments lacking both trees and shrubs.

Comments. Perhaps the commonest of our nesting arboreal warblers, the yellow warbler's song, "*Sweet, sweet sweet, I am sweet*" permeates our summer woodlands, and its flash of golden color confirms its identification. It is often parasitized by brown-headed cowbirds and, unable to expel the cowbird's large eggs, simply adds a new nest lining over its old clutch and starts over. Breeding Bird Surveys between 1966 and 2011 indicate that the species underwent a significant population decline (0.5% annually) during that period.

Chestnut-sided Warbler   *Setophaga pensylvanica*

An uncommon spring and fall migrant in eastern Nebraska, becoming rarer westwardly, but observed as far west as Dawes and Scotts Bluff County. It has bred at least twice in the state, including a 1975 nesting in Scotts Bluff county and a 1894 record for the vicinity of Omaha (*Nebraska Bird Review* 44:10). It breeds in North Dakota and Minnesota, and is a migrant through the Plains States region except for the westernmost areas.

Migration. Sixty-one initial spring sightings are from April 25 to June 4, with a median of May 15. Half of the records fall within the period May 12-19. Nineteen final spring sightings are from May 6 to June 4, with a median of May 23. Six initial fall sightings are from August 17 to September 19, with a mean of September 2. Seven final fall sightings are from September 1 to October 16, with a mean of September 26.

Habitats. Migrants are usually found in thickets along woodland edges, and when breeding the species occurs in low shrubbery, briar thickets, forest clearings or edges, overgrown pastures, and similar low-stature habitat.

Comments. This species is rather puzzling, since it should nest in the state, but there are only two records, and they are situated at opposite ends of Nebraska. There are no nesting records for South Dakota, so perhaps these two records are simply flukes.

Blackpoll Warbler   *Setophaga striata*

A common spring and fall migrant in eastern Nebraska, becoming uncommon to rare in western parts of the state. Migrants occur through most of the Plains States region, mostly in the eastern half. Breeding does not occur south of Canada.

Migration. The range of 120 initial spring sightings is from April 9 to June 2, with a median of May 12. Half of the records fall within the period May 8-18. Forty-seven final spring sightings are from May 1 to May 30, with a median of May 20. Seven initial fall sightings are from August 28 to September 22, with a mean of September 9. Seven final fall sightings are from September 1 to October 21, with a mean of September 26.

Habitats. During migration this species is usually found in tall deciduous trees such as cottonwoods, and generally occurs in streamside forests.

Comments. Blackpoll warblers are one of the two warbler species that are essentially all black and white in plumage; the rather similar black-and-white warbler has darker cheeks and a white stripe above the eyes.

Black-throated Blue Warbler   *Setophaga caerulescens*

A rare spring and fall migrant in eastern Nebraska, observed in at least 11 counties west as far as Garden and Scotts Bluff counties, as well as in Colorado. It has been seen three or more times in Douglas-Sarpy, Lancaster, Adams, and McPherson counties. Breeding occurs in northern Minnesota, and migrants are most common in the eastern half of the region.

Migration. Nine spring records range from April 23 to May 24, with a mean of May 10. Twenty-seven fall records range from August 5 to October 20, with a median of September 23. Half of the records fall within the period September 19 to October 5. The species is apparently more common in fall than during spring.

Habitats. While on migration this species tends to occur in low shrubby areas, such as woodlands, parks, and residential gardens.

Comments. Males of this stunning warbler are dark indigo blue above and contrastingly white below, except for a black throat and upper chest. Like many of the most attractive warblers, it is present in the state for only a few weeks.

Palm Warbler   *Setophaga palmarum*

An uncommon spring and fall migrant in eastern Nebraska, becoming rare westwardly. It has been reported from as far west as Dawes County. Breeding occurs in northern Minnesota, and migrants are mostly found east of the Missouri River.

Migration. Sixty-three initial spring sightings range from April 16 to June 2, with a median of May 5. Half of the records fall within the period May 1-9. Ten final spring sightings are from April 19 to May 24, with a median of May 9. Ten fall records range from September 2 to November 10, with a median of October 5. Half of the records fall within the period October 1-6.

Habitats. Generally associated with brushy fields, open wooded areas, or wooded edges or clearings in woods, where the birds can forage on the ground.

Comments. Palm warblers probably never are found in palm trees except on their subtropical or tropical wintering grounds; They are prone to wagging their tails are they forage, often at ground level.

Pine Warbler   *Setophaga pinus*

An extremely rare migrant or vagrant in eastern Nebraska. Most of the Nebraska records are for Lancaster County. Except for Oklahoma, where it breeds, it is rare to accidental throughout the Plains States. By 2011 there were 21 state records, only seven documented (*Nebraska Bird Review* 79:64). There are at least four Panhandle records (*Nebraska Bird Review* 76: 150).

Migration. Ten spring sightings range from April 17 to May 27, with a median of May 13. Four fall records are from September 7 to September 22, with a mean of September 13.

Habitats. Migrants are associated with a wide variety of forests, especially pine forests, but also utilize deciduous forests and orchards.

Yellow-rumped Warbler   *Setophaga coronata*

A common to abundant spring and fall migrant statewide, and a local summer resident in the Pine Ridge area, including at least Sioux and Dawes counties. Breeding also occurs in Black Hills and northern Minnesota, and migrants occur throughout entire Plains States region.

Migration. The range of 75 initial spring sightings is from February 14 to May 24, with a median of April 23. Half of the records fall within the period April 12-29. Fifty-three final spring sightings are from April 27 to May 29, with a median of May 14. Eighty initial fall sightings are from August 10 to November 1, with a median of September 28. Half of the records fall within the period September 20 to October 3. Seventy-seven final fall sightings are from September 10 to December 18, with a median of October 22.

Habitats. The species is widespread in wooded habitats during migration, arriving well before the leaves appear, and often wintering as far north as southern Oklahoma where it forages on juniper berries. Breeding birds occupy coniferous forests, usually nesting in scattered trees, open plantings or streamside thickets rather than dense, mature forests.

Comments. This species is usually the first warbler to return to Nebraska in spring, usually arriving just as the first hardwood trees are leafing out and during the fall sometimes persisting until late December. In the eastern part of the state most birds are of the white-throated (Myrtle) type, whereas in the Panhandle the majority are of the yellow-throated (Audubon's) race.

Yellow-throated Warbler   *Setophaga dominica*

A rare to occasional migrant in eastern Nebraska, becoming very rare westwardly. A very local breeding population is present in Fontenelle Forest (*Nebraska Bird Review* 62:113). It has been observed west to Scotts Bluff and Sheridan counties, and has been seen several times in Lincoln, Adams, and Thayer counties. It normally breeds from extreme southeastern Kansas southward through Oklahoma. It is accidental in eastern South Dakota and eastern Colorado.

Migration. Twenty-one spring sightings range from April 11 to May 28, with a median of May 8. Half of the records fall within the period May 3-15. Five fall records range from July 14 to October 1, with a mean of September 9.

Habitats. This species is normally associated with rather swampy forests, especially those rich in Spanish mosses. Farther north it occurs in streamside sycamore forests, usually foraging high in the trees.

Comments. Like the northern parula and prothonotary warblers, nesting of this species evidently occurs in an isolated population at Fontenelle Forest. Actual proof of nesting remains to be obtained, however.

Prairie Warbler   *Setophaga discolor*

An extremely rare vagrant in eastern Nebraska. There are two questionable early records of breeding in Richardson and Dakota counties. The species has been reported from as far west as McPherson County, and has also been sighted in Buffalo and Adams counties in south to central Nebraska. There were 13 state records as of 1996 (*Nebraska Bird Review* 64:61), and two during 1996 (Brogie, 1997). It is accidental in South Dakota and unreported for North Dakota, but is a summer resident in eastern Kansas and Oklahoma.

Migration. Eight spring records are from April 21 to June 1, with a mean of May 10. The only fall record is for September 23.

Habitats. The species is generally associated with old pastures, hillsides with scattered woody vegetation, and similar shrubby or woodland habitats, but not true prairie.

Grace's Warbler   *Setophaga graciae*

Accidental. A male was photographed at Crescent Lake National Wildlife Refuge, May 16, 2008 (*Nebraska Bird Review* 77:85).

Black-throated Gray Warbler   *Setophaga nigrescens*

An extremely rare vagrant. It has been observed during May and August in Lancaster, Adams, Scotts Bluff, Cherry, Garden, and McPherson counties. Seen May 1, 1999, at Oliver Reservoir (*Nebraska Bird Review* 67:62), and again September 7, 2001 (*Nebraska Bird Review* 70 69:183). One was seen

August 25, 2002 at Arbor Day farm, and one hit a University of Nebraska–Lincoln window September 1, 2002 (*Nebraska Bird Review* 70:160)

Habitats. Normally associated with dry slopes, thickets and oak or pine woodlands

Townsend's Warbler   *Setophaga townsendi*

An extremely rare vagrant, with at least nine spring and six fall records. It was initially collected in 1911 in Dawes County, but during the 1970s was observed in numerous locations, including at least seven counties. It is a fairly regular migrant in Colorado. It has also been reported in South Dakota, Kansas and Oklahoma, but is accidental in Iowa.

Migration. Six spring records date from April 25 to May 17, with a mean of May 7. Six fall sightings are from August 30 to September 17, with a mean of September 9.

Habitats. Often associated with low oak, juniper or pine woodlands on migration, but found in tall coniferous forests during the breeding season.

(Hermit Warbler)   *Setophaga occidentalis*

Accidental. Photographed at Crescent Lake, National Wildlife Refuge. May 11, 2010 (*Nebraska Bird Review* 78: 9; 56 to 57). Also reported near Creighton, May 15, 2002 (*Nebraska Bird Review* 70:72). There was a sight record for McPherson County in September of 1973 (*Nebraska Bird Review* 42:42).

Black-throated Green Warbler   *Setophaga virens*

An uncommon spring and fall migrant in eastern Nebraska, rarely reported as far west as Lincoln and McPherson counties, but has straggled to Colorado. It breeds in northern Minnesota, and migrants occur in the eastern half of the region.

Migration. Fifty-four initial spring sightings range from April 18 to June 4, with a median of May 9. Half of the records fall within the period May 3-15. Six final spring sightings are from May 9 to May 24, with a mean of May 16. Sixteen initial fall sightings are from August 30 to October 2, with a median of September 18. Sixteen final fall sightings are from September 12 to October 21, with a median of October 5.

Habitats. Associated with a wide variety of deciduous or coniferous woodlands on migration, but most often seen in second growth forest, especially in willows and elms.

Comments. This warbler is not particularly "green," but is instead olive-green above, with a mostly golden face and a black throat and upper breast.

Canada Warbler   *Cardillina canadensis*

An occasional spring and fall migrant in the eastern third of Nebraska, rarely reported from as far west as McPherson County. Breeding occurs in Minnesota, and migrants are regular in the eastern half of the Plains States region.

Migration. Twenty-eight spring sightings range from April 28 to June 6, with a median of May 20. Half of the records fall within the period May 17-25. Fourteen initial fall sightings range from August 10 to October 2, with a median of September 1. Thirteen final fall sightings are from September 3 to October 8, with a median of September 16.

Habitats. Migrants are usually found in brushy areas near streams, but sometimes also range well up into trees at considerable distance from water.

Comments. The attractive black-beaded "necklace" that drapes down over the yellow breast of males provides for instant identification of this species, and even in females a shadowy brown necklace is visible.

Wilson's Warbler   *Cardillina pusilla*

A common spring and fall migrant in eastern Nebraska, becoming uncommon in the western half of the state. Elsewhere, the species is a regular migrant throughout the Plains States.

Migration. The range of 101 initial spring sightings is from April 14 to June 4, with a median of May 12. Half of the records fall within the period May 5-16. Thirty-six final spring sightings range from April 28 to May 30, with a median of May 19. Sixty-nine initial fall sightings range from August 9 to

September 26, with a median of September 1. Half of the records fall within the period August 26-September 7. Sixty-nine final fall records are from September 2 to October 22, with a median of September 26.

Habitats. Migrants are associated with rank stands of weeds and low, shrubby vegetation, often near streams.

Comments. The little black skullcap that sits atop the crown of males is the most distinctive field mark of this species. Like the hooded warbler, it too likes moist to boggy habitats.

Yellow-breasted Chat	*Icteria virens*

Previously a common spring and fall migrant and summer resident statewide in suitable habitats, but in recent years the population of the eastern race in eastern Nebraska (Missouri Valley and eastern Platte Valley) has crashed. It is uncommon in the western parts of the state. Breeding is widespread throughout the Plains States, especially southwardly.

Migration. The range of 120 initial spring sightings is from April 23 to June 7, with a median of May 15. Half of the records fall within the period May 10-21. The range of 63 final fall sightings is from July 21 to October 16, with a median of September 9. Half of the records fall within the period August 21 to September 23.

Habitats. Breeding birds usually favor ravine or streamside thickets, especially those with small trees and tall shrubs, as well as forest edges, dense stands of tree saplings, and clumps of shrubs in overgrazed pastures.

Comments. This is easily the largest and also one of the loudest of all warbler species, and very probably should be removed from the warbler family, although a better location is still uncertain. Breeding Bird Surveys between 1966 and 2011 indicate that the species underwent a significant population decline (0.5% annually) during that period.

Family Emberizidae

Green-tailed Towhee	*Pipilo chlorurus*

An uncommon but regular spring and fall migrant in western Nebraska, mostly in the Panhandle, but rarely recorded east to McPherson, Logan and Lancaster counties. Breeding is limited in the Great Plains region to sage-dominated areas of New Mexico, Colorado and Wyoming, but migrants are regular from eastern Colorado to the Texas Panhandle.

Migration. Nineteen initial spring sightings range from February 18 to May 31, with a median of May 10. Half of the records fall within the period May 3-20. Three final fall sightings are from September 6 to September 29.

Habitats. Migrants are associated with thickets and dense shrubbery in rather arid environments, including sagebrush-covered plains.

Comments. This is a rather dull-colored bird except for its bright brown crown, being mostly olive-green on the tail and upperparts, and grayish below.

Spotted Towhee	*Pipilo maculatus*

Collectively, the eastern & spotted towhees common spring and fall migrants and summer residents in Nebraska. Local breeding by towhees occurs west to Colorado in the Platte and Republican valleys, and to Sioux County in the White River and Niobrara valleys. Breeding is very local in the Sandhills , but extends from the Colorado, Wyoming borders (mainly *maculatus* phenotypes) east in the Platte Valley, where the population is comprised of mainly *erythropthalmus* phenotypes in northeastern and southeastern Nebraska. Many of the summering birds along the Platte and North Platte rivers are apparent hybrids (*Auk* 76:326-338; Brown *et al* 1996). Breeding by relatively typical *erythropthalmus* phenotypes occurs from Manitoba and northeastern North Dakota (Turtle Mountains) south to eastern Kansas and northeastern Oklahoma, Predominantly *maculatus* phenotypes breed from the Missouri Valley of the western and central Dakotas south tithe Nebraska Panhandle and central Niobrara Valley, northeastern Colorado and south into New Mexico. Migrants occur throughout the region.

Migration. Sixty-nine initial spring sightings range from February 7 to May 30, with a median of April 22. Half of the records fall within the period April 10-30. Ninety-three final fall records are from July 24 to December 31, with a median of October 15. Half of the records fall within the period September 30 to October 31. Nearly 20 percent of the records are for December, suggesting that overwintering is fairly frequent.

Habitats. While in Nebraska these towhees occur in brushy fields, thickets, woodland edges or openings, second-growth forests, and city parks or suburbs with trees and tall shrubbery.

Comments. It seems likely that the nomenclature committee of the American Ornithologists' Union will eventually have to reverse itself, and again merge these two "species" of towhees. The zone of hybridization is especially wide in Nebraska; farther south in Kansas there is a geographic break between breeding habitats that make the situation there less confusing.

Eastern Towhee   *Pipilo erythropthalmus*

See previous account. "Pure" eastern towhees breed west to Dawson County, but most birds there are spotted or hybrids (*Nebraska Bird Review 73:*26-18). Unlike the spotted towhee, the eastern towhee rarely winters in Nebraska, except in the extreme southeast. Breeding Bird Surveys between 1966 and 2011 indicate that the eastern towhee underwent a significant population decline (1.3% annually) during that period.

(Canyon Towhee)   *Melazone fusca*

Hypothetical. One individual was reported in Scotts Bluff County in September of 1975 (*Nebraska Bird Review* 44: 30). The record was considered unacceptable by the NOU Records Committee (1997). It is a permanent resident in northwestern Oklahoma, and is accidental (three records) in Kansas.

Cassin's Sparrow   *Aimophila cassinii*

An extremely rare and irregular spring and fall migrant and summer resident in southwestern Nebraska. The species has been reported from a number of counties, but actual breeding records exist only for Perkins and Dundy counties *(Nebraska Bird Review* 42:56; 47:14). Singing males have been seen in Keith and Garden counties (Brown *et al.* 1996) , and probable breeding has occurred near Kilpatrick Lake, Box Butte County (*Birding* 26:416). The species is apparently irruptive, moving north to breed periodically, but normally is restricted to the southern and western portions of the Plains region (*American Birds* 31:133). In 2011 there was a major influx into Nebraska during a drought in the Southwest (*Nebraska Bird Review* 78:960.

American Tree Sparrow   *Spizella arborea*

A common migrant and winter visitor statewide. It is widespread throughout the entire Plains Region during winter and on migration.

Migration. The range of 127 initial fall sightings is from September 3 to December 31, with a median of October 21. Half of the records fall within the period October 12 to November 2. Sixty-five final spring sightings range from January 24 to May 27, with a median of April 6. Half of the records fall within the period March 27 to April 22.

Habitats. During migration and winter periods this species is found in flocks among thickets, brushy areas, shrubby or weedy grasslands.

Comments. Tree sparrows are attractive winter residents in Nebraska; these tiny birds seem to thrive under bitterly cold conditions so long as sufficient food is available and the snow cover is not too great.

Chipping Sparrow   *Spizella passerina*

A common spring and fall migrant statewide, and a common summer resident in all parts of Nebraska except possibly for the Republican River Valley. It breeds widely in the Plains, from North Dakota south to Colorado and eastern Oklahoma, and winters throughout the remainder of the region.

Migration. The range of 100 initial spring sightings is from January 14 to June 3, with a median of April 23. Half of the records fall within the period April 6 to May 2. Ninety-nine final fall records range from July 23 to December 20, with a median of October 2. Half of the records fall within the period September 17 to October 16.

Habitats. While in Nebraska this species is associated with the margins of deciduous forests, parks, gardens, residential areas, farmsteads, orchards and other open areas with nearby or scattered trees and few or no shrubs.

Comments. The sewing-machine-like trill of these birds is a certain sign of spring in Nebraska; they appear with the first warblers and the leafing-out of the trees. Courtship or rival chases among competing males are common then, and the birds lend an air of excitement and optimism to the days of early spring. Breeding Bird Surveys between 1966 and 2011 indicate that the species underwent a significant population decline (0.5% annually) during that period.

Clay-colored Sparrow   *Spizella pallida*

A common spring and fall migrant, and an apparently accidental summer resident in Nebraska, with a record from Hall County in 1973 as the only definite breeding report (*Nebraska Bird Review* 42:9). Probably the species nests locally in northern counties, since it regularly breeds in South Dakota. It also breeds in North Dakota and Minnesota, and appears throughout the rest of the region on migrations.

Migration. The range of 124 initial spring sightings is from March 3 to May 29, with a median of May 3. Half of the records fall within the period April 28 to May 8. Eighty-nine final spring sightings range from April 24 to June 1, with a median of May 16. Forty-one initial fall sightings are from July 23 to November 2, with a median of September 9. Half of the records fall within the period August 30 to September 18. Thirty-nine final fall sightings are from August 27 to December 18, with a median of October 8.

Habitats. Migrants occur in thickets and weed patches among grassland. Breeding birds move to similar habitats, which provide a mixture of medium-stature grasses and scattered shrubs or low trees, or disturbed lands such as cutover or burned woodlands.

Comments. Although rather plain-colored, the species strongly striped head and distinctive gray half-collar allows one to identify this species with ease. Its slow, buzzy songs is rather insect-like, and much lower–pitched than is the chipping sparrow's. Breeding Bird Surveys between 1966 and 2011 indicate that the species underwent a significant population decrease (1.3% annually) during that period.

Brewer's Sparrow   *Spizella breweri*

A common spring and fall migrant in western Nebraska, and a local summer resident in the western Panhandle (from Sioux County south to Kimball County; probably also southwestern Sheridan County). An extralimital breeding record also exists for Howard County (*Nebraska Bird Review* 41:8). Breeding in the Great Plains region is mostly limited to the western parts of the Dakotas as well as the Texas Panhandle and adjacent areas, north locally to extreme southwestern Kansas.

Migration. Twenty-seven initial spring sightings range from April 18 to May 21, with a median of May 5. Half of the records fall within the period April 29 to May 12. Fifteen final fall records range from August 18 to October 12, with a median of September 7.

Habitats. Associated in Nebraska with open scrublands, especially short-grass plains with sagebrush, rabbitbrush, or other semiarid shrubs.

Comments. This is a modestly plumaged sparrow that seems to fit in well with its usual sagebrush habitat. Another ecologically separated form nests at timberline in the western mountains; this "timberline sparrow" may deserve to be considered as a separate species.

Field Sparrow   *Spizella pusilla*

A common spring and fall migrant and a locally common summer visitor almost statewide, excepting the Panhandle. Local nesting occurs at least as far west as the eastern end of Lake McConaughy, Keith County. Breeding occurs widely in the Plains States, excepting the drier southwestern areas and northern parts of Minnesota and North Dakota.

Migration. Eighty-one initial spring sightings range from February 11 to June 6, with a median of April 20. Half of the records fall within the period April 4 to May 6. Eighty-three final fall sightings are from August 1 to December 26, with a median of October 6. Half of the records fall within the period September 23 to October 25.

Habitats. During the breeding season this species occurs in brushy, open woodlands, forest edges, brushy ravines or draws, sagebrush flats, abandoned hayfields, forest clearings, and similar open habitats having scattered shrubs or low trees. It is similar to the chipping sparrow in its habitat, but depends more on shrubs and less on trees for nesting.

Comments. Field sparrows are among the dullest-colored of all grassland sparrows, but their song, a series of whistled notes that increase in pitch and frequency through the series, is unique and may remind one of a ping-pong ball bouncing to a stop. Breeding Bird Surveys between 1966 and 2011 indicate that the species underwent a significant population decline (2.4% annually) during that period.

Vesper Sparrow   *Pooecetes gramineus*

A common spring and fall migrant statewide, and a probable regular but local summer resident over most of the state except that portion lying south of the Platte River. Breeding occurs from North Dakota and Minnesota south to Colorado and Missouri, and migrants are regular in southern portions of the Plains region.

Migration. Eighty initial spring sightings are from March 4 to May 24, with a median of April 18. Half of the records fall within the period April 13-27. Eighty-three final fall sightings range from August 13 to November 24, with a median of October 9. Half of the records fall within the period September 26 to October 18.

Habitats. Migrants and breeding birds frequent overgrown fields, prairie edges, and similar habitats where grasslands join or are mixed with shrubs and scattered low trees.

Comments. The well-named vesper sparrow has a sweet song somewhat like that of a song sparrow, but it usually has only two introductory or "grace" notes. Its white outer tail feathers also help to separate it visually from song sparrows.

Lark Sparrow   *Chondestes grammacus*

A common spring and fall migrant statewide and a common summer resident in grasslands throughout Nebraska, but especially in the Sandhills and Panhandle. Breeding occurs widely through the Plains States, excepting the northeastern areas, where the species is a migrant.

Migration. The range of 125 initial spring sightings is from April 5 to June 10, with a median of May 5. Half of the records fall within the period April 28 to May 13. Seventy-six final fall sightings range from July 23 to November 13, with a median of September 3. Half of the records fall within the period August 22 to September 18.

Habitats. While in Nebraska this species occupies natural grasslands or weedy fields that adjoin or include scattered trees, shrubs, and weeds.

Comments. Lark sparrows are among the most attractive of Nebraska's breeding sparrows. The complex chestnut head markings allow for easy recognition, which is also aided by the white markings on the corners of the tail. Their song is rather lark-like, but always has a few buzzy phrases as if the bird suddenly forgot what it was supposed to be singing and filled in with buzzing interludes. Breeding Bird Surveys between 1966 and 2011 indicate that the species underwent a significant population decline (0.9% annually) during that period.

Black-throated Sparrow   *Amphispiza bilineata*

Accidental or extremely rare. Reported from Sioux County in June of 1972 and Douglas County in the winter of 1973-74 (*Nebraska Bird Review* 40:72; 42:18). Also observed May 26, 1984, near Keystone, Keith County (Rosche & Johnsgard, 1984), and photographed near Wakefield, Dixon County, and in Lincoln, Lancaster County, in the winter and spring of 1993 (*Nebraska Bird Review* 64:33). Also one was banded at Omaha on December 20, 1997 (*Nebraska Bird Review* 65:179) remaining there until April. Another was seen in Antelope County, January 4, 1998 (*Nebraska Bird Review* 66:16). There is a single South Dakota record.

Sage Sparrow   *Artemisiospiza belli*

Accidental. Observed at Sowbelly Canyon, Sioux County, August 6, 1989 (*Nebraska Bird Review* 58:27). Breeding occurs commonly in east to central Wyoming.

Lark Bunting   *Calamospiza melanocorys*

A common spring and fall migrant and summer resident in western and central Nebraska, or generally west of a line from Boyd to Nuckolls counties, with sporadic breeding farther east, and rarely to northwestern Missouri (*Wilson Bulletin* 82:465). Breeding also occurs north to North Dakota and south to central Oklahoma and the Texas Panhandle.

Migration. The range of 104 initial spring sightings is from April 8 to June 10, with a median of May 10. Half of the records fall within the period May 4-16. Sixty-five final fall sightings are from July 20 to October 13, with a median of August 30. Half of the records fall within the period August 20 to September 8.

Habitats. While in Nebraska this species is usually found in mixed short-grass prairie and sage-dominated areas, but it also occurs in areas of taller grasses with scattered shrubs and along weedy roadsides, in retired croplands, and in fields of alfalfa or clover. Outside the breeding season it is highly gregarious, and it is colonial even during the nesting period.

Comments. This is a rather puzzling bird in parts of western Nebraska, such as near Cedar Point Biological Station in Keith County. There it may be very common one year, only to be gone the following one, and return again some years later. Perhaps local precipitation or irrigation patterns cause its periodic appearance and subsequent disappearance. Breeding Bird Surveys between 1966 and 2011 indicate that the species underwent a significant population decline (3.5% annually) during that period.

Savannah Sparrow   *Passerculus sandwichensis*

A common spring and fall migrant statewide, and rare or uncommon summer resident north and west of a line from Scotts Bluff County to the southeastern corner of South Dakota, and mainly in the northern Panhandle region. Breeding in the Sandhills seems to be limited to the western and northern parts of this region. The species also breeds throughout the Dakotas and Minnesota and occurs as a migrant in southern parts of the Plains States.

Migration. The range of 69 initial spring sightings is from March 17 to June 5, with a median of April 22. Half of the records fall within the period April 15-29. Thirty-eight final spring sightings are from April 10 to May 30, with a median of May 10. Thirty-nine initial fall sightings range from July 28 to October 9, with a median of September 19. Half of the records fall within the period September 5-28. Thirty-nine final fall sightings are from October 2 to November 22, with a median of October 19.

Habitats. Migrants are usually found in open grasslands, lightly grazed pastures, and brushy edges. Breeding occurs in wet-meadow zones of wetlands, and in tall to mid-grass prairies.

Comments. Savannah sparrows are poorly named, since their breeding habitats certainly do not consist of savannah. Instead, the species was named after Savannah, Georgia. The birds in Nebraska usually have a yellowish area in front of the eyes (the lores), and the tail is much shorter than a song sparrow's or vesper sparrow's.

Grasshopper Sparrow   *Ammodramus savannarum*

A common spring and fall migrant and summer resident statewide. Breeding occurs widely in the Plains States, excepting the southwestern areas, where the species occurs as a migrant.

Migration. The range of 85 initial spring sightings is from March 14 to June 10, with a median of May 6. Half of the records fall within the period April 27 to May 15. Sixty-seven final fall sightings range from July 26 to November 6, with a median of September 9. Half of the records fall within the period August 12 to September 29.

Habitats. Migrants and breeding birds occur in mixed-grass prairies, pasturelands, short-grass prairies, sage prairies, and to a limited extent tall-grass prairies. Areas that have grown up to shrubs are avoided, but scattered trees in grassland are sometimes used for song perches.

Comments. Few grassland sparrows in Nebraska can be as common as the grasshopper sparrow, but it is so secretive that one can be in the field all day without seeing the species. Yet, its grasshopper–like buzz may be evident almost everywhere, and if seen its rather large beak and striped head pattern is quite distinctive. The birds feed largely on grasshoppers during their time in Nebraska, which might help account for their strong beak. Breeding Bird Surveys between 1966 and 2011 indicate that the species underwent a significant population decline (2.4% annually) during that period, one of the most rapid rates of population decline among grassland birds.

Baird's Sparrow   *Ammodramus bairdii*
        An uncommon spring and fall migrant over most of Nebraska, but probably less common eastwardly and rare in the extreme eastern counties. Breeding occurs in North Dakota and northern South Dakota, and migrants appear throughout the western portions of the region. Probable breeding in Sioux County, Nebraska, occurred in 1996, when three territorial males were seen (*Audubon Society Field Notes* 50:967). A singing male was reported from Banner County in 1996 (Brogie, 1997) and three were found in Sioux County, in 2010 (*Nebraska Bird Review* 78:59.
        Migration. The range of 44 spring sightings is from March 24 to June 8, with a median of April 29. Half of the records fall within the period April 19 to May 5. Fifteen initial fall sightings are from July 26 to October 21, with a median of September 26. Fifteen final fall sightings are from September 10 to November 11, with a median of October 18. Half of the total fall sightings fall within the period September 23 to October 8.
        Habitats. Migrants are associated with prairies and other natural grasslands.
        Comments. This is one least abundant but most attractive of the prairie endemic sparrows. It has been declining in recent years, presumably because of losses in prairie habitats. Breeding Bird Surveys between 1966 and 2011 indicate that the species underwent a significant population decline (2.8% annually) during that period.

Henslow's Sparrow   *Ammodramus henslowii*
        An occasional spring and fall migrant and summer resident in eastern Nebraska (*Nebraska Bird Review* 75: 13–16; 53–60; 116). Most records are for Adams and Webster counties, but the species has been seen west to Lincoln, Logan and Keith counties. Breeding records extend west to Hall County, where the birds are common nesters at the Crane Trust (*Nebraska Bird Review* 75:84). It also breeds in southern Minnesota, western Iowa, and eastern Kansas, and it migrates through eastern Oklahoma.
        Migration. Twenty-one initial spring sightings range from April 6 to May 29, with a median of April 29. Half of the records fall within the period April 25 to May 4. Thirteen final fall sightings are from August 5 to October 23, with a median of September 26.
        Habitats. While in Nebraska this species is found in weedy pastures and meadows, neglected grassy fields, and pasturelands, especially those that are low-lying and rather damp. Scattered low bushes are also often present in breeding habitats, and provide song perches, but nesting is done on the ground.
        Comments. The development of the Conservation Reserve Program in southeastern Nebraska has evidently helped this rare resident. It seems to favor overgrown, weedy fields that result from letting land lie fallow for several years. However, nationally the species has declined by more than 90 percent during the past three decades, and may soon be a candidate for the endangered species list.

LeConte's Sparrow   *Ammodramus leconteii*
        An inconspicuous but regular and probably uncommon spring and fall migrant in eastern Nebraska, rare or absent westwardly. Breeding occurs in North Dakota and northern Minnesota, and migrants are found in the eastern portions of the Plains region.
        Migration. Fifty-four initial spring sightings are from April 1 to June 7, with a median of April 29. Half of the records fall within the period April 21 to May 8. Thirteen final spring sightings are from April 17 to May 19, with a median of May 2. Twenty-one initial fall sightings are from July 25 to October 15, with a median of September 22. Seventeen final fall sightings are from July 26 to November 9, with a median of October 20.
        Habitats. Migrants are found in wet meadows and marshy edges with sedges, cattails, and deep grasses.
        Comments. This is one of those hard-to-see sparrows that are highly memorable. On rare occasions one perches on the tops of marshy grasses long enough to see and appreciate its rich golden eye-stripe and

heavily striped head and back. Breeding Bird Surveys between 1966 and 2003 indicate that the species underwent a probable population increase (1.6% annually) during that period.

Nelson's Sparrow   *Ammodramus nelsoni*

An inconspicuous and seemingly rare spring and fall migrant in eastern Nebraska, with relatively few records available. Most of the sightings are from the eastern half of the state, but it has been seen west to Custer, Cherry, and Sheridan counties. It has been reported more often in Lancaster County than elsewhere in the state. Breeding occurs in North Dakota and adjacent areas, and migrants occur in eastern portions of the region.

Migration. Five spring sightings are from March 29 to May 30, with a mean of May 5. Three of the records are for the month of May. Nine fall records are from September 7 to October 21, with a mean of September 30. Five of the records are for the month of October.

Habitats. Migrants are found along the wet edges of marshes and sloughs, usually in even wetter habitats than those used by the LeConte's sparrow.

Comments. Perhaps even harder to see than the LeConte's sparrow, the Nelson's sparrow is also a bird of dense, marshy vegetation. It is even more golden-tinted than the LeConte's, but has a dark brown crown rather than a strongly striped one.

Fox Sparrow   *Passerella iliaca*

A spring and fall migrant statewide, ranging from common to uncommon in eastern areas to rare or very rare in western parts of the state. Also occurs throughout the Plains States as a migrant or wintering form, becoming vary rare westwardly.

Migration. Fifty-three initial spring sightings are from January 4 to June 4, with a median of March 30. Half of the records fall within the period March 17 to April 18. Twenty-two final spring sightings are from April 1 to April 23, with a median of April 10. Thirty-one initial fall records are from August 2 to November 11, with a median of October 11. Half of the records fall within the period October 5-17. Twenty-eight final fall sightings are from August 18 to December 31, with a median of November 11.

Habitats. Migrants are usually associated with brushy woodlands, streamside thickets and sometimes residential shrubbery.

Comments. The fox sparrow is perfectly named; it has an overall fox-brown plumage cast, and it moves about secretively on the ground, usually in fairly dense cover, where it scratches towhee-like for food. It looks something like an oversized song sparrow, as its breast is patterned in a similar way, and its tail is fairly long.

Song Sparrow   *Melospiza melodia*

A common spring and fall migrant and uncommon winter visitor statewide, and an uncommon summer resident. Breeding is probably limited mostly to the eastern parts of the state. There are recent eastern records for at least Antelope, Cuming, Boone, Polk, Platte, Colfax, Lancaster, Gage and Nemaha counties, and others west to Buffalo, Hall, Valley, Phelps and Webster counties. Breeding occurs from North Dakota and Minnesota southward to Colorado and northeastern Kansas, and migrants are regular to the south of these areas.

Migration. Forty-five initial spring sightings are from January 1 to June 6, with a median of April 8. Forty-five final spring sightings are from January 12 to June 3, with a median of April 30. Seventy-six initial fall sightings are from August 2 to November 2, with a median of September 30. Forty-four final fall sightings are from October 6 to December 31, with a median of December 20. The data suggest that this species commonly overwinters in Nebraska, and that its migration tendencies are very poorly defined.

Habitats. Migrants and wintering birds occur in weedy areas, thickets and streamside woodland edges. Breeding occurs in similar habitats, including forest margins, shrubby swamps, the brushy edges of ponds, shelterbelts and farmsteads.

Comments. One of the most appealing of Nebraska's native sparrows, the song sparrow's typical song begins like Beethoven's third symphony, with three well-spaced introductory whistles, followed by a melodious phrase. It pumps its longish tail in flight, and has a blotchy spot in the middle of its streaked breast. Breeding Bird Surveys between 1966 and 2011 indicate that the species underwent a significant population decline (0.7% annually) during that period.

Lincoln's Sparrow   *Melospiza lincolnii*

A common spring and fall migrant statewide. Also occurs throughout the other Plains States as a migrant or wintering species.

Migration. Ninety-four initial spring sightings are from January 2 to May 29, with a median of April 26. Half of the records fall within the period April 19 to May 7. Sixty-two final spring sightings are from April 20 to May 31, with a median of May 13. Forty-eight initial fall sightings are from September 2 to October 12, with a median of September 15. Half of the records fall within the period September 7-17. Twenty-five final fall sightings are from September 20 to December 29, with a median of October 19.

Habitats. Migrants are associated with streamside thickets, thick weedy areas, and other rather dense grassy or weedy areas close to water, occurring less frequently in residential shrubbery.

Comments. The Lincoln's sparrow was not named after Abraham Lincoln, but instead after a young field assistant of John James Audubon, who thus certainly was one of the youngest persons ever to have a bird named after him. The grayish cheeks of this species help to identify it, and its breast also has a soft grayis-buff breast-band.

Swamp Sparrow   *Melospiza georgiana*

A spring and fall migrant statewide, ranging from uncommon in east to central counties to very rare in western areas. It is a local summer resident in central Nebraska marshes, including Sheridan, Brown, Rock, Loup, Wheeler, Boone, Antelope, Howard, Phelps and Garden counties, very locally in the Rainwater Basin, and perhaps along the Missouri River. Breeding occurs in Minnesota and the eastern portions of the Dakotas, and migrants are regular in eastern portions of the region.

Migration. Thirty-three initial spring sightings are from March 30 to June 6, with a median of April 23. Half of the records fall within the period April 10-30. Fourteen final spring sightings are from April 13 to May 25, with a median of May 7. Nineteen initial fall sightings are from July 21 to October 21, with a median of September 30. Thirteen final fall sightings are from October 2 to December 29, with a median of October 24.

Habitats. Migrants are found in marshy areas, and during the breeding season nesting occurs in marshes or other wetlands having such vegetation as cattails, phragmites, and shrubs or small trees.

Comments. This is a semi-colonial nester whose habitat needs seemingly limit it to only a few known nesting locations in Nebraska. Its song rather strongly resembles a chipping sparrow, but the trills are slower and more melodious.

White-throated Sparrow   *Zonotrichia albicollis*

A spring and fall migrant statewide, common in eastern Nebraska and becoming uncommon to rare westwardly, and a locally common winter visitor. The species breeds in northern parts of North Dakota and Minnesota, and throughout the entire Plains region as a migrant or wintering form.

Migration. Sixty-five initial fall sightings range from September 18 to November 25, with a median of October 3. Half of the records fall within the period September 25 to October 5. Fifty-two final spring sightings are from February 2 to June 4, with a median of May 12. Half of the records fall within the period May 6-17.

Habitats. Migrants are associated with woodland edges, thickets, weedy fields, and sheltered areas near water, sometimes coming to feeding stations during winter.

Comments. People who feed birds through the winter soon come to recognize this rather robust sparrow; in Nebraska many of these white-throated birds have a golden cast in the loral area in front of the eyes. Its beak is pinker and its throat whiter than in the similar white-crowned sparrow.

Harris' Sparrow   *Zonotrichia querula*

A spring and fall migrant statewide, abundant in eastern counties and common farther west. Wintering is regular in the southern parts of the state. The species occurs throughout the entire Plains region as a migrant or wintering form.

Migration. The range of 115 initial fall sightings is from August 13 to December 31, with a median of October 14. Half of the records fall within the period October 4-22. Ninety-five final spring sightings are from February 8 to June 10, with a median of May 12. Half of the records fall within the period May 9-16.

Habitats. Migrants and wintering birds occur in rural, suburban or urban areas having shrubs, low trees and tall weedy plants, often near streamside woodland edges or thickets.

Comments. Nebraskans can count themselves lucky for being in the heart of the migratory route of the Harris' sparrow. It is the largest of the "crowned" sparrows, and one of the prettiest, with a variably black throat during winter (the black gradually increasing in extent during spring), and a bright pink beak.

White-crowned Sparrow   *Zonotrichia leucophrys*

A common spring and fall migrant statewide, and a locally common winter visitor. The species occurs throughout the entire region as a migrant or wintering form.

Migration. Ninety-eight initial fall sightings range from August 25 to December 29, with a median of October 3. Half of the records fall within the period September 21 to October 16. Eighty-two final spring sightings are from February 1 to May 27, with a median of May 15. Half of the records fall within the period May 2-8.

Habitats. Migrants are associated with thickets, woodland edges, and weedy areas, sometimes moving to farmyards and feeding stations in winter.

Comments. About the same size as the white-throated sparrow, this species has a more grayish throat but a whiter beak than does the white-throated sparrow. Both come to winter feeders, but in Nebraska the white-crowned is much rarer under such conditions.

Golden-crowned Sparrow   *Zonotrichia atricapilla*

Accidental. One was banded in Thomas County in May of 1950, one was seen repeatedly in eastern Cherry County in April of 1962, one was reported in Scotts Bluff County in May of 1966, one was observed in McPherson County in October 1966 (*Nebraska Bird Review* 18:68; 35:24; 34:70). Also reported December 18, 1998 in Harlan County (Brogie, 1999).

Dark-eyed Junco   *Junco hyemalis*

A common migrant and winter visitor statewide, and a local summer resident in the Pine Ridge area of Sioux and Dawes counties. The species also breeds in western South Dakota and Minnesota, and occurs throughout the area during migration or winter. The Oregon phenotype (consisting of several races, including the so-called "pink-sided" *mernsi*) is fairly common through the state, and the gray-headed race *caniceps* is an irregular and occasional winter visitor in western Nebraska, sometimes occurring as far east as Lincoln, Webster, Adams and Lancaster counties. The somewhat larger and paler white-winged race is a breeder in the Black Hills and adjacent Pine Ridge.

Migration. The range of 105 initial fall sightings is from September 1 to December 31, with a median of October 6. Half of the records fall within the period September 26 to October 15. Seventy-five final spring sightings are from January 1 to May 20, with a median of April 15. Half of the records fall within the period March 27 to April 25. Four initial fall sightings of *caniceps* are from September 21 to October 21, with a mean of October 3. Twenty final spring sightings are from January 1 to May 18, with a median of March 23.

Habitats. Migrants and wintering birds are widely distributed in woodlands, suburbs and residential areas, foraging on the ground and often visiting feeding stations. Breeding in the Black Hills occurs in coniferous forests, aspen groves and deciduous woodlands in hollows, canyons and gulches, and probably similar habitats are used in the Pine Ridge region.

Comments. One of the commonest of Nebraska's wintering sparrows, the dark-eyed junco often betrays its identity by flashing its white outer tail feathers as it is flushed and disappears into heavy cover. Breeding Bird Surveys between 1966 and 2011 indicate that the species underwent a significant population decline (1.2% annually) during that period.

Family Cardinalidae

Hepatic Tanager   *Piranga flava*
    Accidental; photographed at West Point, Cuming County, January 6, 1999.

Summer Tanager   *Piranga rubra*
    An uncommon spring and fall migrant and summer resident in southeastern Nebraska (especially the Indian Cave area) north to Fontenelle Forest and Platte River Park, and occasionally seen farther west, rarely to as far as Scotts Bluff County. Breeding also occurs in eastern Kansas and eastern Oklahoma.
    <u>Migration.</u> Twenty-nine initial spring sightings range from April 25 to May 31, with a median of May 15. Half of the records fall within the period May 12-20. Two late fall sightings are for September 5 and 15.
    <u>Habitats.</u> Like the scarlet tanager this species favors mature deciduous forests , especially bottomland forests, in Nebraska, often nesting in tall oak trees. Elsewhere it nests in mixed and sometimes open coniferous forests, and in general it may favor slightly lower and more open woodlands than does the scarlet tanager.
    <u>Comments.</u> Perhaps the summer tanager is expanding its breeding range in southeastern Nebraska; Schramm Park is now a nearly certain location for seeing these birds.

Scarlet Tanager   *Piranga olivacea*
    An uncommon spring and fall migrant in eastern Nebraska, becoming rare westwardly, and rarely occurring as far west as Keith, Garden, and Dawes counties. A summer resident in the Missouri's forested valley, westward in the Niobrara Valley to at least Cherry County, and west in the Platte Valley to about Douglas County. It is believed to have bred as far west as Lincoln County. Breeding also occurs in the eastern Dakotas, Minnesota, and eastern parts of Kansas and Oklahoma.
    <u>Migration.</u> The range of 132 initial spring sightings is from April 5 to June 10, with a median of May 10. Half of the records fall within the period May 5-15. Twenty-three final fall records are from July 21 to October 3, with a median of August 23. Half of the records fall within the period August 5 to September 16.
    <u>Habitats.</u> In Nebraska this species is restricted primarily to mature hardwood forests in river valleys, hill slopes, and valleys; less frequently it is found in city parks and mature orchards.
    <u>Comments.</u> Few Nebraska birds are more brilliantly plumaged than are male scarlet tanagers; they are as bright as male northern cardinals and their jet-black wings make them even more memorable, as well as separating them from summer tanagers.

Western Tanager   *Piranga ludoviciana*
    An uncommon spring and fall migrant in western Nebraska, and a summer resident in the Pine Ridge area, possibly extending east in the Niobrara Valley far enough to come into contact occasionally with the scarlet tanager (*Nebraska Bird Review* 29:19). Breeding also occurs in western South Dakota, and migrants are encountered east to western Kansas and western Oklahoma.
    <u>Migration.</u> Sixty-three initial spring sightings range from May 3 to June 8, with a median of May 19. Half of the records fall within the period May 13-24. Twenty-two final fall records are from August 14 to October 10, with a median of September 15. Half of the records fall within the period September 4-23.
    <u>Habitats.</u> In the Black Hills and Pine Ridge areas this species is mainly associated with pine forests, and secondarily with deciduous forests along rivers or in gulches and canyons.
    <u>Comments.</u> Although birders in western Nebraska may long to see scarlet and summer tanagers, the western tanager is a very satisfactory substitute for these. Its bright red head and golden yellow body with contrasting black wings, tail and back, makes for a visual treat.

Northern Cardinal   *Cardinalis cardinalis*

A common permanent resident in eastern Nebraska, becoming uncommon to occasional in western Nebraska. It breeds west at least to Garden County along the North Platte River, and to the Colorado border in the South Platte and Republican Valleys, but is apparently absent from the western Sandhills and the Pine Ridge. It breeds widely in the Plains States region, north to southern North Dakota and locally west to eastern Colorado and the Texas Panhandle.

Habitats. Throughout the year this species is associated with forest edges or brushy forest openings, parks and residential areas planted to shrubs and low trees, second-growth woods, and river–bottom gallery forests in grasslands.

Comments, Nearly everybody in Nebraska is familiar with the northern cardinal except for those living in the northwestern corner of the state. They are among the first birds to begin singing in spring, and are early nesters. They are often parasitized by brown-headed cowbirds. Breeding Bird Surveys between 1966 and 2003 indicate that the species underwent a significant population increase (0.3% annually) during that period.

Rose-breasted Grosbeak   *Pheucticus ludovicianus*

A common spring and fall migrant and summer resident in eastern Nebraska. It breeds west to Holt, Garfield, and Phelps counties, with the western limits confused by hybridization with the black-headed grosbeak. Breeding occurs from central North Dakota south through South Dakota, eastern Kansas, and eastern Oklahoma.

Migration. The range of 134 initial spring sightings is from April 10 to June 3, with a median of May 7. Half of the records fall within the period May 1-10. Seventy-one final fall sightings are from July 23 to November 22, with a median of September 10. Half of the records fall within the period August 23 to September 24.

Habitats. During the breeding season this species occurs in relatively open deciduous forests on floodplains, slopes and bluffs. A denser understory is apparently not so important to this species as it is to he black-headed grosbeak.

Comments. Rose-breasted grosbeaks hybridize fairly frequently with black-headed grosbeaks in the western Platte Valley, which produces some very strange-looking birds. Breeding Bird Surveys between 1966 and 2003 indicate that the species underwent a significant population decline (0.7% annually) during that period.

Black-headed Grosbeak   *Pheucticus melanocephalus*

A common spring and fall migrant and summer resident in western Nebraska. It breeds eastward locally to at least Rock, Garfield, and Hall Counties, but the eastern limits are confused by hybridization with the rose-breasted grosbeak (*Auk* 79:399-424; Wilson *Bulletin* 85:230-6). Individuals have been seen as far east as Douglas County. Breeding also occurs west of the Missouri River in the Dakotas, in western Kansas, and eastern Colorado.

Migration. The range of 114 initial springs sightings is from April 23 to June 8, with a median of May 14. Half of the records fall within the period May 10-19. Thirty-six final fall sightings are from July 20 to September 30, with a median of August 29. Half of the records fall within the period August 20 to September 8.

Habitats. While in Nebraska this species occupies relatively open stands of deciduous forest in floodplains or uplands, especially those with well-developed understories. It also occurs in orchards, brushy woodlands, and parks or suburbs with many trees.

Comments. As noted above, the black-headed grosbeaks of western Nebraska are impacted by rose-breasted grosbeaks, and breeding records of the past were more widespread than more recent ones. Thus the species may be retreating under the influence of competition and interbreeding effects from rose-breasted grosbeaks.

Blue Grosbeak   *Passerina caerulea*

An uncommon spring and fall migrant and local summer resident nearly statewide. It is very uncommon and highly local in the southeastern counties, and rare in the Pine Ridge area. Breeding occurs from central South Dakota and western Iowa southward throughout the Plains States region.

Migration. The range of 129 initial spring sightings is from April 18 to June 10, with a median of May 20. Half of the records fall within the period May 16-24. Eighty-eight final fall sightings are from July 20 to October 13, with a median of August 27. Half of the records fall within the period August 12 to September 6.

Habitats. During the breeding season this species prefers weedy pastures, old fields with scattered saplings, forest edges, streamside thickets, and hedgerows. Like the dickcissel, it is frequently parasitized by brown-headed cowbirds in these habitats.

Comments. This attractive and, in the case of males, sky-blue bird seems out of place on a Nebraska prairie pasture. Males may be easily confused with the smaller indigo bunting, but have bright brown edges on their upper wing-coverts. Breeding Bird Surveys between 1966 and 2011 indicate that the species had a significant population increase (0.9% annually) in that period.

Lazuli Bunting   *Passerina amoena*

An uncommon spring and fall migrant and summer resident in western Nebraska. Breeding is generally limited to an area west of a line from Keith to eastern Cherry counties, and is most prevalent in the Panhandle. Eastern limits are confused by hybridization with the indigo bunting (*Auk* 76:433-63; *Wilson Bulletin* 87:145-77). However, breeding generally occurs in the western parts of the Dakotas, eastern Colorado, western Kansas, and the panhandles of Texas and Oklahoma.

Migration. The range of 113 initial spring sightings is from March 18 to June 9, with a median of May 16. Half of the records fall within the period May 10-20. Twenty final fall sightings are from July 21 to September 30, with a median of August 25. Half of the records fall within the period August 19-30.

Habitats. During the breeding season this species occupies the same habitats as does the Indigo Bunting, namely successional habitats offering a diversity of shrubs, low trees and herbaceous vegetation.

Comments. This sparrow-sized bird is one of several western species that reach the eastern edges of its range in western Nebraska. Females of the two species are almost impossible to distinguish, and hybrids make the matter even worse.

Indigo Bunting   *Passerina cyanea*

An uncommon spring and fall migrant and summer resident in eastern Nebraska. Breeding extends west locally to the Pine Ridge, the central Sandhills, and to the Wyoming and Colorado border along the Platte rivers. It is nearly absent from the Panhandle and western Sandhills, but the range limits there are confused by hybridization with the lazuli bunting. Breeding also occurs widely in the other Plains States, west to the Black Hills and eastern Colorado.

Migration. The range of 99 initial spring sightings is from March 24 to June 8, with a median of May 10. Half of the records fall within the period May 5-16. Fifty-seven final fall sightings are from July 29 to October 28, with a median of August 28. Half of the records fall within the period August 15 to September 10.

Habitats. During the breeding season this species occurs in relatively open forests on floodplains or uplands. It is typically found at forest edges or elsewhere where the shrub density is rather high and the forest canopy is open, and thus is often associated with second-growth or disturbed vegetation.

Comments, Many people gasp involuntarily when they first see a male indigo bunting in bright sunlight; it rivals the blue grosbeak in the intensity of its blue coloration. This coloring is produced by light scattering, just as the "blue" of a clear sky is generated. In shade the birds are transformed into gray tones. Breeding Bird Surveys between 1966 and 2011 indicate that the species had a significant population decline (0.6% annually) in that period.

Painted Bunting   *Passerina ciris*

Accidental. Photographed at the Crane Trust Nature Center, Hall County, May 30-31, 1996. Sight records exist for Scotts Bluff County in May of 1927, Adams County in May of 1962, Kearney County in April of 1960 and Sarpy County in May of 1967. Also reported from Morrill County, May 12, 1996 and Hall County, May 30, 1996 (Brogie, 1997). Nine state records existed through 2003, the latest May 23, 2003 (*Nebraska Bird Review* 73:81).

Dickcissel   *Spiza americana*

A spring and fall migrant and summer resident nearly statewide, excepting the extreme northwestern and southwestern parts of Nebraska, or generally east of a line from Sioux to Dundy counties. It is uncommon to rare in the Panhandle, but a common to abundant summer resident elsewhere in the state. Breeding occurs in all of the other Plains States, but it is rare in the westernmost areas and absent from northern Minnesota.

Migration. The range of 199 initial spring sightings is from April 16 to June 10, with a median of May 16. Half of the records fall within the period May 6 to 24. The range of 105 final fall sightings is from July 21 to October 30, with a median of August 22. Half of the records fall within the period August 10 to September 2

Habitats. While in Nebraska this species is associated with grasslands having a combination of tall grasses, forbs and shrubs, and with various croplands, especially alfalfa, clover and timothy. Although generally abundant in eastern Nebraska, it is heavily parasitized by brown-headed cowbirds.

Comments. Dickcissels are still very common over much of Nebraska, but their numbers have greatly declined nationwide. In part this decline has resulted from poisoning by pesticides on their wintering grounds in South America, and perhaps also because of their sensitivity to parasitism by cowbirds.

Family Icteridae

Bobolink   *Dolichonyx oryzivorus*

A spring and fall migrant throughout Nebraska, fairly common in central Nebraska, but less common in the eastern and western areas. A summer resident throughout most of the state, west to Sioux County in the Panhandle, Garden County in the Sandhills, and with the southern limits occurring between the Platte and Republican rivers. Breeding occurs from North Dakota and Minnesota south locally to central Kansas, and migrants are regular to the south of this area.

Migration. The range of 116 initial spring sightings is from March 20 to June 20, with a median of May 16. Half of the fall records fall within the period July 29 to August 20.

Habitats. While in Nebraska this species is usually found in ungrazed to lightly grazed medium to tall-grass prairies, wet meadows, retired croplands, and occasionally extends to small-grain croplands.

Comments. Breeding Bird Surveys between 1966 and 2011 indicate that the species underwent a significant population decline (2.1% annually) during that period.

Red-winged Blackbird   *Agelaius phoeniceus*

An abundant spring and fall migrant statewide, and a common to abundant summer resident throughout Nebraska in suitable habitats. Overwinters fairly frequently, and large numbers of migrants pass through the state every spring and fall. The species is a migrant or breeder throughout the Plains States.

Migration. The range of 90 initial spring sightings is from January 1 to May 26, with a median of March 3. Half of the records fall within the period February 17 to March 17. Eighty final fall sightings range from August 8 to December 31, with a median of November 21. Half of the records fall within the period November 3 to December 21.

Habitats. Breeding occurs on a wide range of habitats, from deep marshes or the emergent zones of lakes and impoundments, through progressively drier habitats such as wet meadows, ditches, brushy patches in prairie, hayfields, and weedy croplands or roadsides. Migrants often are seen in flocks of other blackbird species, feeding in fields or elsewhere, but roosting is typically done in wet areas rather than in residential locations.

Comments. This is one of Nebraska's most abundant breeding birds, numbering in the tens of millions, and also one of the most attractive. Like several other grassland nesting birds it is impacted greatly by brown-headed cowbirds; few nests of redwings in Nebraska seem to survive without being parasitized. Breeding Bird Surveys between 1966 and 2011 indicate that the species underwent a significant population decline (0.9% annually) during that period.

Eastern Meadowlark   *Sturnella magna*

A common spring and fall migrant in eastern Nebraska, becoming rarer westwardly, and a summer resident in southeastern counties and locally elsewhere. The species is a fairly common breeder east of a line from Gage to Thurston counties, and there is local breeding along river courses and wet meadows as far west as Sioux and Morrill counties, and also is common throughout the western Sandhills. The species also extends west along the South Platte to the Colorado border, where hybridization with the western meadowlark is apparently quite frequent (*Transactions Kansas Academy of Sciences* 75:19). Sometimes it overwinters in the state. The species also breeds in Minnesota, Iowa, eastern Kansas, and most of Oklahoma.

Migration. Fifty-nine initial spring sightings range from January 1 to May 30, with a median of April 8. Half of the records fall within the period March 17 to May 6. Thirty final fall sightings are from August 2 to December 31, with a median of October 10. Half of the records fall within the period September 20 to November 20.

Habitats. Breeding birds are associated with tall-grass prairies, meadows, and open croplands of small grain, as well as weedy orchards and similar open, grass-dominated habitats. At the western edge of its range in the Sandhills and along the Platte River it is limited to low and rather moist habitats around marshes and in wet meadows.

Comments. Although national populations of the eastern meadowlark have decreased by 53 percent since 1966, the birds are still common in eastern Nebraska, and around Lincoln and Omaha the two species of meadowlarks are about equally common. In these areas the eastern species can usually be found on meadows near water, and the westerns on drier hilltops. Breeding Bird Surveys between 1966 and 2011 indicate that the species underwent a significant population decline (1.0% annually) during that period.

Western Meadowlark   *Sturnella neglecta*

A common spring and fall migrant statewide, and a common summer resident virtually throughout Nebraska except perhaps in the extreme southeastern counties. Overwinters in the state fairly frequently. The species also breeds almost throughout the Plains States, excepting the eastern parts of Kansas and Oklahoma.

Migration. Sixty-one initial spring sightings range from January 1 to May 26, with a median of March 4. Half of the records fall within the period February 9 to March 21. Forty-three final fall sightings are from August 20 to December 31, with a median of October 28. Half of the records fall within the period October 10 to November 21. Apparently the western meadowlark is an earlier spring and later fall migrant than is the eastern meadowlark, and is more prone to overwintering than is that species.

Habitats. In Nebraska this species is associated with tall-grass and mixed-grass prairies, hayfields, wet meadows, the weedy borders of croplands, retired croplands, and to a limited extent with short-grass and sage dominated plains, where it is limited to moister situations.

Comments. This is the state bird of Nebraska (and also of several other states), which is a reflection of the affection with which our citizens look upon meadowlarks. The overall range of the western meadowlark is much greater than that of the eastern, and it has not suffered as much from land-use changes. Breeding Bird Surveys between 1966 and 2011 indicate that the species underwent a significant population decline (1.3% annually) in that period.

Yellow-headed Blackbird   *Xanthocephalus xanthocephalus*

A common to abundant spring and fall migrant statewide, and a locally common summer resident in permanent marshes throughout Nebraska. Breeding occurs from North Dakota and Minnesota south locally to Kansas and southern Colorado.

Migration. The range of 103 initial spring sightings is from January 1 to June 5, with a median of April 21. Half of the records fall within the period April 11 to May 1. Eighty-two final fall sightings range from July 23 to December 28, with a median of September 18. Half of the records fall within the period September 4-30.

Habitats. During the breeding season this species occurs in deep marshes, the marsh zones of lakes or shallow impoundments, and elsewhere where there are extensive stands of cattails, bulrushes or phragmites. It is often found breeding in association with red-winged blackbirds, utilizing the deeper portions of the marsh. Migrants are sometimes seen flying or perching with groups of red-winged blackbirds, but more often remain separate from them.

Comments. This very attractive species seems to prefer somewhat alkaline marshes to freshwater ones, and thus it becomes more common in the Sandhills marshes as one proceeds westward.

Rusty Blackbird   *Euphagus carolinus*

A common spring and fall migrant in eastern Nebraska, becoming rarer westwardly, and rare or irregular in extreme western counties. Overwinters frequently in the state. The species migrates through the entire Plains States region.

Migration. Forty-five initial spring sightings range from January 1 to May 19, with a median of March 22. Twenty-one final spring sightings range from January 5 to May 23, with a median of April 14. Twenty-five initial fall sightings are from August 10 to December 17, with a median of November 3. Twenty-one final fall sightings are from October 4 to December 31, with a median of December 26. The large proportion of final sightings in late December suggest that this species overwinters rather frequently in Nebraska.

Habitats. Migrants and wintering birds are usually found in deciduous woodlands near streams, rather than in the open marshlands, grasslands and croplands favored by other species of blackbirds in Nebraska.

Comments. This is the only blackbird that occurs in Nebraska strictly as a winter resident. There is an early report of nesting in Hall County, but this seems rather questionable, considering the known breeding range of this species. Breeding Bird Surveys between 1966 and 2011 indicate that the species underwent a significant population decline (3.6% annually) during that period.

Brewer's Blackbird   *Euphagus cyanocephalus*

A common spring and fall migrant statewide, becoming very common in the Panhandle where it is a summer resident from Sioux to Sheridan counties, and south to Scotts Bluff County, it might also breed southwest of the Wildcat Hills (*Nebraska Bird Review* 78:102). Overwinters in the state infrequently. Breeding occurs from North Dakota and Minnesota south to eastern Colorado, and migrants appear throughout the entire region.

Migration. Sixty-three initial spring sightings range from January 1 to May 25, with a median of April 12. Half of the records fall within the period March 22 to April 24. Forty-five final fall sightings are from September 1 to December 31, with a median of November 5. There are a much lower proportion of late December records than for the rusty blackbird, suggesting that overwintering is rather rare in this species.

Habitats. Migrants are usually seen in pastures, barnyards and grain fields, often in the company of other kinds of blackbirds. During the breeding season the birds favor low-stature grasslands, such as mowed roadsides or burned areas near railroads, residential areas, and farmsteads. Areas that have a combination of grassy habitats, scattered shrubs or small trees, and nearby water are especially favored.

Comments. Although frequent in western Nebraska during summer, there are few records of breeding in the state. However, nesting has been documented in Sioux County (Smiley Canyon, and near Harrison (*Nebraska Bird Review* 73:19). Breeding Bird Surveys between 1966 and 2011 indicate that the species had a significant population decline (2.1% annually) in that period.

Common Grackle   *Quiscalus quiscula*

A common to abundant spring and fall migrant and summer resident statewide, and an occasional winter resident, especially in southern counties. The species breeds throughout the entire Plains States region, excepting the most arid portions of the southwest.

Migration. Eighty-two initial spring sightings range from January 22 to June 7, with a median of March 26. Half of the records fall within the period March 16 to April 6. Ninety final fall records are from August 9 to December 30, with a median of October 28. Half of the records fall within the period September 30 to December 3. Nearly half of the records are for December, so overwintering may occur fairly frequently.

Habitats. During the breeding season this species frequents woodland edges or areas partially planted to trees, such as residential areas, parks, farmsteads, shelterbelts and the like. Tall shrub thickets near croplands or marshlands are also used. Migrants are often seen in large flocks in residential and rural areas.

Comments. Like the other "blackbirds," this grackle is especially abundant during fall migration, when vast mixed flocks appear during late September and October on their way southward. Common grackles are also egg-stealers and nestling-eaters, so they sometimes cause some damage to the reproductive efforts of other nesting songbirds. Breeding Bird Surveys between 1966 and 2011 indicate that the species underwent a significant population decline (1.6% annually) during that period.

Great-tailed Grackle   *Quiscalus mexicanus*

An increasingly regular and now locally uncommon spring and fall migrant, and a local summer resident throughout Nebraska, north into eastern South Dakota. The species was first found breeding in the state in 1976, when nesting occurred in Adams and Douglas counties (*Nebraska Bird Review* 45:18). During the atlasing years nesting was confirmed in Adams, Fillmore, Gage, Lancaster and Otoe counties (Mollhoff, 2001) It was later found nesting rather widely in wetlands south of the Platte River, including Funk W. M. A., Kiowa Springs, near Hastings, and around Grand Island and Ogallala,.

Migration. Five initial spring sightings are from March 31 to May 14, with a mean of April 21. Most breeding birds depart by the end of August; the latest fall record is November 27.

Habitats. Breeding occurs in a wide variety of habitats, but these usually include both open ground and nearby water, so it is common in irrigated croplands.

Comments. It is regrettable that great-tailed grackles have made their way into Nebraska, since they are efficient predators of eggs and young of other species of songbirds. Yet, they are interesting to watch, and probably not nearly so destructive as brown-headed cowbirds. Breeding Bird Surveys between 1966 and 2003 indicate that the species underwent a significant population increase (2.4% annually) during that period.

Brown-headed Cowbird   *Molothrus ater*

A common to abundant spring and fall migrant, and a common summer resident statewide. Breeding also occurs throughout the entire Plains States region.

Migration. Eighty-three initial spring sightings range from January 6 to May 26, with a median of April 17. Half of the records fall within the period April 2 to May 1. Eighty-five final fall sightings are from August 1 to December 31, with a median of October 7. Half of the records fall within the period September 11 to November 27. Nearly 20 percent of the records are for December suggesting some overwintering may occur.

Habitats. Breeding by this socially parasitic species usually occurs in woodland edges, brushy thickets and other habitats where low and scattered trees are interspersed with grasslands. Migrants are often found in fields among cattle. Prairie and edge-nesting host species are most often parasitized , including song sparrow, indigo bunting and field sparrow, but some woodland-nesting birds such as wood thrush are also vulnerable.

Comments. Brown-headed cowbirds are very serious brood parasites for many species of Nebraska's songbirds, with dickcissels, yellow warblers, red-winged blackbirds and northern cardinals being among the species most frequently exploited. Unlike the common cuckoo (*Cuculus canorum*) of Europe, the newly hatched cowbird does not eject the eggs or young of its host species from the nest, but by its constant begging manages to get the majority of the food brought to the nest, often causing starvation of the host's own chicks. Breeding Bird Surveys between 1966 and 2011 indicate that the species underwent a significant population decline (0.6% annually) during that period.

Orchard Oriole   *Icterus spurius*

A spring and fall migrant throughout Nebraska, most common in the eastern half, and a summer resident virtually statewide, becoming less common in the extreme western areas. The species breeds widely from North Dakota and Minnesota south to Oklahoma and the Texas Panhandle.

Migration. The range of 188 initial spring sightings is from March 24 to June 10, with a median of May 9. Half of the records fall within the period May 3-14. The range of 115 final fall sightings is from July 21 to October 9, with a median of August 24. Half of the records fall within the period August 14 to September 5.

Habitats. During the breeding season this species occupies lightly wooded river bottoms, scattered trees in open country, shelterbelts, farmsteads, and residential areas, and orchards. Relatively open rather than closed woodlands are preferred, and areas of low junipers or even grasslands may be used, especially if nearby nest sites are available.

Comments. Orchard orioles are surprisingly abundant along the riparian woodlands that extend west along the Platte Valley to Colorado and Wyoming. At Cedar Point Biological Station they are much more abundant than Baltimore and Bullock's orioles. All of these orioles are prone to nest in trees occupied by nesting kingbirds, since they evidently gain some protection from the highly territorial and aggressive kingbirds. Breeding Bird Surveys between 1966 and 2011 indicate that the species underwent a significant population decline (0.8% annually) during that period.

Hooded Oriole   *Icterus cucullatus*
Accidental. There is a sight record for Columbus, Platte County, for May of 1965 (*Nebraska Bird Review* 33:65). An adult male was also seen by many birders at a feeding station in Garrison, Butler County, over the Memorial Day weekend (May 25–27), 2013.

Bullock's Oriole   *Icterus bullockii*
Collectively, the Bullock's and Baltimore orioles are common spring and fall migrants and summer residents statewide. The eastern taxon (Baltimore oriole) is present over most of Nebraska during summer, but in the Panhandle counties many of the birds are of the western (Bullock's oriole) phenotype, or are apparent hybrids (*Candor* 66:130-150; 79: 335-42; Brown *et al.* 1996). Collectively these two poorly distinguished species breed throughout the entire Plains States region.

Migration. The range of 192 initial spring sightings (both taxa combined) is from April 16 to June 5, with a median of May 6. Half of the records fall within the period May 1-10. The range of 136 final fall sightings is from July 26 to October 25, with a median of September 7. Half of the records fall within the period September 2-13.

Habitats. During the breeding season this species occupies wooded river bottoms, upland forests, shelterbelts, and partially wooded residential areas and farmsteads. In extreme western Nebraska river–bottom stands of cottonwoods and willows are the usual habitat of *bullockii*-type birds or apparent hybrids.

Comments. Breeding Bird Surveys between 1966 and 2011 indicate that the Bullock's oriole underwent significant population decline of 0.6% annually during that period.

Baltimore Oriole   ,   *Icterus galbula*
See previous account. So many of the orioles that breed along the North Platte Valley are apparent hybrids that it is difficult to map the breeding ranges of these two orioles accurately. From the 1950's until 1995 they had been regarded as a single species owing to extensive hybridization, but in 1995 they were "split" taxonomically as evidence accumulated that the rate of hybridization was declining and that they were not as close genetically as once assumed. Breeding Bird Surveys between 1966 and 2011 indicate that the Baltimore oriole underwent significant population declines during that period of 1.2% annually.

(Scott's Oriole)   *Icterus parisorum*
Accidental. Three sight records. The first was for record for Hall County in 1975, when a bird was observed from late May to late June (*Nebraska Bird Review* 43:66). Also observed in McPherson County in 1978 (*Nebraska Bird Review* 46:67), and in Hall County, on July 2, 1997.

Family Fringillidae

Brambling   *Fringilla montifringilla*
    Accidental. Photographed at Scottsbluff in April, 1999 (*Nebraska Bird Review* 67:70; 68:8).

Gray-crowned Rosy-Finch   *Leucosticte tephrocotis*
    A rare and irregular winter visitor to Nebraska, mainly in the Panhandle. Outside of this area, the species has also been seen in Brown, Perkins, and Gage counties. It is a winter visitor in Colorado, and a sporadic visitor to the Black Hills.
    Migration. Six fall sighting range from October 1 to November 6, with a median of October 25. Thirteen spring sightings are from January 1 to March 11, with a median of February 12.
    Habitats. During winter this species is usually found on open plains, fields and weedy areas.
    Comments. This is an alpine-nesting bird that descends to foothills and plains during winter, and so sometimes reaches western Nebraska.

(Black Rosy-Finch).   *Leucosticte atrata*
    Hypothetical. A sight record for Sioux County, 2000 (*Nebraska Bird Review* 68:175).

Pine Grosbeak   *Pinicola enucleator*
    A rare and irregular winter visitor to Nebraska with vagrants appearing at various places in the state, but with few recent records. It had been reported from Douglas, Lancaster, Hall, Brown, Madison, and Antelope counties in earlier years (Bruner Wolcott and Swenk, 1904
    Migration. Fourteen initial fall sightings range from October 21 to December 31, with a median of November 24. Thirteen final spring sightings are from January 15 to May 22, with a median of March 10. There is no clustering of fall or spring records.
    Habitats. During the winter this species is normally associated with seed-bearing trees, including both coniferous and deciduous species.
    Comments. Like many of the other finches, this is an irruptive species.

Purple Finch   *Carpodacus purpureus*
    An uncommon migrant and winter visitor in eastern Nebraska and the Pine Ridge; rare elsewhere in the state. Breeding occurs in northern Minnesota, and during winter the species is rather widespread in northern and eastern areas.
    Migration. Thirty-seven initial fall sightings range from August 14 to December 26, with a median of October 27. Half of the records fall within the period October 15 to November 6. Forty-nine final spring sightings are from January 2 to June 5, with a median of April 23. Half of the records fall within the period April 16 to May 8.
    Habitats. Non-breeding birds are associated with woodland streams, and sometimes also appear at bird feeders during winter.
    Comments. This irregular winter visitor strongly resembles the house finch, and one must look closely to determine the distinctions between them. Females have a more contrasting face pattern than do female house finches, and in purple finch males the raspberry red color extends down the entire back and rump area. The Cassin's finch is even more similar to the purple finch, but is a western species. Breeding Bird Surveys between 1966 and 2011 indicate that the species underwent significant population decline of 1.5% annually during that period,

Cassin's Finch   *Carpodacus cassinii*
    A rare migrant and winter visitor in the Panhandle, but also repeatedly observed in Logan County, and rarely to Boone, Adams and Webster counties. It is also a winter visitor to eastern Colorado and western Oklahoma, but rare or absent elsewhere in the Plains States. Possible breeding has been suggested in the Panhandle (*Nebraska Bird Review* 79:135).
    Migration. The only fall records are for October 26 & 27. Thirteen winter and spring records range from January 1 to May 14, with a median of April 12. Half of the records fall between March 30 and May 3.

Habitats. Normally associated with open coniferous forests during winter, usually foraging on the ground for seeds.

Comments. Compared to the very similar purple finch, males of this species have only their crown area bright red, and females have a less contrasting facial pattern and narrower breast striping. Breeding Bird Surveys between 1966 and 2011 indicate that the species underwent significant population decline of 2.6% annually during that period.

House Finch   *Carpodacus mexicanus*

A locally common permanent resident in both western and eastern Nebraska, as a result of a rapid immigration into the state (mainly through cities) from both directions during recent years. During the atlasing years the species bred east to Hall and Adams counties (Mollhoff, 2001). The entire state is now effectively occupied.

Habitats. Associated with open woods, river–bottom thickets, scrubby vegetation, ranchlands and (in Nebraska) suburbs and towns.

Comments. House finches arrived in eastern Nebraska in the late 1980s from western Iowa, and at the present rate should encounter their western relatives in only a few years, probably along the Platte River. The entire eastern population derives from a few birds released in New York City in the 1940s, when commercial pet dealers dumped their illegally captive birds in order to escape arrest and prosecution. This eastern population has become infected with a bacteria-caused eye disease once carried only by domestic fowl, and which may cause blindness. There have been a few observations of infected goldfinches as well.

Red Crossbill   *Loxia curvirostra*

An irregular winter visitor and migrant throughout Nebraska, probably most common in the Panhandle, and a local but regular breeder in the Pine Ridge (*Nebraska Bird Review* 40:71). It has also bred in Scotts Bluff, Banner and Holt counties (Mollhoff, 2001). Breeding is regular in South Dakota and Minnesota, and erratic in North Dakota. During winter the species occurs south to Texas.

Migration. Thirty-one initial fall sightings range from July 26 to December 29, with a median of November 12. Half of the records fall within the period October 28 to December 14. Forty-four final spring sightings are from January 1 to June 2, with a median of April 1. Half of the records fall within the period March 19 to May 19.

Habitats. During the breeding season this species is primarily associated with coniferous forests. Migrants and wintering birds are also largely confined to conifer plantings or forests, but sometimes flocks also may be found foraging in stands of sunflowers or ragweeds.

Comments. Red crossbills periodically appear in eastern Nebraska, especially around coniferous plantations, where they can pry seeds out of cones using their unique beak tips, which are twisted screwdriver-like to open the seed-containing bracts. Different populations around the country vary in beak shape, flight call and alarm call, suggesting that there may be several "sibling species" now considered as a single species. The form most common is Nebraska (*benti*) is adapted to feeding on the seeds of ponderosa pine (*Nebraska Bird Review* 78:62).

White-winged Crossbill   *Loxia leucoptera*

A rare and irregular winter visitor and spring migrant, mostly in eastern Nebraska. The largest number of records are from Douglas-Sarpy, Lancaster, and Adams counties, but the species has been seen as far west as Scotts Bluff County. There was an incursion into the state in the winter of 2011 2012, with up to 25 seen locally (*Nebraska Bird Review* 80:71) Known breeding is limited to northern Minnesota, but during winter the species appears south as far as Kansas and rarely to Oklahoma.

Migration. Three fall records are from October 16 to November 24. Twenty-two spring sightings range from January 1 to June 14, with a median of March 6. Half of the records fall within the period February 4 to April 20.

Habitats. Associated with coniferous forests or plantations throughout the year, especially pines, in our area.

Comments. This is another irruptive winter finch, feeding in the same manner as the red crossbill. Like other fringilline finches, the young are fed on regurgitated seeds; thus the birds can begin nesting at almost any time of the year, especially after a bumper crop of conifer seeds has matured.

Common Redpoll   *Acanthis flammeus*
An occasional winter visitor statewide. Locally common in some winters, but absent in others. It is generally widespread through the Plains States as a migrant or a winter visitor.
Migration. Twenty initial fall sightings range from August 8 to December 30, with a median of November 26. Thirty final spring sightings are from January 10 to May 30, with a median of March 17. Half of the records fall between March 7 - 26.
Habitats. While in Nebraska this species is associated with conifers, deciduous thickets, and weedy fields, and sometimes visits bird feeders.
Comments. Like most other fringilline finches, this species has a rather short, notched tail and red in the head region, specifically on the forehead in the case of the redpoll. Another finch trait is a high degree of sociality, sometimes even during the breeding season.

Hoary Redpoll   *Acanthis hornemanni*
An apparently accidental winter visitor to Nebraska. Redpolls assigned to this species have been observed in Lancaster, Custer, Scotts Bluff, and Sarpy counties, but intergrades or hybrids with common redpolls also occur and confuse identification (*Nebraska Bird Review* 40:85; 44:35). It is rare in South Dakota and not reported for Kansas or Oklahoma.
Migration. Five sightings range from January (no specific date) to May 20 with the largest number of sightings in February (3).
Habitats. Usually found in the same habitats as, and in company with, common redpolls.

Pine Siskin   *Spinis pinus*
An irregular but sometimes-common migrant and winter visitor statewide, and an occasional summer resident throughout. Regular breeding is limited to the Pine Ridge area, but sporadic nestings have occurred widely in the state, including several eastern and southeastern counties following cold springs (*Wilson Bulletin* 41:77). It regularly breeds in western South Dakota and Minnesota, is an erratic breeder in eastern South Dakota, North Dakota and Kansas. It also occurs widely through the Plains States during migration or winter.
Migration. Sixty initial fall sightings range from July 25 to December 31, with a median of October 16. Half of the records fall within the period October 1 - November 18. Thirty-five final springs sightings range from January 19 to June 9, with a median of May 12. Half of the records fall within the period May 8 - June 1.
Habitats. Non-breeding birds occur in both wooded and treeless areas, often feeding in small flocks on weed seeds. Breeding occurs in both conifers and deciduous trees, including evergreen plantings, ornamental shrubs such as lilacs, vines, and diverse other rural to suburban or urban locations.
Comments. This goldfinch-sized species may be very common at a locality one year and gone the next, in an unpredictable manner. Like goldfinches it has yellow present on its body plumage, but in this case the yellow is mainly located near the bases of the flight feathers, while the breast is heavily streaked. Breeding Bird Surveys between 1966 and 2011 indicate that the species had a significant population decline (3.4% annually) in that period.

Lesser Goldfinch   *Spinis psaltria*
Local summering species in the Panhandle. As of 2000, there were a total of nine state records (*Nebraska Bird Review* 68:126), but since then the species has become regular, with 45 banded at the Wildcat Hills Nature Center in the fall of 2011 *(Nebraska Bird Review* 76:154; 79:135). The first known probable state breeding was in Banner County, June 19, 2010 (*Nebraska Bird Review* 78:103). .

American Goldfinch   *Spinis tristis*

A common permanent resident statewide. Winter populations vary from year to year. Breeding occurs almost throughout the Plains States, excepting the southernmost areas.

Habitats. During the fall and winter flocks of this species may often be found foraging in fields of tall weeds such as ragweeds and sunflowers. Breeding usually occurs in rather open grazing country, farmyards, swamps, weedy fields, and other open habitats where thistles and cattails (the down of which is used for nest lining and the seeds for feeding the young) are abundant.

Comments. Sometimes called "wild canaries" or "thistle-birds," American goldfinches delay their breeding until the latter part of summer, when thistle down (with which they line their nests) and thistle seeds (which they feed their young) are available in quantity.

Evening Grosbeak   *Coccothraustes vespertinus*

An irregular and rare winter visitor, reported from the entire state, but seen most often in the Panhandle. Local breeding occurs in the Black Hills and in northern Minnesota, but during winter the species is widespread in northern areas of the Great Plains.

Migration. Thirty-four initial fall sightings are from September 3 to December 31, with a median of November 9. Half of the records fall within the period October 19 to November 29. Fifty-two final spring sightings are from January 5 to May 28, with a median of April 25. Half of the records fall within the period April 21 to May 20.

Habitats. While in Nebraska this species is usually associated with streamside woodlands having seed-bearing deciduous trees, and it sometimes also appears at bird-feeding stations.

Comments. This large, massive-billed finch is especially fond of sunflower seeds, and can easily crack hard seeds that it encounters. Its bright yellow eyebrows and white wing-patches make identification easy. Breeding Bird Surveys between 1966 and 2011 indicate that the species underwent significant population decline of 1.4% annually during that period.

Family Passeridae

House Sparrow   *Passer domesticus*

An abundant introduced permanent resident throughout Nebraska and the other Plains States.

Habitats. This species is always associated with humans, breeding in cities, suburbs, and around farm buildings. Nesting occurs in almost any kind of cavity or crevice, including those provided by buildings, dense vines growing against walls, tree cavities, old swallow nests, and other diverse locations.

Comments. This familiar species hardly requires any descriptive comments. It is slowly becoming less numerous, as farms are declining in number, and as it is encountering competition from the house finch. Breeding Bird Surveys between 1966 and 2011 indicate that the species had a significant population decline (3.8% annually) during that period.

Eurasian Tree Sparrow   *Passer montanus*

Accidental. Photographed and seen at a feeder near Enola, February 1-4, 2007 *(Nebraska Bird Review* 75:118–120).

References

American Ornithologists' Union (AOU). 1998. *The A.O.U. Checklist of North American Birds.* 7th
    ed. AOU, Washington, D.C. (& supplements in *Auk*: 117:847-856; 119:923–932; 120:923–931;
    121:985–995; 122:1026–1031; 123:926–936; 124:1109–1115; 125:758–768; 126:705–714; 127:726–744;
    128: 600–613; 129:573-588).

Boyle, W, J., & R. H. Bauer. 1994. Birdfinding in Forty National Forests and Grasslands.
    Birding (supplement) 26(2): 186.

Bray, T. E , B. K. Padelford and W. R. Silcock. 1986. *The Birds of Nebraska: a critically evaluated list.*
    Bellevue: Published by the authors. 109 pp.

_____ & M. J. Mossman. 1983. Spring and summer birds of the Niobrara Valley Preserve area,
    Nebraska. *Nebraska Bird Review* 5l: 44-5l.

Brogie, M. A. 2009. The Official List of the Birds of Nebraska: 2009. *Nebraska Bird Review:* 77:112-129.

_____2010a. Nebraska Ornithologists' Union Records Committee: A review of the first 25 years
    (1985–2009). *Nebraska Bird Review* 78: 155–166.

_____2010b. English and scientific alpha codes for the birds of Nebraska. *Nebraska Bird Review*
    78:70–82.

Brown, C. R , M. B. Brown, P. A. Johnsgard, J. Kren & W. C. Scharf. 1996. Birds of the Cedar Point
    Biological Station area, Keith and Garden Counties, Nebraska: Seasonal occurrence and breeding
    data. *Transactions of the Nebraska Academy of Sciences* 29: 91-108.

_____, and M. B. Brown. 2001. Birds of the Cedar Point Biological Station. Occasional Papers of
    the Cedar Point Biological Station No. 1. 36 pp.

Brown, M. B. & P. A. Johnsgard. 2013. *Birds of the Central Platte River Valley and Adjacent Counties.*
    Lincoln, NE: Cons. & Survey Div., Inst. of Ag. & Nat. Resources, U. of Nebraska–Lincoln. 182 pp.
    digitalcommons.unl.edu/zeabook/15. Hardcopies available at www.lulu.com/product/paperback/

Brown, M. B., S. Dinsmore, and C. R. Brown, 2012. *Birds of Southwestern Nebraska.* Lincoln, NE:
    Conservation and Survey Division, Institute of Agriculture and Natural Resources, University of
    Nebraska, Lincoln, NE.

Bruner, L R., H. Wolcott & M. H. Swenk. 1904. *A preliminary review of the birds of Nebraska.* Omaha.

Busby, W. H. and J. L. Zimmerman. 2001. *Kansas Breeding Bird Atlas.* Univ. Press of Kansas,
    Lawrence, KS.

Canterbury, J., and P. A. Johnsgard. 2000. A century of breeding birds in Nebraska. *Nebraska Bird
    Review* 68:89-101. digitalcommons.unl.edu/cgi/viewcontent/cgi?article 1014&content

Ducey, J. E. 1988. *Nebraska Birds: Breeding Status and Distribution.* Omaha: Simmons-
    Boardman Books.

_____2000. *Birds of the Untamed West. The History of Birdlife in Nebraska* 1750-1875. Omaha:
    Making History Press,.

Farrar, J. (ed.) 1985. Birds of Nebraska. *Nebraskaland* (special issue) 63(1). 146 pp.

_____. 2004. Birding Nebraska. *Nebraskaland* (special issue) 82(1). 179 pp.

Faulkner D. W. 2012. *Birds of Wyoming.* Greenwood Village, CO: Roberts & Co. 403 pp.

Fiala, K. L. 1970. The birds of Gage County, Nebraska. *Nebraska Bird Review* 38:42-72.

Haecker, F. W., R. A. Moser and J. B. Swenk. 1945. Check-list of the birds of Nebraska. *Nebraska
    Bird Review* 13:1-40.

Jacobs, B. 2001. *Birds in Missouri.* Missouri Dept. of Conservation, Jefferson City, MO.

_____, and J. D. Wilson. 1997. *Missouri Breeding Bird Atlas.* Jefferson City, MO: Missouri Dept. of
    Conservation,

Johnsgard, P. A. 1979a. *Birds of the Great Plains: Breeding Species and their Distribution.* Lincoln:
    Univ. of Nebraska Press. 2009. 2009 Supplement and Revised Maps.
    http://digitalcommons.unl.edu/bioscibirdsgreatplains/1/

_____.1979 - The breeding birds of Nebraska. *Nebraska Bird Review,* 47:3-14.
    http://digitalcommons.unl.edu/johnsgard/10

_____. 1984. *The Platte: Channels in Time.* Lincoln, Univ. of Nebraska Press. 2nd ed. 2008.

_____. 1996. *This Fragile Land, A Natural History of the Nebraska Sandhills*. Lincoln: Univ. of Nebraska Press.

_____. 2001a. A century of ornithology in Nebraska: A personal view. Pp. 329-55, in *Contributions to the History of North American Ornithology*, Vol. II. (W. E. Davis & J. A. Jackson, eds.) Nuttall Ornithological Club, Boston, MA. http://digitalcommons.unl.edu/biosciornithology/26

_____. 2001b. *Prairie Birds: Fragile Splendor in the Great Plains*. Lawrence: Univ. Press of Kansas.

_____. 2001c. *The Nature of Nebraska: Ecology and Biodiversity*. Lincoln. Univ. of Nebraska Press.

_____. 2007. *The Niobrara: A River Running Through Time*. Lincoln: Univ. of Nebr. Press.

_____.2008. *A Guide to the Natural History of the Central Platte Valley of Nebraska*. http://digitalcommons.unl.edu/biosciornithology/40

_____. 2011. *Rocky Mountain Birds: Birds and Birding in the Central and Northern Rocky Mountains*. 274 pp. Lincoln, NE: Zea E-Books. http://digitalcommons.unl.edu/zeabook/7/. Hardcopies available at www.lulu.com/product/paperback/

_____. 2012. *Wetland Birds of the Central Plains: South Dakota, Nebraska and Kansas*, 275 pp. Lincoln, NE: Zea E-Books & Digital Commons, Univ. of Nebraska-Lincoln Libraries. http://digitalcommons.unl.edu/zeabook/8/, Hardcopies available at www.lulu.com/product/paperback/

_____. 2013. *Wings over the Great Plains: The Central Flyway*. Lincoln, NE: Zea E-Books & Digital Commons, Univ. of Nebraska-Lincoln Libraries. 249 pp. http://digitalcommons.unl.edu/zeabook/13. Hardcopies available at www.lulu.com/product/paperback/

Kingery, H. (ed.). 1998. *Colorado Breeding Bird Atlas*. Denver: Col. Div. of Wildlife,. 600 pp.

Lingle, G. R. 1994. *Birding Crane River: Nebraska's Platte*. Grand Island: Harrier Publ. Co.

Mollhoff, W. J. 2001. *The Nebraska Breeding Bird Atlas*. Supplement and revised maps. 2009. http://digitalcommons.unl.edu/bioscibirdsgreatplains/1/ Lincoln: Nebraska Game & Parks Comm.

Nebraska Ornithologists' Union Records Committee.1987–2011. Reports of the NOU Records Committee. *Nebraska Bird Review* 55:79–85. 57:42–47; 58:90–97; 60:150–155; 64:38–42; 65:115–126; 66:147–159; 67:141–152; 69:85–91; 70:84–90; 71:97–102; 71:136–142; 72:59–65; 73:78–84; 74:69–74; 75:86–94; 76:111–119; 77;80–90. 77:160–168; 79:99–111.

Nebraska Ornithologists' Union Records Committee. 2009. The official list of the birds of Nebraska. *Nebraska Bird Review* 77:112–131.(see also 73:84, 72:108–126; 65:3–16, 56:86–96.)

Orabona, A., S. Patla, L. Van Fleet, M. Grenier, B. Oakleaf & Z. Walker. 2009. *Atlas of Birds, Mammals, Amphibians and Reptiles in Wyoming*. Lander, WY: Wyoming Game & Fish Department. 227 pp. http://wgfd.wyo.gov/web2011/Departments/Wildlife/pdfs/WILDLIFE_ANIMALATLAS0000328.pdf

Peterson, R. A. 1995. *The South Dakota Breeding Bird Atlas*. Aberdeen, SD: So. Dakota Ornithologists' Union,

Pettingill, O. S., Jr. 1981. *A Guide to Bird-finding West of the Mississippi*. 2nd. ed. New York: Oxford Univ. Press.

Price, J., S. Droege, & A. Price. 1995. *The Summer Atlas of North American Birds*. San Diego: Academic Press.

Rapp, W. F., Jr. , J. L. C. Rapp, H. E. Baumgartner, & R. A. Moser. 1958. Revised checklist of Nebraska birds. Lincoln: *Occasional Papers, Nebraska Ornithologists' Union*, No. 5. 36 pp.

Rich, T. C. *et al. (*eds.). 2004. *North American Landbird Conservation Plan*. Ithaca, NY: Partners in Flight and Cornell University Laboratory of Ornithology.

Rosche, R. C. 1982. *Birds of Northwestern Nebraska and Southwestern South Dakota*. Chadron, Nebraska: Published by the author. 100 pp.

_____. 1994a. *Birds of the Lake McConaughy area and the North Platte Valley, Nebraska*. Chadron, Nebraska: Published by the author. 115 pp.

_____. & P. A. Johnsgard. 1984. Birds of Lake McConaughy and the North Platte Valley, Oshkosh to Keystone. *Nebraska Bird Review* 52:26-35.

Sharpe, R. S., W. R. Silcock, and J. G. Jorgensen. 2001. *Birds of Nebraska: Their Distribution and Temporal Occurrence.* Lincoln: Univ. of Nebraska Press,

Tallman, D. A., D. L. Swanson, and J. S. Palmer. 2002. *Birds of South Dakota.* S.D.O.U, Aberdeen.

Thompson, M. C. & C. Ely. 1989, 1992. *Birds in Kansas.* 2 vols. Lawrence: Univ. Press of Kansas.

___, ___, B. Gress, C. Otte, S. T. Patti, D. Seibel & E. A. Young. 2011. *Birds of Kansas.* Lawrence, KS: Univ. Press of Kansas.

U.S. Fish & Wildlife Service. 1981. *The Platte River Ecology Study: Special Research Report.* Jamestown: Northern Prairie Wildlife Research Station. 186 pp.

Distributed by Zea Books, University of Nebraska Libraries, Lincoln, NE 68506

ISBN 978-1-60962-038-7   paperback

ISBN 978-1-60962-039-4   ebook

Electronic (pdf) edition available online at http://digitalcommons.unl.edu/zeabook/

Print edition can be ordered from http://www.lulu.com/spotlight/unllib

Nebraska
UNIVERSITY OF
Lincoln